Casebook
in
Business
and
Society

Casebook in Business and Society

GEORGE A. STEINER

University of California in Los Angeles

RANDOM HOUSE, INC.

First Edition
98765432
Copyright © 1975 by Random House

Library of Congress Cataloging in Publication Data

Steiner, George Albert, 1912-
  Casebook in business and society.

  Includes bibliographical references.
  1. Industry--Social aspects--United States--Case
studies. I. Title.
HD60.5.U5S82   658.4'08   74-22268
ISBN 0-394-31904-4

Manufactured in the United States of America

CONTENTS

Introduction

1) THE STRUCTURE OF BUSINESS ECOLOGY   1
Discussion Guides on Chapter Content   1
Mind-Stretching Questions   2

I) THE ROAD TO TODAY'S COMPLEX
INTERRELATIONSHIPS   3

2) ANTECEDENTS TO CAPITALISM   4
Discussion Guides on Chapter Content   4
Mind-Stretching Question   4

3) THE THEORY OF CLASSICAL CAPITALISM   5
Discussion Guides on Chapter Content   5
Mind-Stretching Questions   5

4) THE AMERICAN EXPERIENCE   7
Discussion Guides on Chapter Content   7
Mind-Stretching Question   8

*Numbers after each case refer to other chapters in George A. Steiner *Business and Society*, Second Edition, to which the case is most related (in order of preference). (RP) stands for role-playing case.

II) TODAY'S BUSINESS SETTING: AN OVERVIEW   9

5) THE CHANGING BUSINESS ENVIRONMENT   10
    A)   Campaign GM (6, 10, 7, 11, 12) (RP)   10
    B)   Big Companies: "Bad Guys" or "Good Guys"
        (7, 24, 10) (RP)   19
    Discussion Guides on Chapter Content   20
    Mind-Stretching Questions   20

6) THE NEW DEMANDS ON BUSINESS AND THE
    CHANGING BUSINESS ROLE   22
    A)   G.E. Faces Society's New Demands (10, 29, 7)   22
    Discussion Guides on Chapter Content   28

7) CORPORATE POWERS: MYTH AND REALITY   30
    A)   The Public Director (6, 10)   30
    B)   Arrow, Inc. (13, 10, 26) (RP)   31
    Discussion Guides on Chapter Content   33
    Mind-Stretching Questions   34

III) BUSINESS AND CHANGING VALUES   35

8) CHANGING VALUES IN SOCIETY   36
    A)   Consolidated Industries Forecasts Changing Social
        Values and Demands (16, 10, 27)   36
    B)   Two-Way Television and Society's Values   37
    Discussion Guides on Chapter Content   38
    Mind-Stretching Questions   38

9) BUSINESS IDEOLOGIES   39
    Discussion Guides on Chapter Content   39
    Mind-Stretching Questions   39

10) THE SOCIAL RESPONSIBILITIES OF BUSINESS   40
    A)   Meeting at Multinational Industries (9) (RP)   40
    B)   South African Apartheid and Polaroid   47
    C)   Role Playing Social Responsibilities of U.S. Steel
        Corporation (RP)   48

D) DuPont's "Give Away" and Social Responsibilities
(12, 7, 26) (RP)   49

E) Excerpts from Ford Motor Company Public Affairs
Policy Statement   50

F) University Proxy Policy   52

G) William Robertson   54

H) DuPont's Refusal to Supply Certain Information   55

I) Elgin Sled Company   57

Discussion Guides on Chapter Content   59

Mind-Stretching Questions   60

11) MAKING SOCIAL RESPONSIBILITIES OPERATIONAL
IN BUSINESS   61

A) The Middle Manager and Company Policies for Social
Responsibilities (10)   61

Discussion Guides on Chapter Content   62

Mind-Stretching Questions   62

12) THE SOCIAL AUDIT   64

A) CGI's Social Audit   64

Discussion Guides on Chapter Content   65

Mind-Stretching Questions   66

13) BUSINESS ETHICS   67

A) B.F. Goodrich Company vs. Donald W. Wohlegemuth
(10) (RP)   67

B) Aerial Espionage or American Entrepreneurship?   68

C) Pension Rights: Law, Economics, and Ethics   69

D) Martin's Campaign Contribution (RP)   70

E) World Charter Airways Systems   72

F) Force Reduction at Machinery Systems (10, 16,
27) (RP)   74

G) Crisis at XYZ (RP)   77

H) Willard Atkinson   78

I) Twelve Basic Armco Policies (8)   79

J) High Wages vs. Shutdown   80

K) The Sweatshop (16)   81

L) An Advertiser Asks a Newspaper a Favor   82

Discussion Guides on Chapter Content   83

Mind-Stretching Questions   84

IV) BUSINESS AND MAJOR COMMUNITY PROBLEMS — 85

14) BUSINESS AND OUR POLLUTED ENVIRONMENT — 86
A) BASF Corporation vs. The Hilton Head Island
   Developers (12, 21, 23, 11) (RP) — 86
B) The Pollution Crisis of Superior Wire Company — 102
C) Birmingham's Pollution Shutdown and Worker Rights
   (28, 13) — 109
D) Do We Need a New Bill of Rights? — 110
Discussion Guides on Chapter Content — 111
Mind-Stretching Question — 111

15) BUSINESS AND CONSUMERS — 112
A) International Foods Industries' Response to
   Consumerism — 112
B) Stocking Snowshovels — 114
C) Home Tool Company Product Liability — 115
D) Puffery or Prevarication in Advertising — 116
E) Smokey Cigarette Company — 117
F) Hypo Pharmaceutical Company Pricing — 118
G) Wisconsin Telephone Company — 119
Discussion Guides on Chapter Content — 119
Mind-Stretching Questions — 120

16) BUSINESS, COMMUNITY PROBLEMS, AND
DISADVANTAGED MINORITIES — 121
A) The Multi-Million Dollar Misunderstanding: An
   Attempt to Reduct Turnover Among Disadvantaged
   Workers (10,22) — 121
Discussion Guides on Chapter Content — 133
Mind-Stretching Questions — 133

17) BUSINESS AND EDUCATION — 134
Discussion Guides on Chapter Content — 134
Mind-Stretching Questions — 134

18) BUSINESS AND THE ARTS   135
   A) Philadelphia Gas Works Adopts Philadelphia Civic
      Ballet   135
   Discussion Guides on Chapter Content   **136**
   Mind-Stretching Question   **136**

19) BUSINESS AND TECHNOLOGY   137
   A) Plane Deal? (25, 21)   137
   B) Technology Assessment of Subsonic Aircraft Noise (16) **141**
   C) Should Government Support Nonmilitary Aviation? (21) **142**
   Discussion Guides on Chapter Content   **148**
   Mind-Stretching Questions   **149**

20) AFFLUENCE, GROWTH, AND THE POST-INDUSTRIAL
    SOCIETY   150
   Discussion Guides on Chapter   **150**
   Mind-Stretching Question   **151**

V) BUSINESS AND GOVERNMENT   **153**

21) GOVERNMENT-BUSINESS INTERRELATIONSHIPS:
    AN OVERVIEW   154
   A) Southern California Edison Tries to Build a Power
      Plant (23, 14)   154
   B) The L-1011 Federal Loan Guarantee   165
   C) Studebaker Closes a Plant and the Pentagon Closes an
      Air Base   173
   Discussion Guides on Chapter Content   **174**
   Mind-Stretching Questions   **174**

22) THE POLITICAL ROLE OF BUSINESS IN
    PUBLIC AFFAIRS   176
   A) The Candidate's Decision (13)   176
   B) Buy American   180
   C) A Triumph for the Pork Barrel (21)   182
   Discussion Guides on Chapter Content   **183**
   Mind-Stretching Questions   **184**

23) THE CONVERGENCE OF BUSINESS AND
GOVERNMENT PLANNING 185
A) Planning for Two-Way Cable TV (RP) 185
Discussion Guides on Chapter Content 186
Mind-Stretching Question 187

24) ECONOMIC CONCENTRATION AND PUBLIC POLICY 188
Discussion Guides on Chapter Content 188
Mind-Stretching Question 189

25) BUSINESS AND INTERNATIONAL POLICY 190
A) The Burke-Hartke Bill (21) (RP) 190
Discussion Guides on Chapter Content 204
Mind-Stretching Questions 204

26) OTHER ISSUES IN GOVERNMENT REGULATION
OF BUSINESS 205
Discussion Guides on Chapter Content 205

VI) BUSINESS AND ITS EMPLOYEES 207

27) THE CHANGING ROLE OF PEOPLE IN
ORGANIZATIONS 208
A) Stan Sheldon and the "Joining Up" Process (RP) 208
B) Whistle Blowing at Hi-Quality Aircraft (13, 10) (RP) 211
C) Conflict of Interest Policy (13) 217
D) Big Companies: Oppressors of Individual Expression
or Sources of Self Satisfactions? (RP) 220
E) The "I Am" Plan: Job Enrichment of Weyerhaeuser
Company (28) 221
Discussion Guides on Chapter Content 232
Mind-Stretching Questions 232

28) LABOR UNIONS AND MANAGERIAL AUTHORITY 233
Discussion Guides on Chapter Content 233
Mind-Stretching Question 234

VII) THE FUTURE   **235**

29) **FUTURE FORCES AND PATTERNS IN THE**
   BUSINESS SOCIETY RELATIONSHIP   **236**
   A) Alternative Environmental Futures for the U.S. (RP)   **236**
   Discussion Guides on Chapter Content   **245**
   Mind-Stretching Questions   **245**

INTRODUCTION

In teaching my courses on the interrelationship between business and society I discovered very early the value of short case studies and provocative questions in stimulating classroom discussion. Over time, therefore, I have accumulated such cases and questions to accompany and complement the second edition of my basic book on *Business and Society*. These are included in this book.

The chapter headings in the table of contents of this casebook are identical with those in *Business and Society*. Included under each chapter heading are, where presented, cases relating to the chapter subject matter. For each chapter there are also questions that may serve as guidelines to classroom discussion of the substance presented in the chapter in *Business and Society*. Finally, "mind-stretching" questions are given for each chapter. These questions raise issues that go beyond the substance of the material in the textbook.

The fundamental purpose of each case in this book is to provide a basis for thoughtful, relevant, and stimulating dialogue about an important issue or point in the business-society relationship. The focus is primarily, although not exclusively, on the way in which environment impacts on the management of organizations (especially business) and the way in which business activity influences environment.

The case studies are concerned for the most part with controversial issues for which there are no single answers. Indeed, a basic purpose of many cases is to make clear to students that equally objective and knowledgeable people can come to different conclusions about specific issues.

Another major purpose of the cases is to emphasize student learning rather than instructor lecturing. In my courses in business and society I do a minimum of lecturing because I think the students get much more out of discussing basic issues among themselves. These cases will help in this learning process.

In an effort to cover a wide span of issues in a relatively short book I have included a large number of very short cases. Many of these could easily be expanded into longer cases, but I find that a short case can also stimulate informed discussion on a vital issue. Some issues, however, cannot be covered well in limited space, and such issues are presented in longer cases.

Since the casebook is meant to supplement the second edition of *Business and Society*, it is assumed that students will have the background in that book to approach specific cases. In a number of instances, however, for better understanding and discussion of the cases, additional background information will be helpful. I have, therefore, suggested specific readings for many cases.

Classical case writers do not like to put questions at the end of their cases because they feel this brings the case writer into the case and destroys the illusion of reality. They say the student becomes aware that the case is only an artificial teaching device. For certain types of cases used in the traditional policy courses I suppose this is so. For teaching and learning in the business-society area, however, I do not think these objections are valid. Many of the case studies in this book are very real and important—and the students know it. Furthermore, it is a time-saver to focus attention on specific issues, and this can be done by asking questions. Thus most cases have questions at the end.

In my classes the cases are used in many different ways. For example, in some instances I elicit a response from any student in the class to the case in general or to a question raised at the end of the case. Following the response there generally is an exchange between students themselves or between the students and the instructor. Sometimes I say nothing about a case, except to correct errors of fact in student discussion, and encourage the students to "go at it" among themselves. For some cases I ask one student or a team of students (usually two) to prepare a presentation to the class on their approach to the case. In other instances students are asked to be knowledgeable about the issues in a case and to act as a resource for general classroom discussion of the case.

One instructor who has used these cases finds the following procedure to be highly effective in stimulating discussion in each group and in class. His classes range between twenty-five and thirty students. Early in the term he separates them into groups of five or six and assigns a number of cases to each group. It is the responsibility of the group to determine how the case can best be presented in class (with the counsel of the instructor) and to arrange the class discussion.

It is stimulating to students to have a businessman visit the class and participate in the discussion. There are, of course, many different ways to make such a visit interesting and useful. For example, the businessman may present his analysis of the case before or after student discussion. He may choose only to respond to student questions. He may use the case to show a specific problem faced by his company. Some cases lend themselves to role playing by students. In role-playing cases the businessman, of course, might be invited to play the role of a businessman.

Sometimes it is helpful for an instructor to present background for a case and to prepare a climate for the discussion. Generally, however, it seems better to stimulate students to debate and engage in dialogue without the instructor standing between them or serving as the "authority" for answers to their individual questions.

Whenever I ask students to make a presentation or to act as a resource, I also request a written statement of their analysis. I find that the discipline of writing not only clarifies their thinking, but also provides the occasion for a different learning experience. To facilitate student thinking in such instances, I suggest readings related to the cases, or ask them to find their own references, or both.

The purpose of adding references to many cases in this book, however, goes beyond this. I think that cases such as those given here alone are not enough for a course in business and society. They should be supplemented by a basic book plus additional readings directly concerned with the issues in the case. For this reason, I have tried to be helpful in providing references, pro and con, for many of the cases. It is only required that students responsible for writing the case read the references. In general, I have tried to locate short articles in the more accessible journals for student reading.

As is evident in the Table of Contents, there are many cases for some chapters but few or none for others. I have tried to provide a number of cases from which an instructor may choose for those subjects that appear to have the greatest current interest in the field. Some chapters in the textbook, for example, Chapters 24 and 26, are composed entirely of case studies. In those chapters where no cases are given, the questions on chapter content and the mind-stretching questions are, hopefully, enough for classroom discussion.

In a typical semester or quarter course, an instructor and his students will not be able to cover all the cases and questions in this text. An instructor, therefore, has an opportunity to pick and choose those issues of particular interest to him and to his students. He may wish to use certain cases not covered in class as topics for a term report.

A special word of appreciation is due Dr. Edward V. Sedgwick of the UCLA faculty, who reviewed this book and gave me some valuable recommendations for its improvement. I thank Miss Sharon Outzen for typing most of the manuscript. Larry Schmid was helpful in preparing cases 13F, 14B, 25A, and 27B; and Jeff Gale was helpful in preparing cases 21A and 21B. A few cases were wholly prepared by others and acknowledgement of their authorship is made in the case.

Analyzing the relationship between business and society has been for me a very interesting and stimulating experience. I hope this book of cases conveys my enthusiasm to those who use it.

Casebook in Business and Society

1

THE STRUCTURE OF BUSINESS ECOLOGY

DISCUSSION GUIDES ON CHAPTER CONTENT———————

1. Define business ecology, business, businessmen, and society.

2. What are some of the paradoxical situations in which business finds itself today?

3. Discuss the range of issues involved in the business-society interrelationship. Does the issue's level of abstraction indicate the difficulty of resolution?

4. Using Figure 1-1 as a guideline, illustrate differences in impact of several major forces on two distinctly different business entities (such as a large and a small company).

5. Do you agree with the author's approach to the study of business-society relationships? Why?

6. When the right issues are identified and all the facts are available, how can reasonable men arrive at vastly different conclusions? Explain.

MIND-STRETCHING QUESTIONS —————————————

1. What curriculum center would be able to give the most comprehensive course on business-society relationships, and with the maximum objectivity? Consider such departments as political science, business management, philosophy, and sociology. Is objectivity the main goal of a comprehensive course in business and society?

2. Do you believe that continuous study of the environment is a necessity for both students and businessmen?

3. Should business constantly try to justify itself?

I

THE ROAD
TO TODAY'S
COMPLEX
INTERRELATIONSHIPS

2
ANTECEDENTS TO CAPITALISM

DISCUSSION GUIDES ON CHAPTER CONTENT————

1. Contrast the role of the businessman in ancient Greece, ancient Rome, the medieval world, and mercantilistic societies.

2. Discuss the implications of the Protestant Reformation for the development of business.

3. What were the major events that led to the decline of mercantilism and the rise of capitalism?

MIND-STRETCHING QUESTION————————

1. Why be concerned with historical patterns and profiles? Is history relevant to current issues? Are there lessons to be learned from a quick review of the history of the business-society interrelationship?

3

THE THEORY OF CLASSICAL CAPITALISM

DISCUSSION GUIDES ON CHAPTER CONTENT ——————

1. Explain briefly the operation of the classical individual-enterprise system and the underlying institutions upon which it was presumed to operate.

2. Define *liberalism* as used in the classical theory of capitalism.

3. What was the function of government from the classical viewpoint?

4. Comment on this quotation: "Adam Smith did not accept a rigorous laissez-faire policy."

5. How valid are the underlying assumptions of the classical individual-enterprise system today? Explain in detail.

MIND-STRETCHING QUESTIONS ——————

1. Why do you think classical capitalistic economics accepted government regulation to protect employers from other employers rather than consumers and employees from employers?

2. The publication of Adam Smith's *Wealth of Nations*, and the Declaration of Independence both occurred in the year 1776. Is this a mere coincidence, or were the two events related?

3. Do you agree with the author that it is important for students of business-society relationships to understand the classical capitalistic theory? Explain.

4

THE AMERICAN EXPERIENCE

DISCUSSION GUIDES ON CHAPTER CONTENT————

1. What major forces led to the rise of the modern corporation?

2. It has been said that the modern corporation is one of the world's great social inventions. Do you agree or disagree?

3. To what extent has business been responsible for the remarkable economic growth of the United States? How has government contributed?

4. What major forces have led government to interfere more and more in the economic sphere?

5. The author discusses a number of social and religious values that have been important in the business-society interrelationship. Which ones have been *most* important in stimulating business?

6. Explain briefly how major economic depressions in our history have affected business.

7. Throughout the nineteenth century and well into the present one, the Supreme Court's decisions have been highly favorable to business. Briefly explain why this is the case. Has this trend changed recently?

MIND-STRETCHING QUESTION ———————————

1. Do you think the pace of change in the business-society interrelationship is more rapid, about the same, or slower today than in previous eras in United States history? Explain.

TODAY'S BUSINESS SETTING: AN OVERVIEW

5

THE CHANGING BUSINESS ENVIRONMENT

A) CAMPAIGN GM

In 1970 the Project on Corporate Responsibility was created by Ralph Nader in Washington, D.C., and leaped into prominence with its "Campaign GM." The broad aims of the Project on Corporate Responsibility concerned such goals as making "corporate decision-makers more responsive to legitimate social demands, such as the need to end employment discrimination and develop the resources of economically disadvantaged communities." The main strategy of the Project was to get proxies from nonprofit institutions to vote proposals prepared by the Project.

Campaign GM was the first significant move of the Project. Two basic demands were made on the General Motors Corporation at its annual stockholders meeting in May 1970, as follows: first, set up a committee on corporate responsibility to study GM's performance in dealing with social and environmental issues and recommend changes "to make GM responsible"; and, second, place three "public interest" directors on the board.

The details of these two proposals as submitted to the stockholders of record, together with management's reasons why stockholders should reject them, are as follows:

The Committee for Corporate Responsibility—Proposal[1]

Whereas the shareholders of General Motors are concerned that the present policies and priorities pursued by the management have failed to take into account the possible adverse social impact of the Corporation's activities, it is

Resolved that:

1) There be established the General Motors Shareholders Committee for Corporate Responsibility.

2) The Committee for Corporate Responsibility shall consist of no less than fifteen and no more than twenty-five persons, to be appointed by a representative of the Board of Directors, a representative of the Campaign to Make General Motors Responsible, and a representative of United Auto Workers, acting by majority vote. The members of the Committee for Corporate Responsibility shall be chosen to represent the following: General Motors management, the United Auto Workers, environmental and conservation groups, consumers, the academic community, civil rights organizations, labor, the scientific community, religious and social service organizations, and small shareholders.

3) The Committee for Corporate Responsibility shall prepare a report and make recommendations to the shareholders with respect to the role of the corporation in modern society and how to achieve a proper balance between the rights and interests of shareholders, employees, consumers and the general public. The Committee shall specifically examine, among other things:

A. The Corporation's past and present efforts to produce an automobile which:

   (1) is non-polluting
   (2) reduces the potentiality for accidents
   (3) reduces personal injury resulting from accidents
   (4) reduces property damage resulting from accidents
   (5) reduces the costs of repair and maintenance whether from accidents or extended use.

B. The extent to which the Corporation's policies towards suppliers, employees, consumers and dealers are contributing to the goals of providing safe and reliable products.

C. The extent to which the Corporation's past and present efforts have contributed to a sound national transportation policy and an effective low-cost mass transportation system.

D. The manner in which the Corporation has used its vast economic power to contribute to the social welfare of the nation.

E. The manner by which the participation of diverse sectors of society in corporate decision-making can be increased including

[1] See, "A Proposal on Corporate Responsibility" (Washington, D.C.: Center for Law and Social Policy, and the Washington Research Project, 20 October 1969.) Reprinted by permission of General Motors Corporation.

nomination and election of directors and selection of members of the committees of the Board of Directors.

4) The Committee's report shall be distributed to the shareholders and to the public no later than March 31, 1971. The committee shall be authorized to employ staff members in the performance of its duties. The Board of Directors shall allocate to the Committee those funds the Board of Directors determines reasonably necessary for the Committee to accomplish its tasks. The Committee may obtain any information from the Corporation and its employees reasonably deemed relevant by the Committee, provided, however, that the Board of Directors may restrict the information to be made available to the Committee to information which the Board of Directors reasonably determines to be not privileged for business or competitive reasons.

The Stockholder has submitted the following statement in support of such resolution:

Reasons: "The purpose of this resolution is to enable shareholders to assess the public impact of the Corporation's decisions, and to determine the proper role of the Corporation in society. Past efforts by men such as Ralph Nader to raise these issues have been frustrated by the refusal of management to make its files and records available either to the shareholders or to the public. Only a committee representing a broad segment of the public with adequate resources and access to information can prepare a report which will accomplish these objectives."

The Board of Directors favors a vote **AGAINST** this resolution for the following reasons:

This resolution and the Proposal for Directors to Represent Special Interests by the same sponsor are parts of an attack on the General Motors Board of Directors and management and on what General Motors has achieved on behalf of its stockholders and the public. In the opinion of the Board of Directors and management the attack is based on false conceptions and assumptions. It was launched by a stockholder (the Project), composed of seven members, which purchased 12 shares of General Motors stock in January 1970 for the express purpose of this attack. The Project has announced that while General Motors is its first target, similar attacks will be made on other large corporations.

The Project is a nonprofit corporation organized this year under the laws of the District of Columbia. Its formation was announced by Ralph Nader. Although he has stated that he is "not a formal participant in the Project" and that the "program" affecting General Motors is one "undertaken by a number of other young attorneys in Washington," he has promoted the Project and the Campaign to Make

General Motors Responsible ("Campaign GM") by press interview, television appearance and otherwise. For many years he has been identified with various campaigns against General Motors and was a prominent participant in a demonstration against the Corporation at the General Motors Building in New York in December 1969.

The names "Committee for Corporate Responsibility" and "Campaign to Make General Motors Responsible" together with this resolution which would establish a Committee for Corporate Responsibility and the statements in support of the resolution suggest that management's decisions "have failed to take into account the possible adverse social impact of the Corporation's activities. . . ." This simply is not true. The true facts in regard to the concern and responsibility with which General Motors has pursued goals of social and public policy are set forth in the enclosed booklet, "GM's Record of Progress." We are proud of this record and all stockholders are urged to read the booklet.[2]

The objective of the resolution is to interpose a body unknown to corporate law or practice (the Committee for Corporate Responsibility)—purportedly investigatory in nature but structured for harassment and publicity—between the stockholders and the Board of Directors. The establishment of such a Committee would seriously hamper the Board of Directors in representing the stockholders and in carrying out its responsibilities to manage the business and affairs of the Corporation.

The proposed Committee, far from achieving "a proper balance between the rights and interest of shareholders, employees, consumers and the general public," is proposed to be appointed "by majority vote" of (i) a representative of "Campaign GM," which is a creature of the proponent of the resolution, (ii) a representative of the United Auto Workers, and (iii) a representative of the Board of Directors. This permits the crucial "majority vote," with power to elect the entire Committee, to be supplied by a representative of "Campaign GM" (which itself owns no General Motors stock) and by a representative of the United Auto Workers. Members of the Committee would not be required to be stockholders of General Motors and would be chosen to represent General Motors management, the U.A.W., environmental and conservation groups, consumers, the academic community, civil rights organizations, labor, the scientific community, religious and social service organizations and small stockholders. It is obvious that the proponent of the resolution seeks this Committee to pursue its special interests.

The proposed method of appointing the proposed Committee makes it clear that its purpose is to harass the Corporation and its management and to promote the particular economic and social views espoused by

[2] *Ed. note:* For a more recent report, see the *1973 Report on Progress in Areas of Public Concern* (Warren, Mich.: GM Technical Center, 1973).

the proponent of the resolution. The Board of Directors believes that this resolution, if adopted, would do serious damage to General Motors and to its stockholders and, in fact, to the general public.

The Board of Directors favors a vote **AGAINST** this Proposal. . . . Proxies solicited by the Board of Directors will be so voted unless stockholders specify in their proxies a contrary choice.

Directors to Represent Special Interests—Proposal

Resolved: That Number 15 of the By-Laws of the Corporation be amended to read as follows:

15) The business of the Corporation shall be managed by a board of twenty-six members (an addition of three).

The Stockholder has submitted the following statement in support of such resolution:

Reasons: This amendment will expand the number of directors to enable representatives of the public to sit on the Board of Directors without replacing any of the current nominees of management. The proponents of this amendment believe that adding representatives of the public to the Board is one method to insure that the Corporation will consider the impact of its decisions on important public issues, including auto safety, pollution, repairs, mass transportation and equal employment opportunities.

The Board of Directors favors a vote **AGAINST** this resolution for the following reasons:

The Board of Directors finds no valid reason why the number of directors should be increased at the present time. Any suggestion that General Motors Corporation has been deficient in considering the interest of the public in such matters as auto safety, pollution, mass transportation and the like is entirely contrary to fact; the Company's record in this regard is set forth in the enclosed booklet.

The Board of Directors believes that each director, in addition to his responsibility to represent all the stockholders, has a very important responsibility to customers, employees, the public and society generally. This is in accord with the development of the modern American corporation and corporate theory to which General Motors wholeheartedly subscribes and in accordance with which it operates. But that is very different from having as members of the Board individuals, no matter how worthy, who would be elected to represent special interests and who would feel obliged to concentrate attention on those special interests whether or not the effect would be to disrupt the proper and effective functioning of the Board.

Moreover, the Board of Directors continues to believe that for a board of directors to be effective each member must feel a responsibility to represent all the stockholders. In fact, representation of special groups introduces the possibility of partisanship among board members, which would impair the ability to work together, a requirement essential to the efficient functioning of a board of directors.

Stockholders should recognize that the resolution to amend the By-Laws to increase the number of Directors is not a simple, innocuous proposal. The real issue posed by this proposal is whether an opportunity should be created to inject into the Corporation's Board of Directors three additional directors who are selected not on the basis of their interest in the success of the Corporation but rather on the basis of their sympathy with the special interests of the proponent of the resolution. This is proposed under the guise that as "representatives of the public" they would insure that the Corporation "will consider the impact of its decisions on important public issues." The proposal is a reflection upon the service rendered to the Corporation and its stockholders by the present members of the Board of Directors who were elected because of their integrity and broad experience in many fields including public service. The suggestion that they have not taken into account the impact of their decisions upon the public has no basis in fact. The objective of this proposal is substantially the same as that of the proposal for the Committee for Corporate Responsibility.

If the proponent should be successful in increasing the number of directors and thereafter electing its nominees, the Board of Directors believes there would be similar internal harassment to the detriment of General Motors, its stockholders and the public.

The Board of Directors favors a vote **AGAINST** this proposal . . . . Proxies solicited by the Board of Directors will be so voted unless stockholders specify in their proxies a contrary choice.*

The Project requested large holders of GM stock to provide proxies to be used at the annual stockholders meeting to enforce its demands. Various university boards of trustees—Harvard, California, Michigan, and Texas, for instance—were requested to give The Project their proxies. Other large holders such as charitable foundations also were solicited. No large holder gave the Project proxies. Some, however, sympathized with its views. The Rockefeller Foundation, for instance, cast its vote with management, but in

*This portion of the article is reprinted with the permission of *The Wall Street Journal*, © Dow Jones & Company, Inc., 1970.

explaining its position criticized the corporation. Some excerpts follow:

> There are constituents other than stockholders to whom corporations are also obligated. There are battles to be waged against racism, poverty, pollution, and urban blight which the Government alone cannot win; they can be won only if the status and power of American corporate industry are fully and effectively committed to the struggle. What is needed from business today is leadership which is courageous, wise and compassionate, which is enlightened in its own and the public's interest, and which greets change with an open mind. In our judgment, the management of General Motors did not display this spirit in its response to the two proposals offered by Campaign GM [a subgroup of the Committee on Corporate Responsibility].
>
> We recognize that these proposals are, from management's viewpoint, unwieldy and impractical; Campaign GM itself conceded the difficulty it encountered in trying to determine a method of selecting members of a Committee for Corporate Responsibility. Because of these inadequacies we are prepared, this time, to sign our proxy as requested by management. But we are not prepared to let the matter rest there.
>
> We do not share the view which was expressed by management that the Campaign GM proposals represent an 'attack' on the corporation. . . We believe the language of the Campaign GM proposals is more reasonable and temperate than the response of management. We also believe the goals of the proposals have been designed to serve the public good by increasing the corporation's awareness of the major impact of its decisions and policies on society at large.*

The demands of Campaign GM were not met because the overwhelming majority of stockholders gave their proxies to GM's management. Reactions in 1970, however, seemed to portend trouble for GM's management in 1971.

In September 1970 the General Motors Corporation announced that it was responding to criticism that the company's decisions sometimes did not take the public welfare into consideration by forming a Public Policy Committee made up of five GM directors. Mr. Roche, chairman of the Board of Directors, said that matters associated with community action and corporate citizenship would as a result, have "a permanent place on the highest level of management." He said that he anticipated the work of the

*From General Motors Corporation, Proxy Statement for Annual Meeting of Stockholders held May 22, 1970. Reproduced with permission.

committee "will demonstrate their understanding of General Motors and its industry, their awareness of the expanding role of business in society and their comprehension of the responsibilities of the board of directors, who are charged with the successful operation of the business." The committee "will inquire into all phases of General Motors' operations that relate to matters of public policy and recommend actions to the full board." None of the members of the committee were officers of GM.

In January 1971 General Motors invited the Reverend Leon H. Sullivan to become the first black member of its board of directors. Reverend Sullivan, in commenting on his appointment, said:

> I told Mr. Roche he should have no illusions about what I am. He knows I'm a man who expresses his opinions, and that I will not be tied to the traditions of the board. I'm more interested in human returns than capital returns. My main concern is helping to improve the position of black people in America. I want to be a voice from the outside on the inside.[3]

At the May 1971 stockholders meeting, Campaign GM advanced new proposals to make GM "accountable to the people their decisions affect." These included a requirement that GM list in the proxy it sends to shareholders the names of suggested directors made by nonmanagement shareholders; a proposal to require GM to disclose in its annual report information about such matters as minority hiring, air pollution, and automobile safety policies so that shareholders "may accurately evaluate the performance of management in meeting public responsibilities in these areas"; and a proposal to permit GM's key constituencies—employees, consumers, and dealers—to participate in the election of three of the directors of the company.

These proposals were overwhelmingly defeated. The Project on Corporate Responsibility held only 12 of GM's 286 million shares of stock and were able to gather together less than 3 percent of the shares voted. This was a smaller percentage than in 1970.

In 1972 The Project on Corporate Responsibility made two new proposals. One would require the directors of General Motors to appoint a committee to study the desirability of dividing the company into several independent corporations. The proposal

---

[3] *Business Week*, 10 April 1971, p. 100.

suggested that GM be broken up because its fear of antitrust action by the government had prevented it from competing for a larger share of the market. The function of the committee, therefore, would be to determine whether breaking up GM was in the best interests of the public and could also maximize profits for the separate companies thus formed. The second proposal called for regular progress reports from GM's Public Policy Committee. These proposals received less than 2 percent of the votes cast.

In three annual meetings, the overwhelming number of stockholders gave GM's management their vote of confidence and flatly rejected the proposals of the Project. By the size of the vote, it is obvious that even the foundations and nonprofit institutions holding GM stock voted with management.

CASE QUESTIONS

1. Identify the fundamental issues raised in this case study about the business-society relationship and the way corporations are influenced and managed.

2. If you were a shareholder in GM, would you give your proxy to management or to the Project? Explain.

3. Argue the pros and cons of the Project's proposal for the Committee for Social Responsibility. (See Henry G. Manne, "Who's Responsible?" *Barrons*, 17 May 1971.)

4. Who is to determine what are the responsibilities of a company like General Motors?

5. Argue the pros and cons of placing special interest representatives on boards of directors of American corporations. (See Harold Koontz, "The Corporate Board and Special Interests," *Business Horizons*, October 1971, pp. 75-93.) For a succinct yet wide-ranging commentary on the challenge to corporate boards of directors see "The Board of Directors Faces Challenge and Change," *The Conference Board Record*, February 1972, pp. 39-54. For an evaluation of the new liability of boards of directors, see Robert M. Estes, "Outside Directors: More Vulnerable Than Ever," *Harvard Business Review*, January-February 1973, pp 107-114.

6. Do you approve the several GM actions that were taken to be more responsive to social interests?

B) BIG COMPANIES: "BAD GUYS" OR "GOOD GUYS"?

David Rockefeller in a speech delivered in January 1972, said: "It is scarcely an exaggeration to say that right now American business is facing its most severe public disfavor since the 1920's. We are assailed for demeaning the worker, deceiving the consumer, destroying the environment, and disillusioning the younger generation."[1]

Yet at the same time, the public speeches and annual reports of many top managers are obvious testimonials to the fact that businessmen today think more about the consequences of their actions than ever before. Role 1) You are a liberal arts major and have heard emphasized in some of your classes the abuses, shortcomings, immoralities, excessive profits, and many other evils of big business. Your role is to collect as many criticisms of big business as you can. Use your own views, attitudes of colleagues and teachers, library research, and any other source you think appropriate. Try to be specific in your allegations. Role 2) You are a business major and feel that large companies are not only inevitable but major forces for good. You are to identify the important reasons why big business has acted responsibly, why it is not deserving of the many attacks on it, and why it is a force for good in society. You also are to be prepared, to the extent that you can forecast criticisms levied in Role 1, to defend big business from its attackers. Your sources are your own knowledge, ideas of your friends and teachers, and, of course, library reading. Role 3) Your assignment is to pick out one large company that has been under attack in the public press for irresponsible action. You are to appraise the attack. You are also to evaluate benefits to society growing out of the company's total effort.

---

[1] David Rockefeller, address to the Advertising Council, reported in the *Los Angeles Times*, January 3, 1971.

———————————————**References**———————————————

Joseph L. Bower, "Planning Within the Firm," *American Economic Review*, May 1970, pp. 186-194.

Elwood N. Chapman, *Big Business: A Positive View*, (Englewood Cliffs, N.J.: Prentice-Hall, 1972).

John K. Galbraith, *The New Industrial State*, (Boston: Houghton Mifflin, 1958).

Neil H. Jacoby, *Corporate Power and Social Responsibility: A Blueprint for the Future*, (New York: Macmillan, 1973).

Morton Mintz and Jerry S. Cohen, *America, Inc.*, (New York: Dial Press, 1971).

Richard A. Posner, "Power in America," *The Public Interest*, Fall 1971, pp. 114-121.

Bruce R. Scott, "The Industrial State: Old Myths and New Realities," *Harvard Business Review*, March-April 1973, pp. 133-148.

DISCUSSION GUIDES ON CHAPTER CONTENT———————

1. What are the major criticisms leveled at today's businessmen? How do they contrast with past criticisms?

2. Are there explanations for criticisms of modern business? Which ones do you think are most creditable?

3. What does the author say are the fundamental, underlying forces that are changing the environment of buisness in a significant way?

4. Explain how these forces are affecting particular business environments.

5. It is said that ours is a pluralistic society. What does this mean with reference to business and its role in society?

6. Do you agree with the author that business success is depending more and more upon how a business relates to its environment? Explain.

MIND-STRETCHING QUESTIONS———————————————

1. Would you accept the thought that today's business environment is making the task of managing a company far more complex than ever before? Explain.

2. Do you agree or disagree with the notion that the very complexity of today's business environment gives the large company an advantage over the small one? Why?

6

THE NEW DEMANDS
ON BUSINESS
AND THE CHANGING
BUSINESS ROLE

A) GE FACES SOCIETY'S NEW DEMANDS

The General Electric Company has been concerned about changing attitudes of society with respect to business in general, and the General Electric Company in particular. It has, therefore, made a number of forecasts concerning the changing business environment. The following is GE's preliminary list of the major demands that society seems to be placing upon business.*

A) Marketing/Financial Power

Federal chartering of corporations, with provision for periodic rechartering

Attacks on "shared monopolies" (re cereal case): restructuring and reorganization of major companies and industries

Limitations on (a) number of businesses one company may engage in, and (b) share of market one company may possess

*Reproduced by permission of the General Electric Company.

Dismemberment of large, diversified companies

Nationalization of some industries (e.g. R.R.)

Prenotification of mergers: all mergers barred to top 200 corporations

Higher corporate taxes; perhaps, excess profits tax or progressive corporate income tax

Prenotification of price increases; permanent wage/price/profit controls on major corporations

Divestiture of finance affiliates

Public control of large corporations because they are either immune from, or (for the public good) they must be shielded from, normal economic and political/legal constraints

B) **Production Operations**

Stringent effluents/emissions standards; fines for violations—and possible plant closings

Internalization of all negative "social costs"

National/regional/state land use planning re plant siting, etc.

Environmental impact statements required for new plants, new processes, etc.

Technology assessment: gov't. approval for introduction of new products/technologies

Elimination/reduction of depletion and depreciation allowances

Require % of recycled materials

Include disposal cost in product price

Strict product safety standards enforced by federal agency

Consumer boycotts, class action suits

Intervention by public interest groups (e.g. environmental protection)

A rapidly increasing share of non-defense R & D done with

government funds, based on political priorities, political choice of recipients

C) **Employee Relations/Working Conditions**

Decline of "success" incentives/economic incentives

Best talent drawn away from large corporations

Deterioration in productivity of employees at all levels

Alienation of blue-collar workers, and to a lesser extent, middle management and professional personnel

More participative management, employee involvement in decisions affecting their interests

Appoint managers capable of dealing with change and "new work force"

Job enlargement/enrichment (team and individual work in plants and offices)

More flexible scheduling of work

Greater employment security (guarantees of income or work): government as "employer of last resort"); massive WPA type programs

Increasing shortages of technicians; craftmen

More attention to career development, retraining; growing obsolescence of skills at all levels

More leisure time; longer vacations; earlier retirement; sabbaticals

Federalization (or federal control) of many benefits, e.g. health insurance, pensions

Affirmative action on hiring, training, promotion of minorities, women (compliance reviews, termination of gov't. contracts)

Equal pay (and benefits) for equal work

Provision (or support) of day care centers

Tighter enforcement of occupational health and safety standards

Due process for employees (ombudsman)

Human assets accounting, to reveal managerial performance re human resources

Special groups—e.g. minorities, women—demand separate collective bargaining rights

Strikes, sit-ins, class action suits to enforce demands

White-collar unionization, including middle-management, professionals

Restrictions on "management rights" (to limit exercise of arbitrary authority)

"Co-ordinated (coalition) bargaining" with major companies/industries

Escalation of labor's bargaining power

Union political power overshadows that of business

D) Governance

Broader representation of other constituencies, viewpoints on Boards; "co-determination" demands by unions

Appointment of public members to Boards

Management should not have right or power to nominate directors

Greater personalization of accountability and responsibility among Board members and top managers; public financial statements to permit identification of any conflicts of interest

Broader, more explicit accounting of corporate performance (economic and social)

Picketing, disruptions at share owner meetings

Large, institutional owners use proxies, bloc voting of stock and other influences for pressure group purposes

Communications

Greater disclosure, breakdown of information (e.g. product line; EEO; pollution control)

Stronger FTC controls on advertising standards; provision for "counter-advertising"

More technical information re products (e.g. contents, performance, life, safety) should be made available

Divestiture of all press and broadcasting outlets (to free press from corporate control)

Stronger SEC backing for share owner resolutions

FCC pressures to dismember communications monopolies

F) Community & Government Relations

More gov't. intervention as a third party in almost every significant area of corporate decision making

A "populist" dominated government

Organization of political power blocs (minorities, consumers, environmentalists, elderly, poor, etc.)

More disclosure, control of businessmen's political contributions

Corporations should work more positively and closely with government in, e.g. establishing national priorities; planning, goal-setting, establishing performance criteria, controlling gov't. expenditures, taxation, policies (VAT, etc.), revenue sharing

More vocal and positive support for social reform programs

Entry into "social needs" markets (products, systems, services), even at some curtailment of profit; participate in "Marshall Plan for the Cities"

Privatizing of some gov't. services; quasi-public corporations, (e.g. COMSAT)

Contribute "know-how" to improve governmental efficiency, productivity

More generous leaves for employees to engage in community and government service

More government control directly (or by tax and subsidy) over amount, location and type of business capital investment

Loyalties among members of the business community could be severely strained by competition for government aid, by customer suits, etc.

Bureaucratic procedures become more burdensome to cope with gov't. regulations

G) Defense Production

Get out of defense work

Shift from defense domination of nat'l. budget

More subcontracting to small business

Tougher agency, GAO controls on costs

Control of profit margins

No title (or no exclusive right) to patents developed under gov't. contracts

Picketing of defense facilities

H) International Operations

Establishment of a "U.S.A., Inc." arrangement with more gov't. help, more gov't. controls

Controls on overseas investment, licensing arrangements, use of technology

Shift toward protectionism

End tax deferrals for offshore profits

Restraints on imports from offshore subsidiaries

Report wage scales paid on offshore manufacturing subsidiaries

Labeling to show country of origin

Federal standards for accounting in multinational operations

Multinational government agreements on control of MNC's; create autonomous internat'l. body to supervise multinational companies

"Coalition bargaining" by multinational unions (e.g. re transfer of operations)

Get out of Angola, South Africa, etc. or reform programs, practices there

World-wide minimum wage standards

Redistribution of corp. profit in low-wage countries

Repeal tariff incentives for creating foreign mfg. subsidiaries

Repeal tax incentives for overseas operations

CASE QUESTIONS

1. Do you have any major additions to this list? Do you feel any of the items are of relatively little significance?

2. In your opinion, which of these items will be of the greatest importance to the General Electric Company? Why?

3. What is your choice of the five demands that will have the greatest impact on the way in which General Electric operates in the next ten to fifteen years? Describe how each will affect company operations.

DISCUSSION GUIDES ON CHAPTER CONTENT

1. The author claims that a major new demand on business is to help society achieve its goals. What does this mean? If a businessman took this seriously, how might he determine what society's goals were?

2. Another major new demand on business is to improve the quality of life. What does this mean?

3. If you were asked by the president of a large company to determine what demands were being made upon his company by its constituents, how would you go about it?

4. Which of the critical public issues of the 1970s do you think will provide the greatest opportunities for GE? Which pose the greatest threats to the company?

5. Do you believe that the expectations most people have about what business should do are unrealistic.

6. How have managerial philosophies changed to keep pace with changing business conditions?

7. Do you think the Bank of America's standards for top executives are ones that all companies should adopt?

8. In what major ways are new managerial philosophies and current demands on business changing the way managers manage?

7

CORPORATE POWERS: MYTH AND REALITY

A) THE PUBLIC DIRECTOR

Robert Townsend, former chairman of the board of Avis and a critic of corporate management, recommends that guardians to protect the public interest should be placed on the boards of directors of all corporations with assets over $1 billion. His suggestion is that the federal government require such full-time board members to be seated.

Each public member would, according to Townsend, be given a fund of $1 million, to be paid by the company in question. The member would pay himself $50,000 annually and would, of course, have enough left over to pay for staff. He and his staff would be responsible for making studies of what the company was doing. Each member would be obliged to call at least two press conferences a year and to report on the company's progress or lack of it on issues of interest to the public.

Each member would have an office in the company and would have access to all meetings conducted by the company.

A group of distinguished national legislators who had occupied vice-presidential positions or higher in nonfamily-owned businesses would choose for these jobs people who met at least four criteria: (1) knowledgeable about large company behavior, with at least ten years' experience in line jobs; (2) wealthy enough to be objective and uncorruptible; (3) energetic; and (4) reasonably intelligent. Once such a pool of people was formed, public directors would be chosen for a particular corporation by lot and at random. After selection, they would rotate each four years.[1]

CASE QUESTIONS

1. Argue the foregoing case pro and con.

2. Are such guardians as Townsend recommends to be viewed as the final word on whether or not the company is serving the public interest? Argue the case pro and con.

3. Can you suggest alternative methods to insure that the public interest is met by large companies?

References

"Arthur Goldberg on Public Directors," *Business and Society Review/ Innovation,* Spring 1973, pp. 35-39: "Responses to the Goldberg Proposal on Public Directors," *Business and Society Review*, Summer 1973, pp. 37-43.

B) ARROW, INC.

Arrow, Inc., is a large conglomerate with major interests in two fields, aerospace and petroleum. Arrow-Jet, Inc., a subsidiary, produces engines for aerospace and defense. Oil & Gas, Inc., also a subsidiary of Arrow, is involved in drilling, refining, and marketing petroleum products.

In 1968, James Sherman, president of Arrow, developed a strategy to strengthen long-range gains. At that time, Arrow's per share earnings were $3.17, the highest ever earned, and the stock was

---

[1] See Robert Townsend,. "Let's install Public Directors," *Business and Society Review*, Spring 1972, pp. 69-70. For a comparable but more conservative proposal, see John A. Patton, "The Working Director— Management Middleman," *The Conference Board Record*, October 1972, pp. 36-39.

trading for $47. From the stockholders' point of view, things looked like they couldn't be better. However, Sherman was concerned about future profits. He knew he had trouble in both of the subsidiaries, and this would affect long-run growth and profits for Arrow.

Sales were declining at Arrow-Jet because of cutbacks both in aerospace and defense spending. The fastest growing market in aerospace was engines for private and executive jets, and this market was desirable because of the lack of competition. The major jet engine producers in the United States were Pratt & Whitney and General Electric, both of which concentrated on big engines for commercial aircraft. Sherman wanted to use the subsidiary's technology to enter into the civilian executive jet and helicopter market. To do this, however, Arrow-Jet would have to develop three advanced jet engines. This program would take five years and cost $50 million. The engines proposed would consume half as much fuel as existing engines, and they would give intercontinental capabilities to the small executive jet. Once certified they would command a sizable share of the market. The problem was that for five years the subsidiary would have to operate at the break-even point and write off the research and development costs for a number of years thereafter. Sherman's strategy was to write off the costs as they were experienced, which would cause a loss in current profits but at the same time take the burden off future earnings.

Oil & Gas, Inc., was also having serious problems in identifying future growth opportunities. The company had been operating primarily in California, but these reserves were declining. New drilling fields had to be developed, and Sherman's plan was to enter into offshore drilling to find new reserves for the subsidiary. At that time, the greatest opportunities were off the coast of Louisiana. After selecting various drilling sites, Oil & Gas spent a tremendous amount of money developing the area. The company made several substantial discoveries, but as of this writing there has been no return on the investment. The wells will start pumping soon and Sherman feels that the future returns will be more than sufficient to merit the expenditure. In the California operation, it was necessary to drill new wells and inject water to force the oil to rise. This, too, was a very expensive program and yielded no returns for two years. To further aggravate matters, the subsidiary had to write down some of its property and assets. All these events reduced current profits.

Sherman made a major decision in 1968 to reorganize Oil & Gas, Inc. The company sold its two refineries and 3,000 service stations. World developments had caused the price of crude oil to rise, thus it was now more profitable to sell the oil unrefined. The service stations were costing $2.5 million a year to operate, and they would not be needed after the refineries were sold. This action provided the needed capital for the offshore project and the California program.

By 1972, because of Sherman's strategy, the price of Arrow's stock had fallen to $18, and the per share earning dropped to a low of $2.68. In a public statement, Sherman declared that he knew in 1968 that the earnings were going to suffer. But, he said, the firm was now in a better position to earn future profits.

CASE QUESTIONS

1. Was Sherman obliged to warn the stockholders in 1968 that earnings were going to suffer if his plans were implemented?

2. Argue the case for and against public forecasts of earnings. See Timothy D. Schellhardt, "The Argument for Profit Forecasts . . . "and John A. Prestbo, " . . . and an Expert Who Says They Won't Work," *The Wall Street Journal*, 11 December 1972. R. Gene Brown, "Ethical and Other Problems in Publishing Financial Forecasts," *Financial Analysts Journal*, March-April 1972, pp. 38-45, 86-87; James Don Edwards and Carl S. Warren, "Management Forecasts: The SEC and Financial Executives," *MSU Business Topics,* Winter 1974, pp. 51-56.

DISCUSSION GUIDES ON CHAPTER CONTENT

1. What is power? What types of powers do large corporations have?

2. It is frequently said that large corporations exercise too much power. Is there any generally acceptable way to measure the power of a large company?

3. Do you think that the classification of the literature on corporate power presented by the author is useful? Explain.

4. A number of writers assert there is a monolithic power in the combination of giant corporations and the government, and that this power completely dominates consumers and individuals. Is this a myth or does it reflect reality? Explain and justify your position.

5. Do you think that the majority of corporations in the United States use what power they have in a reasonably responsible way? Explain.

6. What is the issue of legitimacy? Is it important?

MIND-STRETCHING QUESTIONS————————————

1. The proxy ballot has been alleged to produce "automatic self-perpetuating oligarchies." If this is so, why has it not been replaced as a method of electing management? Can you propose some alternatives?

2. Is the large corporation losing or gaining power today? Explain.

III
BUSINESS AND CHANGING VALUES

8

CHANGING VALUES IN SOCIETY

A) CONSOLIDATED INDUSTRIES FORECASTS CHANGING SOCIAL VALUES AND DEMANDS

Consolidated Industries is one of the largest manufacturing companies in the world. The major products that account for the bulk of its sales are chemicals, steel, aircraft, trucks, and consumer-durable goods. It also produces a wide variety of other commodities. Among these are special metals, light agricultural equipment, small office appliances, medical instruments, and scientific toys.

In recent years, the top management of the company has been attacked with unusual force by such various groups as the Sierra Club, Ralph Nader's "raiders," local communities in which the company does business, and student activists.

This company prides itself on the skill with which it develops long-range plans and has asserted repeatedly that its great success has been due in no small part to the quality of these plans. Top management has decided, however, that if its plans are to be effective in the future it is necessary for the company to have a much better understanding of those changing social values that will particularly affect it.

CASE QUESTION ————————————————————————

You are hired as a consultant to advise the company on how to forecast changing social values and the consequent demands that will be of major concern to the company over the next ten years. What would you suggest? (See Clark C. Abt, "Forecasting Future Social Needs," *The Futurist,* February 1971, pp. 20-21.)

B) TWO-WAY TELEVISION AND SOCIETY'S VALUES

Two-way television with a camera in the home, hooked to a central processing center by cable that permits verbal and visual communications in either direction, is now feasible and is being tried in selected geographical areas. At the present time, however, the costs of such a system are high for the average homeowner. It is estimated, for example, that the costs to a subscriber would be $20 a month for service, with an initial equipment cost to each homeowner of about $1,000.

Suppose, however, that the cost of such a system could be drastically reduced so that the majority of homeowners in the United States could afford such a system. Most of the homeowners could choose, if they wished, to stay home all of the time. A housewife could visit stores, friends, and business associates yet never leave the house. Children could get their education at home. If people became ill they could contact the family doctor and get his diagnosis and prescribed treatment without leaving home. Entertainment, of course, could be had at home. Furthermore, with the use of supplemental monitoring screens and sensors located around the house, automatic warning signals could be relayed to appropriate authorities in case of trouble.

CASE QUESTION ————————————————————————

1. Assuming that such a system was installed in the great majority of houses in the United States, what primary changes in business practice and individual relationships, would you expect? What might be some secondary changes in society's values? Analyze the implications of such changing values for business. (For some thoughts on the impacts of new, cheap communications technology, see J. L. Hult, "Cheap Communications," *The Futurist*, June 1969, pp. 70-72. "The Impact of Interactive Television on Life," *The Futurist*, October 1973, pp. 200-201: For difficulties in making such forecasts, see Richard N. Farmer, "Looking Back At Looking Forward," *Business Horizons*, February 1973, pp. 21-28.)

DISCUSSION GUIDES ON CHAPTER CONTENT————————

1. What is meant by values?

2. Appraise the worth of Figure 8—1 in explaining how values change in a society. Do you think that technology is a basic cause of changing values? How does this happen? What other major forces alter the values that people hold? Compare these forces with those of the past.

3. There is conflicting evidence about the extent to which values have changed in society today. Do you agree or disagree with the author's appraisal of the situation?

4. If you were asked to forecast changing values that might have an important impact on business, how would you go about doing it?

5. What impact will perceptible changing values have on the business-society interrelationship over the next ten to twenty years?

MIND-STRETCHING QUESTIONS————————————

1. What forces do you think could accelerate the changing values of today's youth and which forces could slow down the rate of change?

2. How do you feel about surveys that attempt to describe the attitudes of "average" people? Can values be measured accurately?

3. A survey on the value systems of young people conducted by Louis Harris found that "like their fathers, young people are willing to work, but they want to enjoy what they do and move around less." Do you agree? What is the impact on business?

9

BUSINESS IDEOLOGIES

DISCUSSION GUIDES ON CHAPTER CONTENT————————

1. What are the fundamental distinctions between basic value systems and ideologies?
2. Are business ideologies nothing more than public relations statements, or do they really perform some useful purposes? Explain.
3. Contrast the classical business ideology with the new managerial creed. What are the basic differences between the two?
4. Identify some of the major gaps in the business ideology and explain why they have not been filled.
5. Are there any major inconsistencies and/or conflicts that you have detected among the business ideologies?

MIND-STRETCHING QUESTIONS ————————————

1. Heilbroner thinks that the business ideology is insufficiently inspirational to be of much use in the trying days ahead. What do you think about this?
2. Many businessmen in the latter part of the nineteenth century embraced the doctrine of Social Darwinism, and in their economic activities, they often exploited both people and society. Should they be judged on the basis of values and ideologies that existed at the time or according to our present-day values and modern ideologies?

10

THE SOCIAL RESPONSIBILITIES OF BUSINESS

A) MEETING AT MULTINATIONAL INDUSTRIES

You are about to attend a conference in the New York offices of Multinational Industries. The meeting has been called by the chairman of the board and chief executive officer of the corporation. He opens the meeting with these words:

> Ladies and gentlemen, welcome to Multinational Industries. I have asked each of you to come here today to discuss the social programs of Multinational Industries. At the table in front of each of you is a statement that covers our policies concerning philanthropic giving and the programs that we have supported over the years. As you will see, our cash contributions amounted to approximately $1.5 million in the past year. In addition to this statement you have another that describes those socially oriented programs not handled by our philanthropic committee. As you can see we have been doing many things that, I think, refelct our social concern.
>
> But my purpose in calling you here was not to try to impress you with what we are doing. Nor is it to persuade you that we are doing a good job. We may be or we may not be. I am not sure. Some people tell me we are not doing enough. Others tell me in no uncertain terms we are doing too much.
>
> I have also placed before you our last annual report, which tells you a little about our company. Our total sales last year were over $1.5

billion. We employed over 40,000 people here in the United States and approximately 25,000 in 27 foreign countries. Our principal business is making consumer durable goods like refrigerators, stoves, air conditioning equipment, and so on. But we are an integrated producer, which means we have steel mills, metal refineries, component producers, and so on. I won't bother you with other details now. So, let's move on.

Sitting around this table are the president of our company, several group vice-presidents, the controller, one of our major stockholders, a small stockholder chosen at random from our list of stockholders, the president of the Urban Coalition here in New York, several professors, a member of our board of directors, a representative from Mr. Ralph Nader's group in Washington, two students from Columbia University, our legal counsel, and representatives from several countries in which we do business.

We in business have heard a lot about social responsibilities. Frankly, I am not sure what they are. I think it would be helpful to us if this group would exchange views about what our social responsibilities really are. I personally am convinced we must conduct ourselves in a socially responsible way. I think we are, but there does not seem to be agreement about the matter here in the company or in the various demands made upon us by different groups in the community. This meeting, I hope, will clarify for us what we should be doing.

CASE:

You were permitted to make a tape recording of the meeting. When you returned home, you had a transcription made, and the following are selected excerpts from the tape. The transcriber, of course, was unable to identify the individuals speaking so they are referred to in numerical order.

1) "It seems to me that if your company is going to do business in our country it should make every effort to help us to achieve our aspirations. As you know our per capita income is about $300 per year. Our goal is to raise this to $3,000 a year in ten years."

2) "But Mr. Batu, there is no way our company can do this. We can help by bringing investments and jobs to your country. But our stockholders must insist that the return on investment in your country be as high as or higher than any alternative use of the money. To do otherwise would be financially irresponsible."

3) "There need be no necessary conflict between making profits and pursuing social programs. Indeed, I can conceive of cases where a company's social programs may actually increase short-range as well as long-range profits."

4) "American capitalism is based on the idea that managers' first responsibility is to stockholders. In fulfilling this obligation an intelligent management will give consideration to other elements in society that bear on the task of representing stockholder interests."

5) "That's too simplistic. I say business's first concern must be the consumer. If it can satisfy the consumer, that will take care of stockholder interests. I say the primary goal of business is not profits per se, but freedom to compete in the marketplace in meeting consumer desires."

6) "The word 'responsibility' gives me trouble. Who says that business has a social responsibility? Basically, responsibility means that someone is obligated to do something or give something of value because of value received. There is a sort of implied contract here. I see no contract between business and society other than to produce goods and services for consumers, within the law and the interests of consumers, in such a way as to improve stockholder interests."

7) "You're wrong. There *is* an implied contract. Society gives a business a franchise to do things society wants. If it does not produce, the franchise or implied contract will be changed."

8) "I don't buy that. The purpose of business is to be efficient in using resources at its disposal in meeting the demands of society for goods and services at prices consumers are willing to pay. If it does that well, it will optimize stockholder wealth. The only obligation of business, therefore, is to optimize stockholder wealth."

9) "We have witnessed over the past ten or so years failure after failure in government's efforts to solve our city problems, to clean up the welfare mess, to support black capitalism, to provide minimum housing for our people, to

eliminate poverty, and so on and on. I'm sick of government's ineptness. There is only one resource left. That is business. I say it is business's job to solve society's problems. The people can't. The government can't. There is nothing left but business."

10) "Business has social responsibilities commensurate with its power. The more powerful it is, the greater are its social responsibilities. Business is powerful and should do these things."

11) "Some of you seem to be trying to make business do things it shouldn't. Social responsibilities are nothing but a fad. It is nothing more than the old-fashioned idea of good citizenship. I think business should be a good citizen and that's that."

12) "You're wrong. In Japan, for instance, once you begin work for a company you have a life-time contract. The company agrees to take care of you. That's my idea of social responsibility."

13) "If we push this idea of social responsibility too far, we will encourage executives to indulge their own vanities in doing good for the community, at the expense of the stockholder. If this happens, business will become less efficient. We will lose the goose that lays the golden egg."

14) "That's applesauce! I know of many managers with a high social conscience, and yet their profits are up. Maybe the two go together—both are inherent in better management. In the long run, the best thinking about social responsibilities will also be the best business thinking."

15) "Business should stick to business. If society thinks that business ought to be doing something other than sticking to its own knitting, then pressures ought to be placed on government. If the political consensus says business should do it, it is up to government to tell business what to do."

16) "I don't know what the argument is all about. Business has always been socially responsible and always will be, so long as there is competition and we live in a free society."

17) "Your company does business in South Africa. I don't think you are being socially responsible in being there. Your mere presence there condones apartheid."

18) "I think you are wrong there. We stay in South Africa not only because it is profitable but because we can and have been able to do many things to improve the life of the blacks whom we employ. In addition we have community projects that help other blacks. I can give you convincing details on the benefits of our presence there."

19) "Our company also has contributed mightily to the United States by the mere fact that we have grown from a small company back in 1935 to one with sales over $1.5 billion. We give jobs to tens of thousands of people and provide solid investments for the capital of pension funds, individual investors, and foundations. This is what I call social responsibility."

20) "You also do business with the Pentagon. War is the curse of mankind, and any corporation that directly or indirectly supports it is not being socially responsible."

21) "As a major stockholder in this company, I don't mind if management uses a relatively small amount of my money to undertake "do-good" projects. I don't want it to determine how much of my earnings should be spent on such projects. I want to do that."

22) "Well, what is a small amount? Company profits last year were 12 percent of sales, before taxes. This was about average for your industry. Your philanthropic contributions, however, were only $1,150,000, which was 1.3 percent of net profits. The Revenue Act of 1935 permits you to deduct 5 percent of net profits for charitable contributions. Why did you not contribute up to what the law allows?"

23) "For one reason, profits were very low the year before last, and we did not declare a stockholder dividend that year. We felt that last year we should favor stockholders because of previous lean years."

24) "There is a major dimension to this discussion that has not been mentioned. It is: if a public policy is being debated and the president of the company thinks it will adversely affect his stockholders, even though it may benefit the community generally (e.g. pollution standards are excessively high in the judgment of the president), is the president being socially responsible if he takes a strong stand against the measure? To take an extreme position, suppose adherence to the regulation will lodge such a heavy burden on the company that it has no recourse but to close its doors."

25) "I believe the corporation has no business in politics. It should take no stand on public issues, one way or another. To do so distorts our very system of government. But people in the corporation acting as individuals, and not as representatives of the company, should be active in politics."

26) "Everyone seems to be missing the point about social responsibilities. You all are talking about making some incremental changes in the way business operates. I say we need a complete and thorough change in the entire business structure. Small changes are not going to erase the almost criminal disregard for consumer safety, the bias against minorities in hiring, the vast unemployment when business conditions are low, massive poverty, excessive profits, brutal use of power, and so on. There has got to be a complete house cleaning. Solving our social problems will not be met by business without really radical, if not revolutionary, change in the way business operates."

27) "I can't let that go unchallenged. I do not know what you have in mind. But the radical surgery you seem to demand will make things worse, not better."

28) "We have been talking at high levels of abstraction for the most part. OK, business does have social responsibilities. But what are they in a specific instance? Who decides? The chairman of the board? Ralph Nader? You? Me? Our biggest customer? The FTC? The SEC? Dissident stockholders?

Majority stockholders? And, furthermore, once we do something that is supposed to be in the realm of social responsibility—whatever that is—who is going to measure whether we have been performing our social responsibilities acceptably? Again, go over the list of names I have just mentioned. Whose appraisal shall we accept?"

29) "There is here today a misunderstanding of the meaning of an abstract principle and an operational imperative. There is nothing inconsistent with saying that there is a general consensus that business does have social obligations, but there is no consensus about what they are in operational terms. That is something for each individual business to decide in light of many factors."

30) "I'm not too concerned about social responsibilities. This is a big flap today, much confusion, much uncertainty, a fad. Once managers figure out how to institutionalize social responsibilities so as to satisfy the public and also the stockholders, which they will, the issue will disappear."

31) "Whatever the outcome of the issues discussed here today, I insist that we must not allow the drive for efficiency in our business institutions to erode. The demands for business productivity, with labor, are too great. We have an affluent society, but it won't be affluent very long if business becomes a social club instead of an efficient productive machine."

CASE QUESTIONS

1. What major different philosophies about the role of business in society do you detect in this discussion?

2. Who do you think is right and who do you think is wrong in the above discussion?

3. What is the case for business having no social responsibilities? See Milton Freidman, "The Social Responsibility of Business Is to Increase its Profits," *New York Times Magazine*, 13 September 1970, pp. 33, 122-126.

4. Can you make a case for business having social responsibilities? *Social Responsibilities of Business Corporations* (New York: Committee for Economic Development, June 1971).

5. What do you consider to be an acceptable definition of business's social responsibilities for the present? What do you think the generally acceptable definition will be in twenty years?

B) SOUTH AFRICAN APARTHEID AND POLAROID

On January 13, 1971, the Polaroid Corporation ran a full page statement in the *Los Angeles Times* (Part 1, p. 8) responding to critics who condemned the company for selling its products in South Africa. It had been asserted that so long as Polaroid sold in South Africa, its very presence there supported the South African government and its policies of racial separation and subjugation of the blacks. A number of other American companies doing business in South Africa had been similarly condemned.

Polaroid's South African sales amount to less than one-half of 1 percent of its worldwide business. At the time of the article Polaroid sold its products in South Africa through an independent firm, Frank and Hirsch. Sales of this company were around $1.5 million a year, and it hired 210 white and 155 black workers. Polaroid formed a committee of both black and white employees to study this question: Is it right or wrong to do business in South Africa? The newspaper statement said the first conclusion was arrived at quickly and unanimously, namely: "We abhor *apartheid*, the national policy of South Africa." The committee visited South Africa and, after talking with many people, came to the conclusion that Polaroid should stay in South Africa but undertake the following experimental program. First, the company would take steps with its distributors and suppliers to improve dramatically salaries and benefits for nonwhite employees. Second, Polaroid's business associates would be obliged "to initiate a well-defined program to train nonwhite employees for important jobs within their companies." Third, the company would use some of its profits earned in South Africa to encourage black education. Fourth, Polaroid (which does not have investments in South Africa and does not at present intend to change that policy) would investigate "the possibilities of creating a black-managed company in one or more of the free black African nations." The statement concluded:

> How can we presume to concern ourselves with the problems of another country? Whatever the practices elsewhere, South Africa alone articulates a policy exactly contrary to everything we feel our company stands for. We cannot participate passively in such a political system. Nor can we ignore it. That is why we have undertaken this experimental program.

CASE QUESTIONS

1: Argue the case for and against Polaroid's decision to stay in South Africa. See John Blashill, "The Proper Role of U.S. Corporations in South Africa," *Fortune*, July 1972, pp. 49-52, 89-92.

2. Can you suggest any guidelines for American companies doing business in foreign countries to follow in attempting to change major government policies without alienating their hosts?

C) ROLE-PLAYING SOCIAL RESPONSIBILITIES OF UNITED STATES STEEL CORPORATION

Divide the class into groups to develop the following positions on the subject: What are the major social responsibilities of the United States Steel Corporation?

A. Your position on this question is that of the chairman of the board of directors of U.S. Steel.

B. Your position on this question is that of Ralph Nader.

C. Your position on this question is that of Senator Proxmire.

D. Your position on this question is that of a prominent black leader.

E. Your position on this question is that of Alexander Devarro, a twenty-year foreman in the Gary, Indiana sheet-strip mill.

D) DUPONT'S "GIVEAWAY" AND SOCIAL RESPONSIBILITIES

Not long ago, *Fortune* magazine published an article entitled "DuPont 'Gave Away' Billions—and Prospered," by Gilbert Burck.[1] The article was written to offset an attack on DuPont in the book *The Company State*, written by two of Nader's "raiders," namely James Phelan and Robert Pozen. The report bitterly criticized DuPont's relations with the State of Delaware and complained that financial help from the company should have been far greater than it was.

In the article, Burck noted that from 1960 through 1972 the national consumer price index rose 41 percent and the wholesale price index advanced 25 percent, but the averge price of DuPont products declined 24 percent. Now, said Burck, if the prices of DuPont's products had not fallen but had moved upward with national price indexes, the volume of DuPont's sales in 1972 would have been $5.5 billion. As a matter of actual fact, DuPont's sales in 1972 were $4.2 billion. "The $1.3 billion gap," said Burck,

> represents the latest installment of a vast transfer of productivity-created wealth, a true social dividend paid to consumers of clothing, carpeting, synthetic rubbers, plastics, fungicides, pharmaceuticals, and other products. Compared to the myriad benefits from its "parochial" business, anything the company could do to ameliorate Delaware's social problems, impressive as such an effort might be, pales into insignificance.[2]

CASE QUESTION

1. Argue the case pro and con for *Fortune*'s point of view. (For further details see James Phelan and Robert Pozen, *The Company State*. New York: Grossman Publishers, 1972.)

[1] Gilbert Burck, "DuPont 'Gave Away' Billions—and Prospered," (*Fortune*, January 1973, pp. 68-75; 164-168).

[2] *Ibid.* p. 68.

E) EXCERPTS FROM FORD MOTOR COMPANY PUBLIC AFFAIRS POLICY STATEMENT

Ford Motor Company policy in the public affairs field is based on three fundamental premises:

First—"The Company recognizes that a democratic form of government, a free enterprise system, and a healthy and improving free society are essential to the accomplishment of its corporate objectives and that governmental actions and social and economic developments vitally affect the Company's operations and interests."

Second—"The Company also recognizes that a basic premise of our democratic system is the acceptance by all citizens, individual and corporate alike, of a responsibility to participate in its functions."

Third—"The Company believes, therefore, that it is essential to its own interests and to the proper discharge of its responsibilities as a corporate citizen to participate actively in maintaining a sound social, economic and political environment."

These principles underlie Company policy in four closely related areas—Civic Affairs, Governmental Relationships, Urban Affairs, and Contributions.

Civic Affairs

"The Company will maintain an active interest in the general welfare of our society and participate in programs and citizen efforts concerned with social and civic improvement. The Company is particularly interested in the social, civic and physical betterment of the communities in which it operates. The Company's community relations committees, which consist of key members of management in each plant community, have important responsibilities in this respect. They are the chief medium at the local level for expressing and implementing (Company public affairs) policies. . . . "

Governmental Relationships

"The Company will maintain an active interest in governmental affairs and will give effective expression of its position on public issues affecting its interests. Its position on such issues will be

Reprinted from the National Industrial Conference Board, Studies in Public Affairs, No. 5 and used with permission.

determined on the basis of an assessment of both its own legitimate interests and the requirements of sound public policy. The Company will take no partisan political position nor will it employ its resources for partisan political purposes. . . . "

(MANAGEMENT AND EMPLOYEE PARTICIPATION). "Members of management are expected to maintain an active interest in public affairs and, as appropriate, to participate in the formulation and representation of Company positions on issues affecting its interests. Management members are also expected to do their part in fulfilling the Company's responsibilities as a corporate citizen and to consider participation in constructive civic and community activities on behalf of the Company as part of their management responsibilities. . . . The Company encourages its employees, as individual citizens, to participate in social and civic improvement efforts and in political and governmental affairs."

Urban Affairs

"Our goal is to do all we realistically can to give people who have been held back by prejudice and poverty a chance to earn a decent life. This goal is entirely consistent with our responsibility to conduct our businesss soundly and profitably. . . . By helping people to help themselves, we can help to cure a social cancer that threatens the vitality and peace of the communities where we do business, to reduce the costs of welfare and crime and the taxes we all pay, and to enlarge the markets for our products. . . . Our Company and our country will face far greater problems if we and other employers fail to do what we can to help disadvantaged people overcome the barriers that keep them from sharing in the abundance of the American economy. . . . The achievement of genuinely equal opportunity is the most urgent task our nation faces."

Contributions

"It is the policy of the Company to contribute to selected charitable, educational and civic improvement organizations and to give financial assistance to selected trade or business organizations. . . . The Company regards itself as a citizen of the communities in which it maintains facilities and employs people. As such it recognizes the importance of supporting worthy community institutions, programs, and endeavors."

CASE QUESTIONS————————————————————————

1. Mr. Henry Ford II, chairman of the Ford Motor Company, asks you to review this policy statement and make recommendations to him for change where you think change is appropriate. What would you recommend?

2. Develop for the company more detailed policies covering each of the three main areas covered in the statement.

F) UNIVERSITY PROXY POLICY

In April 1971 Stanford University trustees agreed to consider social, economic, and political factors, as well as rate of return, in making investments in, and giving proxy for, decisions concerning corporate securities. A number of other universities have also decided to do the same thing. In mid-1971 the Regents of the University of California decided to form a committee to consider whether corporate practices in such questions as minority hiring, pollution, and consumer product quality, should influence the university's investment policies. On one side were those who agreed with the student who observed: "I find it intolerable that the Regents of this tax-supported institution uncritically back the policies of a corporation guilty of vast environmental pollution and other socially deleterious actions in this state." One Regent said, however, that the Regents were responsible to see that university investments were financially sound and yielded the highest rates possible consistent with risk. He added further that the investment policies of the university had been questioned because the returns were not as high as they should have been. Another Regent said he was delighted to see pressures being brought on corporations to be more socially responsible, but that he was bothered on two counts: (1) Should a university use its investment influence in this fashion? and (2) Could the university make a proper evaluation of each proposal brought before it?

In October 1973 the committee rejected the proposal to consider moral and social factors in voting stock proxies on securities owned by the university. As a result of the negative conclusion, the university now automatically votes all its proxies with management and expresses its displeasure with a company only by selling stock in the firm.

Two issues apparently were uppermost in the decision. First, there was the assumption that application of social concerns in decision-making costs the investor money, and this, thereby, reduces return on the investment. As one Regent put it, the university has a "fiduciary responsibility" to insure that investments earn the maximum profit possible, regardless of a corporation's social policy. Other Regents who favored the proposal said that a healthy business community will exist and flourish only where there is a healthy social community.

The second issue concerned methods to evaluate social performance of companies. President Charles Hitch recommended that a Regents investment committee be formed to hold open hearings to solicit opinions from faculty, staff, students, and others on proxy issues that related to broad public interest and/or questions of corporate social responsibility. Those Regents who opposed the proposal said that corporations should be given an opportunity to speak on issues where they were concerned and that to assure this would create an unwieldy process.

CASE QUESTIONS

1. What major issues do you discern in the question the Regents asked its committee to answer?

2. Argue the following case pro and con: A university should use its investment power to influence corporations to act in a socially responsible fashion. (See Burton G. Malkiel and Richard E. Quandt, "Moral Issues in Investment Policy," *Harvard Business Review*, March-April 1971, pp. 37-47. John G. Simon, Charles W. Powers, and Jon P. Gunnemann, *The Ethical Investor* (New Haven: Yale University Press, 1972). Eli Goldston, "A Review of 'The Ethical Investor,' " *Foundation News*, July-August 1972, pp. 30-36. "University Investments—The Ethical Endowment," *Business Today*, May 1973, pp. 19-25.)

3. If you are in favor of a university using its portfolio to exert moral pressure on corporations, what criteria and what type implementation process would you suggest?

4. Is your position in questions 2 and 3 the same for a private investment fund?

G) WILLIAM ROBERTSON

William Robertson, a senior vice-president for the Chicago Steel Corporation, wrote an article for a national magazine deploring the fact that his company, together with other corporations in the Chicago area, had not done enough to avoid polluting Lake Michigan. Furthermore, Robertson declared, they ought to take the lead in really getting everyone involved to clean up the lake. He mapped out a clean-up program costing hundreds of millions of dollars.

Some of the customers of the corporation became annoyed at this blast, because they felt the net result would be demands by the government to undertake costly antipollution programs that the customers could not afford. The more disgruntled customers actually canceled orders.

The top management of the corporation felt that Robertson had gone much too far. They felt they had done much to avoid polluting the lake and that this publicity denigrated what they had done. Moreover, it promised not only to get them involved in very costly programs but to embroil the company in all sorts of unnecessary political and social battles. As a result, the chairman and chief executive officer asked Robertson never again to comment publicly without clearing his statement in advance with him.

Robertson resigned, saying that he refused to give up his responsibilities as a citizen. This action was considered too drastic by the top management, who suggested that Robertson manage for a year or so a new plant in France, which the corporation had recently acquired under his leadership. Robertson refused the position, saying that his conscience would not permit him to evade the issue in this fashion.

Robertson's friends viewed the matter in different ways. One executive said: "I have devoted my life to this corporation and its well-being is a matter of major significance to me. If I have to give up a few things to support the company, that is a small price to pay. My compensation is high and covers many things I may not like." Another said: "As long as Bill works for the company, it seems to me he ought to accept the company position and not stick a knife in its back." Another took a more philosophical position, saying: "No one has forced Bill to take his job. But, so long as he has the job, he cannot, as a major officer of the company, separate himself from it. He enjoys free speech under the Constitution, but the Constitution does not protect his job. The company has a right to defend itself from public statements of its officers if it wishes to do so."

CASE QUESTIONS

1. To what extent should a corporation protect its image? Should an executive be asked to follow a prescribed company position on a public issue, even if it deprives him of his right to speak out as he sees fit?

2. Comment on the moral issues raised in viewpoints expressed by Robertson's friends.

H) DUPONT'S REFUSAL TO SUPPLY CERTAIN INFORMATION

February 11, 1972

TO: Subcommittee on Monopoly of the Senate Select Committee on Small Business

FROM: Ralph Nader

Re refusal by the DuPont Company to provide certain information.

Jim Phelan, director of the student task force that produced the report, "DuPont in Delaware: The Company State," had the following experiences in seeking information from the company as a stockholder and a citizen:

1. DuPont refused to provide any data on air emissions and water effluent either in the aggregate or on a plant-by-plant basis, on the grounds that the former was confidential; the latter not collected. Note that in order to complete a permit application under the 1899 Refuse Act, plant-by-plant data on water effluents must be filed and must be public.

2. DuPont refused to provide any data on minority employment even though aggregate data is supplied to the Equal Employment Opportunity Commission. Company spokesmen maintained that they do not keep the data on a plant-by-plant basis. Two plant managers, apparently unaware that they did not keep those figures, provided them to the task force.

Reprinted from U.S. Senate Select Committee on Small Business, *Role of Giant Corporations: Hearings Before the Subcommittee on Monopoly,* 92nd Cong., 1st Sess., Part 2A, 9 & 12 November 1971, pp. 1218-1219.

3. DuPont refused to supply the company telephone directory.

4. DuPont refused to reveal the total of company deposits in state banks.

5. DuPont refused to give a list of major stockholders and foundations with company stock, even though virtually all corporations with more than 500 stockholders are required to file at least a partial list of major stockholders with the Securities and Exchange Commission.

6. DuPont refused to disclose its membership in trade associations on the grounds that it would be too burdensome to compile the data.

7. DuPont reported aggregate figures on frequency of work accidents, but refused to report it on a plant-by-plant basis.

8. DuPont refused to reveal the number of employees in each plant, but did so in two cases. Company spokesmen indicated that this could enable competitors to discover secret manufacturing processes (e.g., by learning the number of engineers at work on a given project).

9. DuPont refused to disclose the value added per plant on the double grounds that it was a trade secret and that, in any case, the information was not kept.

10. DuPont refused to provide any information on the employment of women other than to say that their promotion policies with respect to women were the same as for all other employees.

11. DuPont would not disclose the company's policy statement containing guidelines for employee political participation.

12. DuPont refused to provide a list of company investments in Delaware on the grounds that the information was not maintained on a state basis. When asked the capitalized or book value of their lands and buildings in Delaware, company spokesmen said these figures are confidential.

CASE QUESTIONS

1. Should DuPont be forced to supply this type of information to anyone wanting it? Argue the issue pro and con.

2. What specific information should United States companies be obliged to make public that they are not now required by law to disclose publicly? (For some details, see Hearings.)

3. Through library research, support this assertion: American businesses disclose to the public far greater and more detailed operational information than businesses located in any other country of the world.

I) ELGIN SLED COMPANY

I. C. Slope inherited a small sled company from his father, who in turn, had inherited the plant from his father. Not content to simply continue the production of children's sleds, Slope decided to move into the production of snowmobiles. He was a graduate of the School of Engineering of Iowa State University, and with the help of two classmates who also were engineers, he developed a highly successful line of snowmobiles.

The headquarters of the company were located in Bristol Creek, Iowa, a comparatively small town of 50,000 people that had not grown very much in the last decade. The town had only two very small parks, no museums, no live theaters, and few other recreational facilities.

Elgin Sled's sales in 1972 were $25 million, and profits were a hefty 20 percent of sales after taxes. The company had not failed to earn money after World War II and had consistently paid dividends throughout this period. The board of directors was composed of seven officers of the company besides Slope, plus the president of a small insurance company with headquarters in Bristol Creek and the president of a small quarry located in the area. Both were old family friends of the Slope family, but neither held much Elgin Sled stock.

I. C. Slope was a public-spirited individual and decided that his company, because it was the largest employer in town, should do something about the "cultural attractions" of the town. While he himself had a sizable fortune, he felt that both he and his company should assume more social responsibilities. One of the first things he did was to build a recreational facility for youngsters, to which he personally contributed $1 million, and Elgin Sled gave an equal amount. He then decided that it would be beneficial to the citizens of Bristol Creek if they had a modern museum of art. To this he contributed $1 million and the Elgin Sled Company gave $2 million. Following these two moves, he was acclaimed a local hero, and the Elgin Sled Company received national attention for its public spiritedness. This was followed by a pledge to build a modern opera house, which was to be a gift from the Elgin Sled Company and its employees. The gift of $6 million was made by the company, but the employees were not asked to contribute; the gift was made in their name. To eliminate substandard housing in the town, Elgin Sled decided to build small, prefabricated houses that would sell at or slightly below cost.

Entranced with these activities, Slope spent more and more of his time and money—and that of his company—on public affairs. As a result, his snowmobile sales, which accounted for the bulk of the company's sales and profits, fell drastically. While Slope was engaged in public affairs, the distribution system of Elgin Sled deterioriated, and its revitalization became an obvious need to everyone but Slope. In addition, competitors had introduced new features in their snowmobiles that made their products more attractive than Elgin's. To make matters worse, the Prefabricated Housing Division proved to be a major cash drain on the company.

The net result was that Elgin's cash position fell to alarming levels, and the company was forced to borrow heavily from banks and to float bonds. Although Elgin was able to secure this financing, it could not do it on terms favorable to Elgin. To conserve cash and to cut costs, the company reduced employment for the first time since the depression. The work force reduction amounted to around 20 percent of total employment.

To conserve cash further, the company reluctantly decided to sell its Prefabricated Housing Division. A buyer was found, but the sale was made under terms that forced Elgin to write off a sizable loss. Stockholder's equity was reduced by 25 percent as a result.

Some dissident stockholders threatened to sue the board of directors for failure to act as trustees in their interests. There were many who felt that Elgin Sled probably could not survive its current difficulties without going into bankruptcy. Others, however, put their faith in the brilliance that I. C. Slope and his top managers had displayed in the past. And there were those in Bristol Creek who continued to praise the public spiritedness of I. C. Slope and the Elgin Sled Company.

CASE QUESTIONS

1. What is your view of the way I. C. Slope pursued his public affairs program?
2. How do you think different "stakeholders" in the Elgin

Sled Company might appraise Slope's "social responsibilities"?
3. Assuming that the Elgin Sled Company survives and once again becomes a profit-making concern, what specific policies would you suggest that it adopt to guide its public affairs programs?

DISCUSSION GUIDES ON CHAPTER CONTENT ————————

1. "It is often said that the old classical managerial responsibility was to maximize profit in the short run. The idea that managers had to balance the interests of constituents was accepted because this was needed to maximize profits in the long run. So also is the idea of social responsibility accepted, since it is necessary to assure long-range profit maximization." Do you agree with this statement? Explain.

2. What is meant by the "social responsibility of business"? Which of the many definitions in the text do you think is most useful in dealing with the problem today?

3. Argue the case against business's assumption of social responsibilities.

4. Argue the case for business's assumption of social responsibilities.

5. How do you assess the two sides of questions 3 and 4? Explain.

6. What is the concept of voluntarism? Of what significance is it in this argument?

7. Do you agree with the basic purpose of the Project on Corporate Responsibility? Do you think the proposals that the project made at GM's stockholder meeting in 1970 were acceptable?

8. What are the pros and cons of institutional investors using their portfolios to influence companies in which they own stock to take social actions the investors consider desirable?

9. What are "social costs of business"? Is it possible to determine how much social cost a business should bear?

10. What bearing does the decision of the judge in the A. P. Smith case have upon business's social responsibilities?

11. The textbook sets forth major criteria for determining the social responsibilities of business. Do you think they are acceptable? Explain your position.

MIND-STRETCHING QUESTIONS——————————————

1. Is it right for society to expect business to help further national goals, even though the result might be that a corporation loses money in the process? For example, is it right for the federal government to ask a company not to make foreign investments so as to ease the balance of payments problem?

2. Do you think the question of social responsibilities for business will have much to do with the preservation of individual political and economic freedoms in the future?

3. "One of the greatest problems that the United States must face today and in the near future is this: Shall private enterprise function in a comparatively free market within a broad framework of law? Or shall business be considered an instrument to be used by the state to achieve social objectives that people generally feel have the highest priority?" What are your reactions to these statements?

11

MAKING SOCIAL RESPONSIBILITIES OPERATIONAL IN BUSINESS

A) THE MIDDLE MANAGER AND COMPANY POLICIES FOR SOCIAL RESPONSIBILITIES

Michael Goodman is the general manager of the Metal Stamping Division of the Atlantic Manufacturing Company. His division is the largest in the company and is responsible for 65 percent of the corporate net profits. He is sitting at his desk—angry, frustrated, and puzzled. A delegation of employees has just left his office threatening a strike if his production line is not slowed down. Yesterday, he became embroiled in a losing battle with the government's pollution supervisor because his air emissions were above allowable levels. Over the past six months, he has watched the productivity of his plant decline because central headquarters has forced him to employ increasing numbers of hard-core unemployed who, without requisite skills for their jobs, cannot meet productivity standards.

What bothers Goodman most is, on the one hand, being forced to take action that will reduce productivity and profits, while, on the other, being judged strictly on the returns on investment of his division. To make matters worse, he cannot seem to impress the president of the company with the fact that his speeches about all the great things the company should do to meet its social obligations are putting great pressure on Goodman to do things that will reduce his ability to achieve his profit goals. For instance, in a speech to the Local League of Women Voters last week, the president said: "Our company is and will continue to be on the forefront of those that stand as good citizens in the community. We recognize our obligations to help those with whom we are associated, inside as well as outside our company, to lead the good life." Goodman thinks there is a direct connection between such rhetoric and the increasing demands made upon him to do things which reduce his profits. The president disagrees with Goodman and points out that if the environment of a business, internally and externally, is vibrant and healthy the profits of the company will expand.

CASE QUESTIONS

1. Identify some of the basic problems in this case. How do you account for the dichotomy between presidential rhetoric and Goodman's problems in implementing social programs? (See Philip T. Drotning, "Why Nobody takes Corporate Social Responsibility Seriously," *Business and Society Review*, Autumn 1972, pp. 68-72.)

2. You are hired as a consultant by this company to make recommendations for specific policies and plans to put the president's fundamental social aims into operation. What do you recommend? (See George A. Steiner, "Social Policies for Business," *California Management Review*, Winter 1973, pp. 17-24. Terry McAdam, "How to Put Corporate Responsibility into Practice," *Business and Society Review/Innovation*, Summer 1973, pp. 8-20. Robert W. Ackerman, "How Companies Respond to Social Demands," *Harvard Business Review*, July-August 1973, pp. 88-98.)

DISCUSSION GUIDES ON CHAPTER CONTENT

1. What is meant by institutionalizing social values in the decision-making process of a business?

2. Explain whether you think it is easy or difficult to inject social values into the decision-making process of a typical large company? A very small company?

3. What methods may a top manager of a company use to get his managers to consider the social point of view in their decisions? Which do you think are the preferred methods?

4. Evaluate the set of social policies for a company that the textbook presented. Do you strongly approve of any of them? Do you disagree with any of them?

MIND-STRETCHING QUESTIONS

1. Draw up a set of social policies for the Product Development Department of the Inland Steel Corporation. Defend your proposals.

2. Precisely where and in what ways do you think business can increase short-term profits while at the same time helping society resolve some of its pressing problems?

3. The chairman of the board of the General Motors Corporation asks your advice in answering this question: Which urban problems can I act on to ease and at the same time demonstrably increase the corporation's long-run profits?

12
THE SOCIAL AUDIT

A) CGI'S SOCIAL AUDIT

Conglomerate Growth International is one of the largest companies in the United states, with sales of around $2 billion. During the past ten years, the company has been moderately successful, with earnings at or slightly above the average for most industries in which the company has important interests. In some of its product divisions, however, earnings have not been too satisfactory, and the company is having difficulties in meeting competition.

At the present time, the company is engaged in the following lines of business. Its aircraft division, which is responsible for approximately one-quarter of its total sales, makes small, executive aircraft, wing assemblies for Boeing and McDonald-Douglas commercial aircraft, and helicopters for the U.S. Army. The Architectural and Construction Division has contracts around the world in port development, dam construction, and oil pipelines. The company also has wide-ranging interests in other areas, including paper and pulp mills, electronic assembly in Hong Kong and Taiwan, glass containers, and food containers.

Not long ago, the president of the company became concerned about social responsibilities and asked his principal managers to give him a report on what individuals in CGI were doing in this area. He was astonished to learn of the many activities in which his managers were engaged on their own. He felt that not only should such activities be encouraged, but that they ought to be accompanied by similar efforts on the part of the company.

Each year principal officers of the company from all over the world gather to review the performance and long-range plans of each of the affiliated companies and divisions and to discuss major company problems. The president felt that it would be useful if this year he asked a professor from a local university to talk with his managers about the subject of social responsibilities for companies. Following this talk, the president and managers decided that the company should make an audit of its social affairs.

CASE QUESTIONS

1. What is a business "social audit"?
2. Why do larger companies make social audits?
3. What type of social audit would you suggest to the president of CGI?
4. Should the social audit be made mandatory? (See John J. Corson and George A. Steiner, *Measuring Business' Social Performance: The Corporate Social Audit*. New York: Committee for Economic Development, 1974, Raymond A. Bauer and Dan H. Fenn, Jr., *The Corporate Social Audit*. New York: Russell Sage Foundation, 1972.)

DISCUSSION GUIDES ON CHAPTER CONTENT

1. What types of social audits have been made?
2. In your judgment, does the social audit respond to what many people say is today's corporate accountability?
3. If your answer to Question 2 is "yes," then explain what ought to be included in the social audit.
4. If a corporation is accountable to society, as the textbook suggests, then how is the corporation to determine what society wants from it?
5. "The whole thrust of business social audits will not get very far until there are creditable measures of the social

performance of business, and they will not be developed very soon." Comment on this quotation.

6. Evaluate the model for the social audit suggested in the textbook.

MIND-STRETCHING QUESTIONS————————————

1. Even assuming that someday the social audit will be mandatory for business, do you think it will be as uniform as today's financial audit?

2. What do you think the social audit of General Electric Company will look like in the year 1985?

13

BUSINESS ETHICS

A) B. F. GOODRICH COMPANY VS. DONALD W. WOHLGEMUTH

Donald W. Wohlgemuth worked in the spacesuit department of B.F. Goodrich Company, in Akron, Ohio. He had joined Goodrich in 1954, after earning a degree in chemical engineering at the University of Michigan. In 1962 he became the general manager of the spacesuit division and, of course, knew intimately the details of Goodrich's spacesuit technology for the Apollo flights.

Wohlgemuth became dissatisfied at Goodrich, mainly because he felt his salary was too low. He then joined Goodrich's competitor, International Latex Corporation in Dover, Delaware, where he received a substantial increase in salary and was made manager of engineering for the industrial products area, which includes making spacesuits in competition with Goodrich. After concluding these negotiations, he notified Goodrich he was leaving. Goodrich asked him if he thought his action was moral and legal. He observed: "Loyalty and ethics have their price and International Latex has paid the price." Goodrich thereupon sought a restraining order.

The case was heard in 1963 by the Court of Appeals of Ohio on an appeal from a lower court decision that had denied Goodrich's request for an injunction to restrain Wohlgemuth from disclosing trade secrets. The Court of Appeals upheld the lower court decision.

CASE QUESTIONS

1. Do you think Wohlgemuth acted ethically? How about International Latex? Defend your position.

2. What were the reasons the court gave for not restraining Wohlgemuth? (See Michael S. Baram, "Trade Secrets: What Price Loyalty?" *Harvard Business Review*, November-December 1968, pp. 66-74. For a thorough, yet short treatment of the law concerning trade secrets, see Joseph Schneider, "Protecting Trade Secrets," *Trial Magazine*, January-February, 1972.)

3. Courts of law are faced with two difficult questions in dealing with trade secrets: To what extent is a corporation entitled to protect its secrets from being taken to other companies by departing personnel? And to what extent should an individual be restrained from using information learned on one job in another job? (Consult William Bowen, "Who Owns What's in Your Head?" *Fortune*, July 1964, pp. 175ff.)

B) AERIAL ESPIONAGE OR AMERICAN ENTREPRENEURSHIP

One sunny day in 1969, in Beaumont, Texas, a small airplane was seen circling over a plant being constructed by E. I. DuPont de Nemours & Company. Once finished, this plant would produce methanol, a chemical used in making antifreeze by a secret and unpatented process. There was a photographer in the airplane who freely admitted taking pictures of the plant and delivering them to a third party.

DuPont sued the photographer and others, alleging that trade secrets had wrongfully been obtained, and asked for damages and an injunction from the use of the photographs. DuPont said that since the plant was under construction, a skilled person could tell from the photographs the secret process that would be used in making methanol. It claimed the process had been developed at great expense in time and money and gave DuPont a competitive advantage over other producers.

The defendants claimed there was no wrongdoing. They said the photographs were all taken in airspace in the public domain. No government aviation laws or standards were violated, and there was no trespass or breach of confidential relationships. Indeed, they asserted, there was nothing more involved than good old American entrepreneurship.

The court agreed with DuPont, and observed:

> Our devotion to freewheeling industrial competition must not force us into accepting the law of the jungle as the standard of morality expected in our commercial relations. . . . One may use a competitor's process if he discovers it by his own independent research; but one may not avoid these labors by taking the process from the discoverer without his permission at a time when he is taking reasonable precautions to maintain its secrecy. To obtain knowledge of a process without spending the time and money to discover it independently is *improper* unless the holder voluntarily discloses it or fails to take reasonable precautions to ensure its secrecy.[1]

CASE QUESTIONS

1. In your view, was the photographer acting unethically?

2. In the case, the judge said: " 'Improper' will always be a word of many nuances, determined by time, place, and circumstances. We therefore need not proclaim a catalogue on commercial improprieties. Clearly, however, one of its commandments does say 'thou shall not appropriate a trade secret through deviousness under circumstances in which countervailing defenses are not reasonably available.' " Name some practices that you think are improper ways to obtain trade secrets. Name some that go on in industry which you think may be proper. (See, Michael S. Baram, "Trade Secrets: What Price Loyalty?" *Harvard Business Review*, November-December 1968, pp. 66-74.)

3. What can an employer do to protect himself from such espionage? (See William F. Glueck and Robert A. Mittelstaedt, "Protecting Trade Secrets in the Seventies," *California Management Review*, Fall 1973, pp. 34-39.)

C) PENSION RIGHTS: LAW, ECONOMICS, AND ETHICS

A tiny union of Manhattan shoe salesmen and a huge copper corporation said Tuesday they were sorry but Murray Finkelstein, 60, and Mrs. Iris Kwek, 48 had lost their right to pensions after 30 years on the job.

[1] E. I. DuPont de Nemours and Company vs. Christopher (431 F. 2d 1012, 1972.)

The Anaconda Corporation and the Retail Shoe Salesmen Employee's Union testified as the Senate Labor and Public Welfare Committee resumed hearings on legislation to set national minimum standards for private employee pension plans.

Last summer Finkelstein, of Rego Park, New York, told the committee how after 35 years in the shoe business, the store he was working for folded, and the union pension plan to which his employer had contributed for 19-1/2 years told him he was entitled to no retirement.

Mrs. Kwek, from Detroit, said Anaconda laid her off after 30 years in the billing department and she lost her right to retirement benefits, receiving only a small lump-sum severance.

Anaconda's director of personnel, Douglas Monroe, and Finkelstein's union chief, Irving Tuckman, said at the present hearings that employees of neither pension fund were entitled to a dime if they were terminated before retirement age. To give employees a vested right in their pension fund after a certain length of service, they said, would increase the cost of contributions beyond their reach.

But Senator Jacob K. Javits (R-N.Y.) said the countless "personal tragedies" like those of Finkelstein and Mrs. Kwek showed the need for legislation to control pension plans, which are "designed and operated in ways directly in conflict with the interests of the worker."

Monroe said that vesting employees with an irrevocable right to an Anaconda pension after 10 years of service would cost the company $890,000 a year. He said Anaconda could not afford it because of the government seizure of mines in Chile, huge union wage settlements and the fact that many Anaconda employees were staying on to collect their pensions.

Tuckman and other officials of the shoe union said they had little sympathy for Finkelstein, since he "voluntarily" relinquished his pension rights by going to work in a store not covered by the union plan.

D) MARTIN'S CAMPAIGN CONTRIBUTION

Jack Martin is speaking to his wife Mary. "Yesterday I had lunch with Ed Wilson. You remember him. You saw him at the country club party last year."

Mary: "Yes, but very vaguely. What did you talk about?"

Jack: "Oh, mostly business. But did you know he is backing Bill Smith for mayor?"

Mary: "Bill Smith! How could he? Smith is a crook, and you know it."

From the *Los Angeles Times*, October 13, 1971. Copyright, United Press International. Reproduced with permission

Jack: "Yes, I know it. That's why I am backing Joe Donaldson."

Mary: "Our League of Women's Voters' Committee on Candidates is backing Donaldson, and I'm going to campaign actively for him."

Jack: "That's good. But try to maintain a low profile, would you?"

Mary: "Why?"

Jack: "Well, Ed Wilson feels pretty strongly about Bill Smith. I don't want to offend him because he's my biggest customer. He just gave me another $100,000 contract. As a matter of fact, he asked me for a contribution to Smith's campaign, since he is treasurer of the businessman's committee for Smith."

Mary: "Jack, how could you? You don't want Smith for mayor, so why help with a campaign contribution?"

Jack: "Mary, you don't understand. We talked about the new order before talking about Smith. Ed was all set to sign the contract when he raised the question about a $100 contribution for Smith's campaign. I gave him a check right there and then. Having him agree on the contract after that was as easy as silk. This means a great deal to the company and to us. I don't see how we could break even during the next six months without this contract."

Mary: "If you had been honest with Ed Wilson, I am sure he would have accepted the fact that you don't want Smith and don't want to help him campaign. This is a democracy. Why should Ed Wilson resent your views? Why should he hold it against you if you don't contribute to Smith's campaign?"

Jack: "Mary, I'm sorry I mentioned the matter. You don't understand. If I had refused to contribute, Ed would have smiled and said, 'Jack, I fully understand and respect your views.' But, he would as likely as not have also said he wasn't quite ready to sign the contract, that he had a few details to check out before making the commitment. There are others in this business who can fill his order as cheaply as our company can. We would have parted with a friendly handshake, and Ed would have said to call him in a few days. I would call, and Ed would say that he wasn't really ready yet. A few weeks later, I would call again but be unable to reach him. Then I would learn through the grapevine that he had given the contract to my competitor. Mary, this is a dog-eat-dog business. It was a 'come-across-or-lose-my-contract' situation. I could tell by Ed

Wilson's way of speaking. We simply could not risk losing his business. I would have given him $500 had he asked me."

Mary: "You should have stood up to him. What kind of a man is Ed Wilson? I wouldn't do business with him. If he is that stubborn and indifferent to the rights of others, let him take his business elsewhere. Jack, you are not the man I thought you were. Where is your moral backbone?"

Jack: "Oh boy! Why did I ever mention it?"

Mary: "Something is very wrong with business when you have to submerge your real convictions to get a contract. Something is wrong with business, when you are forced to choose between your family's well-being and your moral convictions! If this is possible then business is immoral."

CASE QUESTIONS

1. Compare Mary's viewpoint to Jack's. Is there a difference between business ethics and ethics in other walks of life?

2. Can you support Jack's action?

3. It has been argued that doing business is often like playing poker. Do you agree? See Albert Z. Carr, "Is Business Bluffing Ethical?" *Harvard Business Review*, January-February 1968, pp. 143-153. (This case was drafted from the article. See also Timothy B. Blodgett, "Showdown on 'Business Bluffing,'" *Harvard Business Review*, May-June 1968, pp. 162-170.)

E) WORLD CHARTER AIRWAYS SYSTEMS

World Charter, like a number of other airlines, has adopted a strategy of acquiring and building hotel accommodations in the various cities to which its line flies. It decided to build a large hotel and extensive recreation complex in Padre, located in the chain of islands off the Costa Rica coast. When the company was about ready to conclude a purchase agreement for land, the company negotiator was subtly told that a small "gift" would expedite matters. The negotiator yielded, but said nothing to company management since the amount involved was small and could easily be covered in other expenses associated with the transaction.

When World Charter was ready to begin construction of the hotel and recreation complex, it ran into a series of roadblocks because it had not engaged in Padre's time-honored practice of making petty gifts. Will B. Strong, chairman of the board of World Charter, finally heard of the delays and the reasons for them and went directly to the president of Padre. In no uncertain terms, Strong told the president that if World Charter was forced to get involved in this sort of petty bribery it would abandon the project. The net loss to Padre would be enormous in tourist dollars and jobs. The president told Strong that the practice was deeply entrenched in business life and was not considered dishonest in his country. It simply was an accepted condition for facilitating business transactions. Strong said, however, that this sort of thing was not tolerated in the United States except in rare cases, and that so far as he was concerned United States standards of ethics would apply anywhere his company did business. The president of Padre yielded to Strong's persuasion, and there was no delay through the construction phase of the operation.

Strong appointed one of his hotel managers, who had been very successful in the United States, to administer the complex in Padre. Operations seemed to be going smoothly and, after a short period, was even more profitable than World Charter had expected.

It was not long, however, before Strong discovered that Edward Peterson, the complex general manager, was going along with the Padre custom of buying favors by giving favors. Peterson not only gave free rooms to local government officials, but paid for lavish banquets for government officials' families and friends. The transactions of the hotel and recreation complex were riddled with handouts having nothing to do with the real cost of services provided. When Strong confronted Peterson with what he had heard, Peterson did not deny the situation. "This is the only way to do business here. *Mordidas* is the way of life," explained Peterson. "If we do not go along, we will lose everything. You have no idea the many ways in which things can be sabotaged, delayed, and increased in cost by local businessmen, workers, government officials, and the ordinary citizen." "Well, I'll be damned if I will go along with it," stormed Strong. "It must stop or we will close down." "That will be expensive," said Peterson. "The write off will seriously affect our earnings."

Strong closed the complex, and the loss did seriously affect his profit picture for the year. A number of stockholders complained bitterly. One of them said; "Strong is not a realist. He's trying to apply his standards of ethics throughout the world. You just can't do it and stay in business. Why should we tell the Padrians what their ethics ought to be? Who knows, maybe their standards are just as acceptable as ours."

CASE QUESTIONS————————————————

1. Do you think Strong was right? Or was Peterson right?
2. How have multinational companies coped with the problem of differing ethical standards in different parts of the world? (See Howe Martyn, "Bribery and Corruption in International Business," *Essays in International Business*, Institute of International Business, Georgia State University, Atlanta, Georgia, Fall 1969.)

F) FORCE REDUCTION AT MACHINERY SYSTEMS

Bill Paust, manager of the Engineering Department of Machinery Systems, was responsible for three sections: Design Engineering, Production Engineering, and Drafting. His department did all of the engineering for Machinery Systems (MS). MS was a division of International Business Systems, (IBS), a large company that did world-wide business.

Business within the division had been good, but, recently, things were slowing down because of the economic recession. Paust knew it was only a matter of time before adjustments in expense and products would be necessary. So, when Paust and the other department heads of MS were informed that IBS wanted a 10 percent cutback in costs, he was not totally surprised.

When Paul Stevens, MS's president, read the directive to his managers, he included an additional 5 percent cutback. As one of the senior managers within the division, Paust objected to the addition, but Stevens was determined to exceed the demands of the parent and held his ground. Now it was up to Paust and the others to find ways and means to implement the reduction. The following morning, Paust informed his section heads of the cutback and requested each of them to submit to him a proposal for reducing expenses.

Paust now sat at his desk reviewing the three proposals. The task was rather routine and impersonal, for each manager had worked out an operating schedule and a budget. Each had indicated which projects he was cutting back and how many people were to be laid off. A footnote on the proposal from Design Engineering caught Paust's eye. It read: One of the seven engineers I have to lay off is Terry Moore, the only black engineer I have in the design section."

This troubled Paust for two reasons. First, he had long been an advocate of civil rights and had strongly supported the IBS program of minority hiring. Second, his division had major government contracts and was subject to periodic review to insure that equal employment policies were followed. At that time in Paust's department, 7 percent of the nonprofessionals and 2.8 percent of the professionals were black. Laying off Moore would cause a significant drop that would be noticed. Paust wanted to find a way of keeping Moore.

Paust had previously requested the personnel records of those employees to be laid off. He thumbed through the folders, selected Moore's, and read the personal data sheet. "Two years with the company. Thirty-three years old. Married with two children. B.S. in electrical engineering. Grades average. Previous work experience satisfactory." He turned to the comments made when Moore was hired. "Attitude seemed good, and has potential to do work within standards of this division." He then turned to the supervisors' quarterly assessment and selected various comments. "Moore is well liked in the department, he is a pleasant fellow and gets along well with his co-workers. He is learning the procedure, and at present there seem to be no problems." Another comment read: "Having complaints from manufacturing on Moore's work. He is catching his mistakes too late, and has had to put through a number of modification notices. Spoke to Moore and gave him suggestion to improve." Another read: "Still too many modification notices on Moore's work. Is now attending a refresher course in New York. Plan on assigning him to Mason on the advanced program circuit project when he returns. Should give him some help." These comments indicated to Paust that Moore was able to adjust and willing to work to improve his performance. But the notes, together with what he knew about the other engineers in his department, left no doubt in his mind that Moore was not as capable as the others.

Paust thought of some alternatives for keeping Moore. He could go to Stevens and explain the situation: He quickly rejected this because he knew that Stevens would not yield on a decision. Paust would have to find another way of solving the problem.

He considered not cutting back on the advanced program circuit project; again, he rejected this because a cutback here would not affect the present schedule nor create future problems.

Could he have Gene Howell, the design section head, lay off someone else? He reached for the phone and dialed Howell's extension. "Hi, Gene," said Paust, "I'm reviewing your proposal for the cutback and wanted to discuss the possibility of moving Moore to a current project in place of another man."

"I considered that possibility, Bill, but right now I'm behind schedule and will be short seven men. If I move Moore instead of a more experienced man, I'm afraid he won't be able to cut it. And, with the present situation, that's something I can't afford to do," replied Howell.

"Why couldn't he cut it?" questioned Paust.

"It would take any man a few months to know the project as well as a man who'd been working on it for nine months. Furthermore, consider the backlash I would encounter if I replaced a white fellow with Moore. There would be talk of preferential treatment. To be perfectly honest, I need all of the morale I can muster to meet my schedule with a reduced staff."

"Do you see any alternatives?" asked Paust.

"No, not really," answered Howell.

"I understand," said Paust.

Paust knew he could not move Moore to Production Engineering, because he had asked that section head to cutback, too. Moving Moore around within the department was not feasible either, because he had no experinece with the other engineering programs.

Paust removed a booklet from his desk that contained the IBS minority employment requirements. He turned to the last page and read the concluding paragraph: "A manager should recognize that he is expected to fulfill the above equal employment requirements within his Department, while at the same time achieving his profit goals. It is not an either/or situation, and one does not give relief to the other."

Paust knew his decision would have to satisfy both rules and that he would have to make it before tomorrow, when he was to meet with Stevens.

CASE QUESTIONS

1. What realistic alternatives are open to Paust? (This case was suggested by Theodore V. Purcell, "Case of the Borderline Black," *Harvard Business Review*, November-December 1971, pp. 128-133; 142-150. Timothy B. Blodgett, " 'Borderline Black' Revisited," *Harvard Business Review*, March-April 1972, pp. 132-140. Colin Barrett, *Harvard Business Review* January-February 1972, pp. 161-163.)

2. If you were Paust, what decision would you make? What justification would you give for your decision?

3. What policies would you suggest to prevent future problems of this nature?

Reference

For a good short and operational statement of what one company is doing about equal opportunity and minority relations see "General Electric's Commitment to Progress in Equal Opportunity and Minority Relations," (Corporate Business Environment, Equal Opportunity/Minority Relations Operation) New York: (General Electric, N.D.).

G) CRISIS AT XYZ

National Electronics Company, the parent of many subsidiaries, was embarrassed by having to report substantially lower earnings than had been previously forecast to the public. Shortly after the report, XYZ Company, one of National's subsidiaries, announced the selection of a new president and a new vice-president of finance (replacing the controller). John Smith, former president of XYZ, and George Logan, former controller, had been withholding information from the parent company about the poor financial condition of XYZ.

Smith had made a decision to go after two large contracts. Smith's managers disagreed on his optimistic estimate of the probabilities of getting them, but he persisted and became more and more committed financially. Finally, XYZ failed to get the contracts, and the poor financial position of the company had to be made known to headquarters. Had XYZ won the contracts, Smith would have been a hero. As it turned out, he resigned under pressure and his resignation was accepted.

One director of National said that out-and-out fraud was involved, while another thought this was a situation directly attributable to the pressures on men like Smith to make profits. In such instances, this director felt, they tended to take the optimistic view.

A major question that arose was why a number of top managers at XYZ, who had close affiliations with men at National, did not go above Smith and make the situation known. Investigaation showed that loyalty to Smith was high, and, as a result, his staff accepted his position.[1]

CASE QUESTIONS

1. Was there a violation of common standards of ethics in this situation?
2. Who was to blame for the fiasco?
3. What would you have done had you been the controller?

H) WILLARD ATKINSON

Willard Atkinson has been with the Tiller Container Corporation for forty years and is now in charge of production for a very large division. When Atkinson first worked for the company, he was quite capable of dealing with the problems of production that he encountered, but he has not bothered to keep abreast of new production techniques. However, he was successful in hiring two bright young MBA's who are highly competent in production techniques and excellent general managers as well, and he has tended to delegate more and more of his responsibilities to these men. There is little if any doubt that he could not manage the affairs of his

---

[1] For a detailed discussion, see John J. Fendrock, "Crisis in Conscience at Quasar," *Harvard Business Review*, March-April 1968, pp. 112-120. John J. Fendrock, "Sequel to Quasar Stellar," *Harvard Business Review*, September-October 1968, pp. 14ff.

department without the talents of these young men. Unfortunately, they have made it known that they may leave unless brighter opportunities are opened for them, and the management knows they would be extremely difficult to replace. About the only place they would fit in the company would be in Atkinson's job.

Atkinson is now sixty years of age. The voluntary retirement age at the company is sixty-five, and the mandatory retirement age is seventy. Atkinson has made it known that since he is in good health he intends to stay until mandatory retirement. The president is thinking seriously of asking him to take early retirement in order to save one of the two young men on his staff whose talents are sorely needed in the company. Early retirement will give Atkinson 40 percent of his salary, whereas voluntary retirement at sixty-five would give him 50 percent.[1]

CASE QUESTIONS

1. Do you think Atkinson is behaving ethically?

2. If the president of the Tiller Container Corporation forces Atkinson to take early retirement, do you think he is acting ethically?

3. If you were one of the younger men, what would you do?

I) TWELVE BASIC ARMCO POLICIES

In 1919 Armco Steel Corporation adopted a set of business policies. The following, updated version is virtually identical to the original:

1) To do business guided and governed by the highest standards of conduct so the end result of action taken makes a good reputation an invaluable and permanent asset.

2) To insist on a square deal always. To make sure people are listened to and treated fairly, so that men and women really do right for right's sake and not just to achieve a desired result. For everyone to go beyond narrowness, littleness, selfishness in order to get the job done.

---

[1] Arthur L. Svenson, "An Augean Stable—The Case of Management Featherbeds," *California Management Review*, vol. 4, Summer 1963, pp. 17-22.

Reprinted by permission of the Armco Steel Corp.

3) To develop and maintain an efficient, loyal, aggressive organization, who believe in their company, to whom work is a challenge and to whom extraordinary accomplishment is a personal goal.

4) To create and maintain good working conditions . . . to provide the best possible equipment and facilities . . . and plants and offices that are clean, orderly and safe.

5) To adopt "Quality and Service" as an everyday practice. Quality will be the highest attainable in products, organization, plant, property and equipment. Service will be the best possible to customers, to shareholders, to city, state and nation.

6) To employ people without regard to race, sex, religion or national origin. To encourage employees to improve their skills by participating in available educational or training programs. To provide every possible opportunity for advancement so that each individual may reach his or her highest potential.

CASE QUESTIONS

1. Do you approve of such creeds or philosophies for a company?

2. If you were asked to revise this statement of policy to reflect your own values, what would you recommend? (See Stewart Thompson, *Management Creeds and Philosophies*, Research Study No. 32. New York: American Management Association, Inc., 1958.)

References

For a short resume of different types of business creeds and philosophies see George A. Steiner, *Top Management Planning* (New York: Macmillan 1969), pp. 144-150.

J) HIGH WAGES VS. SHUTDOWN

Lester Weber is president of the Superior Cabinet and Hardware Company. The business was begun by his grandfather in 1910 and has always been located on a little creek outside of town. Hardware is a highly competitive business, and Weber has watched his profits dwindle because he cannot cut his costs sufficiently to meet competition from mass producers. Much of his work has a high labor content, and he hires predominantly unskilled labor. The cabinets and hardware he produces are principally in the low-price range.

He was visited recently by a representative of the local

Environmental Quality Administration and was told that he was violating both air and water emissions standards and would have to comply or be fined stiffly. He wanted to comply but found that to do so would put him in the red. He could, however, make ends meet by laying off older workers who received high wages and replacing them with cheap labor at around minimum wage levels. He knew that only a few of his 110 employees could get jobs elsewhere in town. Many of them would be forced to move if they were laid off. However, since Weber's is not a union shop, he can act without facing union reprisals. He felt the layoff was his only alternative, and he discharged 80 of his older workers.

CASE QUESTION

Do you approve or disapprove of Weber's action? How strongly do you feel about it? Give your reasons for your position.

K) THE SWEATSHOP

Martin the Shirtmaker has been in business for thirty years. Jim Martin's father started the firm in Philadelphia, and it has manufactured mostly low- and medium-priced dress shirts, undershirts, and shorts for men. Competition from the Orient, especially Hong Kong, has been getting stiffer and stiffer, and Martin has found it difficult to operate at a profit. The area where his plant is located was once a very respectable neighborhood, but now it is a ghetto. Because of competition, Martin feels forced to pay the minimum wage established by law. At this wage he can do a little better than break even. He has strongly advocated the abolition of the minimum wage, especially for teenagers, because he feels he can meet foreign competition at a lower wage and hire many more people in the ghetto. He is concerned about the 30 percent unemployment rate among teenagers in his area as well as the precarious profit position he sees ahead.

Recently, a Concerned Citizens' group visited Martin's establishment and accused him of exploiting labor by paying low wages and maintaining sweatshop working conditions. Martin replied that conditions of work in his shop were far from ideal, but at least he gave jobs to people who wanted to work and could not find employment elsewhere. To raise wages, he said, or improve working conditions would erase his profit.

CASE QUESTIONS ———————————————————————————

1. Do you approve or disapprove Martin's position? Defend your position.
2. What is the case for and against the minimum wage?
(See Burton W. Teague, "The Minimum Wage—How Minimum Should it Be?" *The Conference Board Record*, January 1974, pp. 21-26. John M. Peterson and Charles T. Steward Jr., *Employment Effects of Minimum Wage Rates*. Washington D.C.: American Enterprise Institute, 1969.)

L) AN ADVERTISER ASKS A NEWSPAPER A FAVOR

The Clean Sweep Lawnmower Company is a small enterprise with headquarters in a small town west of Chicago. Its principal market is the Chicago area, although it ships some goods to other areas of the country. Total sales last year were approximately $4.5 million. Although it has been making a profit during the past three years, it recorded deficits in six of the past ten years. In none of the past ten years did the company earn over 8 percent on stockholder equity after taxes.

Two years ago, when profits of the company were at the breakeven point, a new electric lawnmower was introduced into the market. This mower was tested and found to be as safe as any the company had ever produced. However, it seemed to cause an unusually large number of accidents. The trouble lay in the type bolts used to secure the metal housing over the blades. If the mower had hard wear and the bolts were not tightened, the housing came loose and had a tendency to throw rocks and other hard substances caught by the blades. There were no recorded fatalities, but there were a number of rather painful cuts and bruises.

One woman was cut deeply in the legs by a piece of metal thrown by the mower. She sued, but the courts held that the company was not liable. Its brochure describing the machine and its use specifically said that the housing bolts had to be kept tight for safety. It cautioned all users to check the mowers in this and a number of other prescribed ways.

There was a strong demand among retailers of the mowers, as well as among the purchasers, to recall the machines and have the company apply new self-locking bolts that would not easily work loose. The company refused to do this, however. It said it was not liable: the mower would be perfectly safe if maintained as specified. To recall the mowers would reduce a small profit for the year to a substantial deficit.

Mark Wells, the president of the company, discovered that the local newspaper was preparing a story on local business firms and their relations with consumers. He called Jim Publicker, an old friend and editor of the paper, to make sure that the recall story was not included in the series. Clean Sweep was an important advertiser for the little paper, and Publicker did not want to offend an old friend and good advertiser. He therefore agreed that the defective bolt story would not be printed in the series.

CASE QUESTIONS

1. Do you approve or disapprove of Publicker's action? How strongly do you feel? Support your position.

2. Are there any generally accepted rules that would tell Publicker whether he should or should not publish the incident?

DISCUSSION GUIDES ON CHAPTER CONTENT

1. In a recent survey, almost all the executives questioned disagreed with this statement: "The businessman exists for only one purpose, to create and deliver value satisfactions at a profit to himself. . . . If what is offered can be sold at a profit . . . then it is legitimate. . . . The cultural, spiritual, social, and moral consequences of his actions are none of his concern." Do you agree with the majority opinion? How do you think the vote might have gone one hundred years ago?

2. What are some of the major reasons why ethical problems arise in business?

3. Identify the guides for ethical business conduct presented in the textbook and comment on the strengths and weaknesses of each.

4. The possibility of business becoming more ethical is bound up with the possibility of its professionalization. Comment.

5. What can and should a company do to improve the ethical and moral conduct of people working for it?

MIND-STRETCHING QUESTIONS————————————

1. Critics often say that the managers of a business, unlike members of other professions, primarily seek cash and emphasize materialistic values. Other professions, on the other hand, seem to have fine primary purposes and high ideals of public service from which, as a side-line, money flows. Comment.

2. The president of a local construction company asks your advice in developing a code of ethics that may be used to guide the actions of all employees in his company. What would you suggest? (You might consult Stewart Thompson, *Management Creeds and Philosophies* New York: American Management Association, Inc., 1958).

3. Draw up a code of ethics that you would like to follow when you enter the business world. Do you think you will be permitted to follow it? Explain.

4. What connection do you see between technical morality and consumer complaints over product quality?

IV
BUSINESS AND MAJOR COMMUNITY PROBLEMS

14

BUSINESS AND OUR POLLUTED ENVIRONMENT

A) BASF CORPORATION VS. THE HILTON HEAD ISLAND DEVELOPERS* [1]

Introduction

From 1966 to 1969, foreign investment in the United States rose from $9 billion to $12 billion, partially alleviating the balance-of-payments problem. One firm expanding in the United States was a German chemical firm, Badische-Analin and Soda Fabrik Co. (hereafter referred to as BASF). This firm had sales of $2.4 billion in 1969 and property assets of over $550 million. The company produced over 5,000 products for sale in over 130 countries. The firm, which had plants in New Jersey, expanded its operations in the United States in 1969 by acquiring the Wyandotte Chemical Co., located near Detroit, and by acquiring land and announcing plans to build a $100-million petro-chemical plant in the Southeast, in Beaufort County, South Carolina. The Southeast appeared particularly attractive to BASF as a location site because of its proximity

---

[1]*Copyright 1972, by John E. Logan and Sandra P. Logan Reproduced with permission.

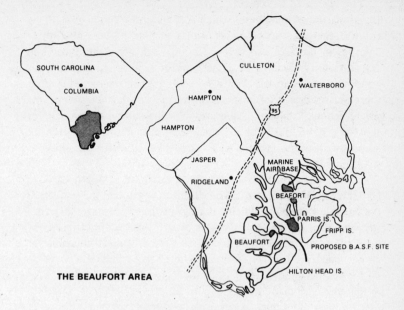

Fig. 14.1. The Beaufort Area

to many petro-chemical and dyestuff customers, and because there were no major petro-chemical plants between Philadelphia and Miami.

The company examined sites in 20 states, especially in Georgia, North Carolina, and South Carolina, over a two-year period, and talked with state developemnt board officials in many states. BASF had many requirements: 1,800 acres of land, five million gallons of fresh water per day, close proximity to a railroad and the seacoast, a free-trade area for the tax-free importation of chemical inputs, and an adequate labor force available at competitive prices. An area in the southeastern part of South Carolina, in Beaufort County, appeared to meet their requirements.

State officials, including the then Governor Robert E. McNair and officials of the State Development Board, and many other people in South Carolina badly wanted BASF to locate in Beaufort County because of the poverty and economic imbalances in the area. Although per capita income in Beaufort County was above the national average, due to military installations (including the Parris

Island Marine training base) which accounted for about 68% of the county's personal income, per capita income in the other three counties in the area was below $2,000, with per capita income in Jasper County standing at $1,192 in 1968. Further, the area was steadily losing agricultural jobs and population at the same time that there was a dearth of manufacturing jobs. A further sign of the severe economic plight of the area was the substantial amount of substandard housing. For example, according to the 1960 census, 55.5% of all housing units in Hampton County were classified as substandard.

BASF was attractive to officials of the State of South Carolina for several other reasons. The Beaufort area had just received unfavorable national publicity during hearings on hunger before a subcommittee of the United States Senate. Also, state officials had been trying to interest industry in state-owned land in this area for about a decade. Further, it was predicted that a business recession might well occur in 1970. The location of such a large facility as the proposed BASF plant would help the South Carolina State Development Board continue its five-year record of having new plant investment in South Carolina exceed $500 million annually.

Initial Plans

By June 1969, BASF representatives were convinced that Victoria Bluffs in Beaufort County best met their requirements. At this time, the South Carolina State Pollution Control Authority received a copy of the petro-chemical company's proposed plans for the site. Although these plans were incomplete, Dr. Hans Lautenschlager, President of BASF in the United States, saw no reason to fear that they would violate South Carolina's pollution laws.[2] In June, the Beaufort County Development Board held a confidential advisory meeting with invited representatives of various businesses to discuss BASF's possible location in Beaufort. On June 17, 1969, Charles Fraser, President of Sea Pines Plantation Co., one of the major developers of the Hilton Head Island resort area, wrote a letter to the Beaufort County Development Board stating that pollution from

[2] "Why in South Carolina: BASF Needed Area, Water, Labor Force," *The State*, 25 January 1970.

the proposed BASF plant could impair the Hilton Head resort industry and affect thousands of jobs.[3]

On October 1, 1969, officials of the German company and the South Carolina State Government publicly announced plans for the construction by BASF of a dyestuffs plant at Victoria Bluffs. Company officials, at this time, claimed that the investment in this new facility would be approximately $100 million and that this plant would employ about 1,000 people in the production of styrene, polymers, dyestuffs, and pigments. In addition, to help lure BASF to South Carolina, the state had already promised to construct a 13-mile railroad, a four-lane highway and new docking facilities, and to dredge the Colleton River, subject to approval by the Army Corps of Engineers. South Carolina would also grant the company a five-year exemption from State corporate income taxes. The United States Chamber of Commerce forecast the effect of the plant on the Beaufort economy as follows:

> . . . the influx of 1,000 employees in Beaufort will result in a population increase of 3,590; more than $3,000 more in personal [per capita] income; 30 more retail establishments; 1,000 more households; 970 more passenger car registrations; $3,310,000 more retail sales per year; 910 more school children; $2,290,000 more in bank deposits; and 650 more jobs over and above what the plant will employ.[4]

On October 15, 1969, BASF officials announced that their long-range total investment in the site might well be in the neighborhood of $400 million. The dyestuffs plant, to be constructed first, would cost $25 million. The next step would involve the establishment of a $98-million petro-chemical plant. In late December, when full details of this second phase were announced, company officials revealed that the petro-chemical plant would be constructed only if they could obtain a free-foreign-trade zone for Port Victoria in Beaufort and permission to import 40,000 barrels a day of naphtha, a chemical used to produce ethylene, which in turn is used in the production of plastics.

In November 1969, BASF purchased an 1,800-acre site at Victoria Bluffs from the State Ports Authority for $980,000. The

[3] Letter from Charles Fraser to the Beaufort County Development Board, 17 June 1969.

[4] "Beaufort Getting New Industry," *Columbia Record*, 1 October 1969.

company then announced that it would not lower the quality of the water of the Colleton River, into which its wastes would be dumped. All wastes would be treated, both at the plant itself and at the water authority treatment facility, before being released. At this time, neither officials of BASF nor of the South Carolina State Pollution Control Authority publicly expressed any fear that the new plants would violate state pollution laws. Some state officials suggested that the plants would be a boon to the depressed economy of the area.

Charges and Countercharges

The dams of controversy burst on December 2, 1969, when Fred Hack and Charles Fraser, the developers of Hilton Head Island, claimed that the proposed chemical plant would pollute the Colleton River and pose a very serious threat to the existence of the $100-million resort community on Hilton Head Island. Fraser pointed out that the chemical plant could legally pollute the water in the Beaufort area because of the loopholes in the present South Carolina pollution laws.[5] He suggested further that BASF be forced to post a $25-million performance bond which would be forfeited if its plant polluted. Governor Robert E. McNair responded to Hack and Fraser the next day.

> We have assurances from BASF . . . that the company is vitally concerned about the ecology and beauty of the area and that steps are being taken to satisfy all legal, environmental and industrial requirements in safeguarding the air and water from pollutants.[6]

Hack and Fraser also explained why they had not protested the proposed plant location in October when it had been announced.

> Hack and Fraser said they withheld judgment for eight weeks after the plant was announced to study the company and the background and experience of other communities that had become the site of chemical plants.[7]

---

[5] Robert E. Brownlee, "Pollution Prevention Urged for Beaufort," *Columbia Record*, 9 December 1969.
[6] "McNair Assures Pollution Control," *Columbia Record*, 10 December 1969.
[7] "Group Meets to Plan Action Against BASF," *The State*, 4 December 1969.

They also stated they would be willing to buy the Victoria Bluffs land from BASF to develop it as a recreation center, and offered to attempt to find light industry more compatible with the area.[8]

Later that same month, various other groups began to actively oppose the construction of the BASF plant in Beaufort County. Among these were the Citizens Association of Beaufort County, Inc., headed by Vice-Admiral Rufus L. Taylor, USN (Ret.), and the Environmental Quality Control Council, headed by Franklin Rouse. The Board of Directors of the Hilton Head Chamber of Commerce also announced its belief that the location of a chemical plant would be a serious threat to the recreation and seafood industries in the area.

Relative peace reigned for the next 10 or 15 days, after which time controversy boomed forth again. On December 23, Charles Fraser, in response to the announced plans for the petro-chemical plant, claimed that a naphtha import quota of 40,000 barrels a day would allow BASF to escape paying Federal import taxes of $20 million a year. On the same day, Dr.Hans Lautenschlager attempted to refute the various accusations against his firm by stating, "BASF intends to be one of the industrial leaders in resolving problems of pollution." He said that his company would continuously measure the quantity and quality of its effluents and that it would make this information public. However, Fraser doubted that these provisions would prevent pollution.

> We are alarmed that there are indications that BASF is planning to budget only one million dollars for air and water pollution control equipment. We have received private word from executives within the petro-chemical industry that a budget of seven or eight million dollars would be a more realistic figure if they genuinely intend to install the most modern and efficient control equipment.[9]

A few days later, company officials announced that construction work at the Victoria Bluffs site would begin in 1970. It was estimated that 800 workers would be employed in construction efforts in 1970 and that the payroll would be $6 million. In 1971, roughly 1,300 construction workers would be needed, with a $9

---

[8] Ibid.

[9] "BASF Tells Details of Second Beaufort Plant," *The State*, 23 December 1969.

million payroll, while 1972 would see a $12 million payroll for 1,500 construction workers. Skilled, semi-skilled, and unskilled laborers, the latter in abundant supply in the Beaufort area, as well as managerial workers, would be needed. BASF representatives announced also that, by 1975, 1,000 people would be employed in the Port Victoria complex. (However, throughout the dispute, many observers were skeptical as to how many jobs would actually be created and how many of these jobs would actually go to poor residents of the Beaufort Economic Area.)

According to BASF estimates and the analysis of Dr. Robert Rosen and Professor David Pender of what has happened where similar petro-chemical plants were built and complexes resulted, operating labor at chemical facilities at Victoria Bluffs would increase from a little over 600 employees in 1974 to over 3,000 in 1976, and to over 6,815 in 1978. Even more important, the number of unskilled jobs generated would amount to about half of this total.

In the last week of December, Hilton Head Island conservationists announced their intentions to meet during the first week of January 1970 to examine the pollution problem; BASF representatives were not invited. While the pollution symposium was taking place, BASF and State Government officials agreed to study the problem of pollution in the Victoria Bluffs area with the state's Water Resources Commission and an independent firm engaged by BASF to conduct separate studies. Meanwhile, conservationists were busy drawing their own conclusions.

> Dredging—which the state had promised to do in the Colleton River so ocean-going vessels could dock at Victoria Bluffs—could damage Beaufort County's water supply and severely impair the area's seafood industry.
>
> 1) Oyster beds form on sloping river banks. The dredging would upset this slope and ruin the beds.
>
> 2) Dredging could alter the pattern of surrounding marshbanks, thereby forcing shrimp to move elsewhere.[10]

Dr. John O. Withers said "changes in the life cycle of one form of sea life could alter the entire ecological balance [of the area]." He argued that, as no study of the tidal flows in the area had ever been

[10] John David Spade, "Group Warns Against Plan to Dredge Colleton River," *The State*, 7 January 1970.

undertaken, it was possible that the water in the Colleton River at Victoria Bluffs never went into the ocean.[11]

Other conservationists were upset by the company's plans. Conservationist and geographer Alan Ternes pointed out in an April 1970 article in *Natural History*:

> If, when it says preserve the ecology, the BASF corporation means to maintain the existing ecosystem, it is proposing to do the impossible. The daily effluent of some 2.5 million gallons from the plant, no matter how it is treated, will change the ecosystem. So will the dredging of a channel to the site.[12]

However, Ternes was equally critical of Hilton Head developers and "conservationists," claiming that they were also guilty of tampering with the environment.

> Labor crews and tractors with brush-cutting rigs are constantly assaulting the undergrowth [on Hilton Head Island] so that the landscape will have a parklike appearance. . . . Dredging equipment has cut deep channels through many parts of the island, changing the drainage and destroying wet sites and their distinctive biota. Other areas are filled in with the spill from dredging. . . . Ultimately one-tenth of the island will be occupied by golf courses, which may be pretty by some tastes, but which certainly are not examples of natural beauty. . . . Charley Fraser and other developers of Hilton Head Island are concerned about saving an environment, but it is an environment they have created, and it is as far removed from the natural environment as the conceptions of BASF.[13]

By January 9, 1970, BASF had announced plans to proceed with construction on schedule, and the conservationists had recommended a complete ecological study of the area before construction took place. Orion Hack, the brother of Fred Hack, accused Representative Brantley Harvey of Beaufort of conflict of interests, claiming that Harvey had helped BASF acquire the land under dispute. Harvey denied that his actions created any conflict of interest.

[11] John David Spade, "Biologist Worries While Local Groups Argue," *The State*, 10 January 1970.

[12] Alan Ternes, "An Introduction to the Setting and Characteristics of the Tragical Farce or Farcical Tragedy of Victoria Bluffs, South Carolina," *Natural History*, 79 (April 1970), p. 12.

[13] Ibid., pp. 12*ff.*

Charles Fraser also pointed out that BASF could hurt employment in the area. He estimated that, for every non-high school graduate hired by the new plants, there would be three high school drop-outs employed in the seafood and recreation industries who would lose their jobs.[14] Although Fraser did not give any reason for his statement concerning loss of jobs, he may have been estimating a decline in employment in these industries because of the threat of pollution. Conservationists also pointed up the possibility of accidental spills from tankers in the Colleton River, a danger which BASF officials admitted they could not prevent.

Dr. Hans Lautenschlager saw little competition between his company and the seafood and recreation industries for labor because "we won't employ many maids or cooks in the plant." Dr. Lautenschlager also pointed out that 600 people—a somewhat lower estimate than before—would be employed at the plant, with half the jobs going to unskilled workers. He thought opposition to the proposed plant was ill-founded.

> He said opposition to the plant was confined to a minority of a well-organized and economically independent group of people who know how to use the news media and are well acquainted with industry. He said the plant could become a laboratory in which man could learn how to have industry without pollution.[15]

Later in January, a State Pollution Control Authority investigation on the Tenneco Corporation plant in the Beaufort area revealed that Tenneco, in spite of promises to the contrary, was indeed polluting the stream into which its effluent poured.[16] In explanation, officials of the State Pollution Control Authority said that, due to a lack of funds, they were severely understaffed, and, thus, could not effectively monitor all industry. (The South Carolina Legislature subsequently turned down a request by the State Pollution Control Authority for 87 new positions and $800,000 more for the 1970-1971 fiscal year.)[17]

In late January, opponents of the BASF project began to

---

[14] John David Spade, "Legal Action Considered to Halt BASF Construction," *The State*, 11 January 1970.

[15] William D. McDonald, "Advantages of BASF Plant Listed," *The State*, 21 January 1970.

[16] Ternes, "The Tragical Farce of Victoria Bluffs," p. 17.

[17] "Prospects Dim for More Enforcement of Pollution Laws in South Carolina," *The State*, 18 February 1970.

exclaim that of more importance than the company's promises not to pollute were the facts that the BASF operations in West Germany and Belgium had polluted the Rhine and Schelde Rivers, respectively. In defense of BASF policies and practices, Dr. Lautenschlager claimed that the parent company was only one of many firms dumping waste into the Rhine, but the pollution in this river would be reduced due to the strengthening of laws. The company was to invest $45 million over the next four years to cleanse its operations on the Rhine River. As for the Schelde River, he said it was "dead" before BASF began to dump wastes in it.[18] In defense of BASF operations in New Jersey, the State of New Jersey's pollution controllers asserted that this company was obeying their anti-pollution laws.[19]

In February 1970, South Carolina officials discussed pollution problems. H. J. Webb, Associate Director of the South Carolina State Pollution Control Authority, said the biggest pollution problem in the state might be the hundreds of small sewerage and waste plants built for small real estate developments throughout the state. There were more than 500 of these plants in existence in 1970, and officials estimated that this figure would double by 1980. John C. West, then Lt. Governor of South Carolina, pointed out that over 21 million gallons of waste per day were pumped by the city of Columbia into the Congaree River or about 10 times the waste it was estimated the new BASF plants would release into the Colleton River, and that air pollution was already a severe problem in North Charleston. The State Legislature began to consider various anti-pollution bills designed to strengthen existing laws. Strom Thurmond, Senator from South Carolina, requested that the Department of the Interior study the BASF plant proposal in order to settle the conflict concerning the plant's ecological effect on the Beaufort County area.

Meanwhile, citizens of Beaufort County presented BASF officials with a petition welcoming them to Beaufort: it contained 7,488 signatures. A Beaufort pharmacist observed: "I would say 80% of the people in Beaufort County are in favour or BASF. Those who aren't are rich."[20]

[18] McDonald, "Advantages of BASF."
[19] "New Jersey's Tough-Minded Pollution Controllers Give a Clean Bill of Health to BASF's Operations in their State. . . ." *The State*, 1 February 1970.
[20] William D. McDonald, "Youth Corps Looking for Jobs," *The State*, 23 February 1970.

Controls on BASF

The State Legislature considered various proposals designed to combat pollution, including a moratorium on construction of the proposed plants, during February. Representative J. Wilson Graves of Beaufort County asked for a concurrent one-year moratorium on inshore fishing and crabbing in Beaufort County in order to help equalize costs between the disputants. This conflict was settled in March, with agreement on a one-year moratorium on granting additional waste permits in Beaufort County until a one-year study on pollution in that area could be completed by the South Carolina Water Resources Commission. This study of the effects of industry on the tidelands area was to involve 16 Federal and State agencies and would cost about $156,000.[21] After this compromise had been agreed upon, Representative Graves dropped his proposal for a moratorium on fishing. In February, the South Carolina House of Representatives had enacted a bill enabling the South Carolina State Pollution Control Authority to appeal to the court for an injunction against any individual or industry polluting the air to the extent that it hampered a person's enjoyment of his own property. The South Carolina State Pollution Control Authority also was reorganized to give it more strength.

The controversy entered another arena in February—the Federal courts. On February 10, the Hilton Head Fishing Cooperative Inc., Blue Channel Corporation, and the Ocean, Lala, and River Fish Companies filed suit in the United States District Court in Aiken, South Carolina, against BASF[22] The defendant responded that, since it had done no business in South Carolina, the United States District Court at Aiken had no jurisdiction over it. BASF contended

[21] William D. McDonald, "Study of Effects of Industry on Tidelands Unveiled," *The State*, 25 March 1970.

[22] Fishing and the packaging of fish was a fairly significant industry in Beaufort County, with the manufactured value of fish in the country reaching $2.7 million in 1967, while the value of shellfish harvest, primarily oysters and crabs, was $1.3 million. These totals were about 75 percent and 46 percent of South Carolina's total, respectively. The six seafood-processing firms employed about 400 people during peak season, while it was estimated that the "fishing cooperatives" in the county employed over 200.

(From Oliver G. Wood, "Economic Profile of the Beaufort Economic Area," unpublished manuscript, 1971, p. 28.)

also that the service of the suit was insufficient. About the same time, opponents of the proposed project began to question the cost to taxpayers of the South Carolina State Ports Authority's promises to BASF, i.e., the 13-mile railroad, the new docks and watersheds, the four-lane highway, and the five-year State tax exemption.[23]

In March 1970, the South Carolina Collegiate Press Association sponsored a symposium on pollution problems. Among the speakers was Miss Marion Edey of the Washington, D.C. office of the Friends of the Earth. Miss Edey said, "South Carolina must choose between making an effort to halt pollution and having an industrialized area as unliveable as New York City, which I fled long ago.[24]

Later in March, a survey taken in neighboring North Carolina revealed that chemical workers were the highest paid industrial workers in the state, with average weekly earnings of over $146, as compared with apparel workers in the textile industry in North Carolina, who averaged less than $72 a week.[25] (Over 50% of South Carolina's manufacturing workers were employed in the textile industry and received similar wages. Many people have argued that, if South Carolina is to improve its per capita income levels, more high-wage industries must be attracted to the state.)

In spite of the one-year moratorium mentioned previously, the furor continued. The Beaufort Junior Chamber of Commerce joined the forces opposing the location of the plants in Beaufort County. One spokesman for the Beaufort Jaycees said he could see no dearth of employment opportunities in Beaufort County, noting that his "classmates" from school appeared to be employed.[26]

On March 18, 1970, the Hilton head Company, the Sea Island Development Corporation, and Port Royal Plantation, Inc.—the major developers of Hilton Head Island—filed suit to enjoin BASF permanently from engaging in construction at Victoria Bluffs. One of the principal attorneys for this group later stated that, the longer construction could be delayed, the lower the probability that the

[23] Advertisement in *Sea Islander*, 26 February 1970.

[24] Jay A. Gross, "South Carolina Pollution Controversy Called Possible 'Test Case,' " *The State*, 1 March 1970.

[25] "Chemical Workers Top Wage Earners in North Carolina," *Charlotte News*, 10 March 1970.

[26] "Groves: Anti-BASF Forces Ignore Congaree Pollution," *Beaufort Gazette*, 12 March 1970.

plants would ever be built on that site, since time was extremely important to the company if it were to remain in the vanguard of the chemical industry.

In late March, Secretary of the Interior Walter Hickel warned BASF officials not to change the composition of the estuarine waters of the Colleton River. This was interpreted by many observers as a radical change in Federal environmental control policy. Others saw it as a dangerous encroachment by the Federal Government in local and state affairs. Later, most observers felt this was the straw that broke BASF's back. Several days later, company representatives sent a letter to Hickel stating that they would abide by any government regulations. A company spokesman also said that the Federal Government must set pollution standards and insure that it protects the public interest. Company officials decided to delay all construction at the Victoria Bluffs site until the appropriate Federal agencies could formulate these standards. Robert E. McNair, then Governor of South Carolina, expressed concern that the Department of the Interior had become involved in an internal state problem. He wondered whether South Carolina was to become "the guinea pig for a new Federal policy on air pollution."[27]

Fraser and the Hack brothers were also busy during late March and April, proposing the possible development of the Victoria Bluffs site into a recreation area to be known as "Seven Flags Over Port Royal," which they envisioned as being similar to the "Six Flags Over Georgia" operation. Although they offered to buy the site from BASF, the three men also said that perhaps they could find another suitable location in the area if the BASF plants did not pollute.[28] Fred Hack said further that the state had sold the Victoria Bluffs site to BASF much too cheaply ($200 per acre). He charged that the company had had to pay about $4,000 an acre for the rest of the land at Victoria Bluffs. Hack argued that, if BASF had paid $4,000 per acre for the whole package, the State treasury would have been $4.5 million richer.[29] However, his estimate of the total purchase price—approximately $250,000—disagreed with the

[27] "BASF Delays Building of Plant at Beaufort," and "Hickel Statement Blasted," *The State*, 8 April 1970.

[28] "Developers' Plans Depend on BASF," *The State*, 2 April 1970; and "Hilton Head Island Region Could be Model for World," *The State*, 3 April 1970.

[29] "Opponents Say BASF Benefits Gotten at Taxpayers' Expense," *The State*, 3 April 1970.

$980,000 purchase price publicly announced by the State of South Carolina and BASF the previous November.

Proponents of the proposed project were also busy during April. State Senator James M. Waddell, Jr. urged conservationists to be equally concerned about poverty, and the NAACP called for more opportunities for Negroes in non-traditional fields.

> Isaiah Williams [Field Secretary for the state conference of NAACP branches] said further recreational development of Beaufort County would result in the employment of poor people in traditional jobs as maids, janitors and servants for the wealthy, with no hope of upgrading themselves in the future.[30]

James A. Moore, Chairman of the Committee for the Advancement of Poor People, pointed out that there would be relatively few employment opportunities under present conditions for about 200 youths, black and white, graduating from high school in Hampton County, who were not going on to college.[31] Governor McNair, in noting substantial poverty problems on a state-wide level, said that more than 200,000 families in South Carolina had incomes of less than $3,000 per year.[32]

In early May, a controversy arose over the legality of funds ($8,500) donated by Beaufort County to the Beaufort Chamber of Commerce, when it became known that the Chamber had used part of these funds in its campaign against the proposed BASF plants. The County Government was a proponent of the project.

At this time, the State Development Board, in conjunction with a consulting firm, issued a new economic profile of Beaufort County. The analysis indicated that the Beaufort area would probably suffer economically if the BASF plant did not locate there. According to these statistics, by 1980 there would be 36,000 jobs in Beaufort without the new plant, while there would be 58,00 jobs with it. Fred Hack argued that these statistics were inaccurate. The Hilton Head Island developers engaged the consulting firm of Skidmore, Owings, and Merrill to draw up a master plan for Beaufort and Jasper Counties. One proposal of the study was a series of agricultural cooperatives in both counties. Skidmore's report also

[30] "NAACP Backs BASF: Reports Jobs Needed," *The State*, 22 April 1970.

[31] "Rally Set to Support BASF Plant," *The State*, 22 May 1970.

[32] "McNair Hits Opposition to BASF," *The State*, 25 April 1970.

recommended the establishment of more recreation industry and "compatible" light industry, such as a building components plant. The firm estimated that, if a mere 130 conventions were held yearly, roughly 20,000 jobs could be created.[33]

However, according to some experts, even "compatible" light industry could be difficult to lure into the area.

> ... the image of South Carolina in industrial circles was not enhanced by the long bitter fight by those who felt BASE's pollution potential would ruin one of the few unspoiled marine estuarial areas left in the United States. State officials ... say that industrial developments in the Coastal Plains amounting to many, many millions during the next five years will be lost. A number of firms not wanting to get caught in the crossfire that hit BASF are said to be shying away from the coastal region of South Carolina.[34]

Another aspect in the controversy surfaced in July 1970 when Paul J. Holmes, operator of a Beaufort County landscaping service, filed a class action suit against State Development Board members in the Courts of Common Pleas in the counties where the board members lived. The suit asked that the State Development Board be prohibited from issuing news releases supporting the proposed BASF plant. Holmes charged that using state funds to support BASF constituted a violation of the State constitution, since the legislature had not appropriated funds for that purpose. Holmes argued further that the board was going beyond "the limit of its authority and violating the very spirit and purpose for which it was created." The board countered by claiming that Holmes's charges were not within any court's jurisdiction. A spokesman for the board stated, "The issues raised by the complainant are of a purely political nature, which should be resolved by the legislature and over which the court has no jurisdiction."[35]

In late November 1970, speculation arose, after the removal of Walter Hickel as Secretary of the Interior, that the United States Department of the Interior might change its stand against BASF.

---

[33] John David Spade, "Beaufort-Jasper Co-ops Proposed," *The State*,[25] August 1970.

[34] "Alternative to BASF: Natural Development," *The State*, 3 September 1970.

[35] Ginny Carroll, "Development Board Denies Politics Charge over BASF," *The State*, 7 August 1970.

However, no formal change in policy was announced. Further, no BASF spokesmen made any significant comments concerning possible attempts to begin plant construction.

In January 1971, BASF announced that it would not locate at Victoria Bluffs. The primary reason cited was the decline in the demand for chemicals as a result of the recession. Others felt, however, that BASF's increased financial problems, the expansion room at its recently acquired facilities at Wyandotte, Michigan, and the degree of opposition offered by conservationists and resort developers also affected this decision.

In late January, the State of South Carolina was notified that a major oil company had decided to build a $1/2 billion oil refinery at Wilmington, North Carolina, instead of Charleston, South Carolina, and that the Hilton Head developers would not build the major amusement park-resort area they had proposed if BASF did not locate at Victoria Bluffs. The reason for this latter change in plans was that the developers believed the noise from such facilities would disturb guests and residents of Hilton Head Island. This announcement, however, occasioned some strong comments. Charles W. Jones, Jr., of Estill, South Carolina, in a letter to the editor of *The Columbia State*, argued:

> This [the decision not to build the amusement park] was exactly what I expected. Pollution was only an excuse so they could pay lower wages for their workers in order to survive.
>
> May God help our country when a few men of wealth can determine the fate and well-being of people whose only desire is to work and earn an honest living.
>
> I hope these men will think of the cold and hungry people who are in that condition because of their selfishness.[36]

In the meantime, it is not at all certain that the Hilton Head developers have won their battle. J. Bonner Manly, the recently appointed Director of the State Development Board, indicated that the state badly needs an oil refinery and other petro-chemical facilities if the state is to break its bonds of poverty. He stated that the primary sites for such developments were at Charleston and Victoria Bluffs. He noted that there was ample technology to

[36] Letter to the Editor, *The State*, 1 February 1971.

prevent pollution, but argued, "Even if it were not, we would have to take cognizance of the fact that men remain morally more important than birds, animals, and fishes."[37] Two weeks after this statement was made, Orion Hack received an award for being South Carolina Conservationist of the Year.

CASE QUESTION

What major issues in the buisness-society interrelationship are raised in this case? What is your position with respect to each? (For additional facts about this case see Oliver G. Wood, Jr., John E. Logan, Sandra P. Logan, Robert W. Rosen, and David R. Pender, *The BASF Controversy: Employment vs. Environment*, Essays in Economics, No. 25, Bureau of Business and Economic Research, College of Business Administration, the University of South Carolina, 1971.)

B) THE POLLUTION CRISIS OF SUPERIOR WIRE COMPANY

Foreword

Superior Wire Company is a small industrial firm located in Norwalk, a small city in Los Angeles County, California. Norwalk is primarily a residential community, with a number of small industrial firms scattered around its periphery. Several of the firms are in the same general area as Superior, which has easy access to the freeway to nearby Anaheim and Los Angeles, only fifteen miles away. This present location is ideally suited for business with many of the large aerospace firms. The Orange County Flood Control Channel to the Pacific Ocean, Long Beach, is behind the Superior Wire Company's facilities.

Superior's principle business is associated with the chemical processing and mechanical working of hot rolled steel wire pur-

---

[37] Edward D. Harrill, "Petrochemical Industry Seen as Answer to Poverty," *The State*, 6 February 1971.

Reprinted by permission of Branford Pacific Wire, Inc.

chased from the large steel mills. The firm improves the dimensions and surface characteristics of the wire. It in turn sells the processed wire to metal-fabricating manufacturers, of which the fastener industry is the principle customer. The company currently commands from 10 to 15 percent of the wire market among fastener manufacturers in southern California. Its principle customers are the aerospace companies.

Entrepreneurs Start Superior

In 1966, Bob Smith (now the president of Superior) and some associates began what is now the Superior Wire Company. These men had worked in the industry for a number of years, either at large steel mills or in the local wire-processing plant located in the Santa Fe Springs area. Smith liked the idea of being in business for himself. This desire, coupled with an intimate knowledge of the industry and substantial capital raised within southern California, led him to be very optimistic about his probable business success. He felt that through high-quality products he could compete with local firms, the large mills throughout the United States, and foreign processors. Superior was incorporated on January 1, 1968.

As a southern California resident for many years, Bob was intimately aware of the pollution problems faced in that area. His approach was to establish his operations in a way to minimize their effect on the environment while remaining competitive in the industry. He incorporated techniques that he felt were equal, if not superior, to those utilized by his former employer, the original wire-processing mill in the area. Much to his surprise, this was not enough.

Enter the Pollution Controllers

The primary pollutants of a wire mill are associated with the chemical "milling" operations of the firm. Chemicals such as sulphuric acid, hydrochloric acid, nitric acid, and various caustic sodas are used to remove the scaling and impurities on the surface of the wire. The chemicals themselves then must be removed from the wire to prevent further corrosion. This is done through the use of rinse water. While some vapors are given off within the plant, water pollution via the rinse solution and the chemicals themselves are viewed as the major problem.

During 1968 Bob attempted to obtain approval to dispose of spent acids and rinse water into the Los Angeles Flood Control Channel. The Los Angeles County Flood Control District granted Superior a master permit to use the channel, at a cost of $100. However, it developed that the permit carried with it no usable benefits. Approval to exercise the permit had to be obtained from the U.S. Army Corps of Engineers, since it had authority over the use of the channel.

A major interest of the Corps of Engineers was to assure the proper design of the entrance inlets to the flood control channel. The Corps approved the design that Superior proposed and issued a permit (cost, $50) to construct. Construction of the entrance then began and was completed nine months later. But, still another permit was required to allow the company to use the inlet.

The State of California Water Quality Control Board has jurisdiction over the injection of industrial effluents into state waterways. In this instance, the waterway was the flood control channel. After some discussion with representatives of the board, it was determined that Superior had to install a water clarifier. The type and specifications of the equipment, however, could not be obtained from the board. The board simply stated its requirements that the water entering the channel must be clear, contain less than five-parts-per-million of undissolved solids, and have a Ph[1] rating of from seven to ten. Superior also was informed that it would not be permitted to dump acid wastes into the channel. These were to be disposed through the County Waste Disposal Facility. Only the treated rinse water could be pumped into the channel.

The Water Control Board refused to become involved in the approval of this proposed equipment to clarify the rinse water at the design or construction stages. The board said it would simply monitor the effluents entering the channel and cite the company if irregularities were found. The clarifier was built and, fortunately, produced effluents acceptable to the board.

The construction and installation of the clarifier cost approximately $22,000. This was not, however, a one-time expenditure. A

[1] Ph is a chemistry measure indicating the degree and extent of a solution's acid or basic characteristics, e.g., 7 is neutral, < 7 acidic and > 7 basic. Total range is 1-14.

clarifier utilizes caustic soda, through which the acidic rinse water is passed to provide the neutral to slightly basic Ph rating. It also contains filters for removing undissolved particles. The clarifier must be completely cleaned twice a week, and the spent soda replaced. The wastes from the clarifier, like the acids used for cleaning the wire, cannot be dumped into the channel.

All solid waste and untreatable solutions must be shipped to the County Waste Disposal facility. This is accomplished by transferring the materials into fifty-five gallon drums and trucking them to the dump. Because of the quantities involved, three to four trips per week are necessary, with all the requisite costs including that of a dumping permit (approximately $35 depending on the volume to be dumped). After providing for waste disposal, the firm was finally ready to begin operation. It should, however, be noted that prolonged dumping "privileges" are not guaranteed, and more costly locations may be required in the future.

One other point on waste removal deserves mention. Because of the arrangement of the county facility, the acid and caustic solutions are directed to one location, while solid wastes must be segregated and transported to a separate location. Dumping and transportation costs for the firm average $18,000 per year.

Air Pollution Harassment?

After about a year of operations, the problems of controlling water pollution effluents appeared to be behind Superior, even though the costs were a constant reminder of the situation. Air pollution was never considered a relevant strategy problem. However, in 1970 Superior began to receive visits from the Air Pollution Control District of Los Angeles County. The investigators claimed that they had received complaints from the surrounding residential neighborhood about persistent obnoxious fumes emanating from Superior. Smith doubted the validity of the claims, since the only claimant's address supplied by the district was actually located two miles away. He felt the investigators were really summoned as a result of fictitious reports filed by other processors who were beginning to feel Superior's competitive strength and who themselves were polluters. The upshot of the APCD investigations was that Superior had to install equipment which would eliminate all possible air pollution or face fines of $500 per day or plant closure.

Again, the type or extent of equipment was not specified. But it was concluded that it would be necessary to install hoods over each of the acid tanks (eight tanks) and that a fume scrubber would be required at a cost of approximately $50,000. A formal permit of compliance was to be issued on an annual basis, at a fee of $100. In addition, all equipment would be subject to periodic inspection.

A fire inspector happened by in 1971 to check the building fire precautions. Upon discovering that acids in bulk storage were on the premises, and that an ammonia tank was also in use, he ruled that a permit had to be purchased annually to comply with fire regulations. The fee was $25 a year.

Profits Less Pollution Controls Equals Loss

In its three and one-half years of operation Superior has yet to show a profit. Table 14.1 shows the sales and losses for these years. While the net losses may not be entirely attributable to pollution problems, there can be little doubt that the heavy costs of pollution control devices have certainly limited profit potential.

───────────────────**TABLE 14.1.**───────────────────

SUPERIOR SALES AND PROFITS SUMMARY

Year	Sales	Profits
1968	$ 339,000	($136,000)
1969	1,352,000	($137,000)
1970	1,600,000	($ 65,000)
1971	2,136,000	($ 52,000)

Table 14.2 is a summary of the approximate costs in pollution restrictions for each of those years.

The wire milling industry is fiercely competitive, and even small increases in price may cause buyers to change to other producers. Consequently, Superior has had to absorb almost all the added costs of pollution controls. Superior was able in the past to offer its customers the advantage of quick local supply. Now, however, large Eastern steel mills and foreign competitors have set up local distributors to compete with Superior.

—————————— TABLE 14.2. ——————————

POLLUTION CONTROL EXPENDITURES

	One-time (Amortized) Costs	Annual Costs: Accumulative
Disposal of Rinse Solutions		
Permits: (L.A. County Flood Control district;		$ 100.00
U.S. Army Corps of Engineers;		50.00
State of California Water Quality Control)		50.00
Flood Control Channel effluent entrance	$ 1,500.00	
Clarifier design and installation	22,000.00	
Neutralization chemicals (caustic sodas)		6,000.00
Clarifier maintenance (3 hrs./day)		5,000.00
Acid and solid waste disposal		
Dumping permits and hauling		18,000.00
Fume scrubbing equipment		
Design and installation of fume scrubber		50,000.00
Scrubber maintenance (3 hrs./wk)		750.00
Annual permits (APCD and Fire Dept.)		125.00

Future Prospects

Smith confidently predicts that 1972 will be the first year that Superior will show a profit. The company's sales have climbed rapidly since its first year of operation, which indicates that there is a demand for its services. Incidently, he insists that other local producers are not burdened with the added costs of antipollution devices and have thus far been able to avoid detection.

Smith is not very optimistic about the future, however, because he feels that a company such as his does not have community support (indeed, the community would like it to leave). Superior has studied the possibility of relocation to other communities, but thus far it has received very little encouragement except from locations in Mexico. Smith puts it this way: "Even my family fails to see the economic implications of pollution problems. My daughter recently voiced her feelings with; 'Let the pollutors clean up the mess.' " Smith's own feelings are decidedly mixed. He said, "If I lived next door to the company I would raise hell to stop the pollution. But I don't live next door. I run the company, and when I enter the front door my job is to make money. The big question for me is: Can we afford to pay for the antipollution costs?"

Smith doesn't believe that his firm or others like it can afford to bear the entire costs of pollution controls. He feels that some type of aid must be made available through federal, state, or local financing. Government guarantee of long-term, low interest bonds and even tax-exemption credits for pollution controls would go a long way to help ease the costs burden, he says.

CASE QUESTIONS——————————————————————————

1. What major pollution issues are contained in this little case—for business generally, governments, and society as a whole? (List only.)

2. Argue this case pro and con: Government should help little companies like this to survive and still meet pollution standards. (See Henry C. Wallich, "How to Live with Economic Growth," *Fortune*, October 1972, pp. 115-122.)

3. In the general election of 1972, California voters approved a proposition that authorized the state legislature to provide for the issuance of revenue bonds not secured by the taxing power of the state to finance the acquisition, construction, and installation of environmental pollution control facilities, and for the lease or sale of such facilities to persons, associations, or corporations other than municipal corporations. The lease rentals on the antipollution facilities would be used to pay the principal and interest on the revenue bonds, and the operating costs of the authority set up to administer the legislation. Assembly Bill No. 1925 was passed and approved by the governor on December 19, 1972, to implement the proposition approved by the voters. It established the California Pollution Control Financing Authority and authorized it to issue up to $200 million in revenue bonds for the purposes stated in the proposition. Do you favor this type of legislation to aid companies like Superior? What would you include in a cost benefit analysis of such a law from the point of view the people of California? (See Paul W. Barkley and David W.

Seckler, *Economic Growth and Environmental Decay*. New York: Harcourt Brace Jovanovich, 1972, chapter seven.)

4. Do you think that the uncoordinated governmental regulatory actions in this case add up to "harassment" as far as Superior is concerned?

C) BIRMINGHAM'S POLLUTION SHUTDOWN AND WORKER RIGHTS[1]

On November 18, 1971, the Environmental Protection Agency obtained a court order shutting twenty-three plants in Birmingham, Alabama, until an air pollution crisis caused by a temperature inversion had passed. The authority for this action was the Clean Air Act of 1970.

Birmingham is a steel center with a record of air pollution. The inversion began on Monday morning, and by Tuesday, the pollution count had reached 771 micrograms of particulate matter per cubic meter—three times the danger level which affects children, the elderly, and those with respiratory problems. It was the 60th time in 1971 that the danger level had been exceeded.

County health officials, in response to the situation, sent telegrams to the 23 largest emissions sources requesting a cutback of 60% in emissions for the duration of the crisis. However, the emissions were down only 20% on Wednesday.

EPA officials were not satisfied with the results of the voluntary cutback and obtained the court order on Thursday. By Saturday, the crisis had passed.

Labor union officials said that the plant closings idled about 5,000 workers who lost approximately $400,000 in wages. Following the crisis some union officials were quoted as wanting contract provisions which would "protect" workers when polluting plants were forced to close down.

CASE QUESTIONS——————————————————————

1. Do you think that when a company is forced to shut down temporarily because of a pollution crisis workers should not lose wages as a result?

[1] *Business Week*, November 27, 1971.

2. Suppose the shutdown is permanent?

3. If you think workers should be protected, what types of contract provisions would you suggest as reasonable, equitable and operable from management's point of view?

D) DO WE NEED A NEW BILL OF RIGHTS?

"For years you have accepted this principle that where there are two or more parties at interest sharing the same resource or parcel of land, but for different purposes, there had to be some sort of accommodation that preserved the rights of each. So the farmer, the rancher, the pipeline company, the producer, and the community downstream all co-existed, maybe not altogether peacefully, but co-existed, on the basis that each had rights to be respected by others.

"Move the scene to a prized recreation area of great scenic beauty and scientific interest. Is there any difference, really, between the right of the farmer and the rancher to go about their business secure from harm resulting from oil operations, and the right of the motel owner, the marine operator, the marine biologist, the commercial fisherman to be secure from the same hazards? What of the right of the tourist to expect a clean beach; the right of the sports fisherman to expect fish where fish normally are to be found; the right of the marine biologist to make his observations in a habitat undisturbed by pollutants? Is there any difference, in principle, in responsibility for operations that on one hand leave a dead steer on the range and, on the other, a dead bird on a beach?"

CASE QUESTIONS

I. What is your reaction to this quotation?

2. If you think we need a new bill of rights covering the environment, what would you put in it and how would you implement it? (See Hans F. Sennholz, "Controlling Pollution," *The Freeman*, February 1973, pp. 67-77.)

Speech given by Russell E. Train, then Under Secretary of the Interior, at the Fiftieth Anniversary Meeting of the American Petroleum Institute, Jesse H. Jones Hall, Rice Hotel, Houston, Texas, November 11, 1969. Reprinted by permission.

DISCUSSION GUIDES ON CHAPTER CONTENT ──────

1. What are the major types of environmental pollutions today, and why be concerned about them?

2. Who or what is to blame for these major pollutions?

3. Identify and explain the "schools of thought" concerned with the pollution problem.

4. Do you think the "issue-attention cycle" identified by Downs has been working in the United States? Explain.

5. Our society is a complex of systems within a system. In this light, the establishment of pollution standards may conflict with other systems. Illustrate a few conflicts.

6. What major tools are available to help decision makers be more rational in establishing pollution standards? Do you think the tools are as powerful as they should be?

7. Who should bear the costs of pollution control?

8. What are environmental impact studies, and of what consequence are they to business? To society?

9. Identify the Clean Air Act. Appraise its significance.

MIND-STRETCHING QUESTION ──────────────

1. Many people think it is time that an international agreement be made to assure cooperative action on the part of all nations of the world to reduce the pollution of the oceans. What major problems exist in trying to do this? How would you suggest trying to get needed cooperation?

15
BUSINESS AND CONSUMERS

A) INTERNATIONAL FOODS INDUSTRIES' RESPONSE TO CONSUMERISM

Martin Masterson was congratulating himself on his leadership in International Foods Industries. He had been president and chief executive officer for four years, during which time he brought IFI out of a deep deficit to become the most profitable company in the industry. This had not been easy. His predecessor had gone on an acquisition spree and had accumulated a number of money losers that Masterson had to make profitable or divest. At the same time, he was faced with a serious problem of declining productivity in his work force, lax production controls, and a decline in share of market for most of his major products. He was able to correct these problems and achieve his present enviable financial success by setting tough-to-achieve financial- and market-share goals for all divisions, serious formal corporate planning, tight control, and "hardnosed" management.

IFI earnings last year were the highest ever recorded. New records had also been established for profit margin, earnings after taxes, return on stockholder's equity, and earnings per share. To further brighten the picture, there had been dramatic increases in market shares in most of the areas in which IFI did business.

IFI is a dominant producer of a number of food products, including cheese, coffee, bakery products (fresh as well as pre-mixed), wine, beer, soft drinks, a line of canned goods, and dog food. The company also has a large service subsidiary that markets its products. It has a chain of restaurants as well as retail stores. The latter are particularly important in the overseas operations of IFI.

Masterson has long asserted that the success of IFI is based upon a strong devotion to the basic philosophy defined by its founder—to which he, Masterson, has added his own ideas. Wilber Knutson, the founder, had a bronze tablet made and placed in the cornerstone of his headquarters, a building that is still used by IFI. It reads: "Our policy is to think first of a quality product and service to consumers. Profits will then take care of themselves." Masterson never had the tablet removed, but in all his discussions about company policy and activities related to company management, he has eliminated the last sentence and inserted in its place: "If we meet this policy fully we shall maximize profits."

Masterson's illusions on his successful management of IFI were shattered one day last winter, when a series of problems seemed to arise all at once. One was a class-action suit for $150 million brought by a beer drinker. This customer claimed that he had spot-checked the contents of IFI's standard beer and found that instead of ten ounces the can checked had only nine ounces. Multiplying the output of the company's beer during the time of the test, times the overcharge to consumers, the suit claimed customers had been defrauded of the sum mentioned. On the very day of the suit, the FTC issued a cease and desist order, together with demands for corrective advertising, because of alleged deceptive advertising claims made for IFI's dog food. A few days later, customers were up in arms in Philadelphia because some defective bottles of catsup had turned up. This is just a sampling of consumer complaints that Masterson suddenly faced.

The vice-president of Marketing claimed that the current troubles were merely coincidences. IFI's public image, he said, was as high as any in the industry, and IFI was merely the victim of excessive consumer expectations. On the other hand, several members of the board of directors felt that Masterson's vigorous drive for improved financial performance was motivating managers down the line to pay less attention to quality than to profits.

Masterson reviewed company policy and programs concerning product quality, consumer services, and profit planning. He concluded that IFI perhaps was not responding as it should be to consumer demands.

CASE QUESTIONS

1. Mr. Masterson asks you to lay out for his consideration a set of basic policies and programs that IFI should adopt to be fully responsive to the legitimate—as well as the excessive—demands of consumers. What would you suggest? (See David A. Aaker and George S. Day, "Corporate Responses to Consumerism Pressures," *Harvard Business Review*, November—December 1972, pp. 114—124.)

2. What is meant by "consumerism"? What are its root causes?

3. Do you believe that consumerism will result in more or fewer demands on business in the future?

B) STOCKING SNOWSHOVELS

Wilbur Goodpaster is owner-manager of a department store in Stroudsburgh, Pennsylvania. For years he has prided himself on finding good buys for his customers and making the products available as promotional items. The great majority of his customers have been well satisfied with Goodpaster's promotions, although, occasionally, a product has proven to be less useful than it seemed to be at first. At any rate, the price of Goodpaster's promotions have generally raised no question. The most common complaint has been that the values are so attractive the stock available disappears before all the customers can get to the store to make their purchases.

Last September Goodpaster bought a quantity of snowshovels and was able to price them very low. The very day that Goodpaster advertised the snowshovels, Stroudsburgh and its vicinity was struck with an early, and completely unexpected, heavy snowfall. One result was a rush to buy the durable and low-priced shovels at Goodpaster's store. Within one hour, all the promotion stock was sold.

The next day, much to his surprise, Goodpaster was sued by Peter Crier on behalf of a local consumer activist group called

SCAAT, an acronym for Stroudsburgh Consumers Arise and Fight. Crier filed a class-action suit with the local courts charging that Goodpaster deceptively induced people into his store with the snowshovel promotion, but did not stock a reasonable quantity for sale. The suit asked for damages and costs of $50,000, of which $15,000 was for 5,000 customers who might have bought the shovels and had to pay for new shovels that were $3 more expensive than the promotional shovels.

The people of Stroudsburgh were divided on the merits of this case. Some felt rather strongly that if Goodpaster promoted an item he surely had to keep enough on hand to take care of reasonable consumer demand. Others felt, however, that Goodpaster was doing his customers a service in finding useful merchandise at low prices. They had been well satisfied in the past and felt that Crier and SCAAT were assuming prerogatives on their behalf that they wanted to carry themselves. They did not, in other words, want SCAAT speaking for them, especially in this particular case.

CASE QUESTIONS————————————————————————

   1. What would you consider to be a "reasonable" supply in a case such as this?

   2. This case raises a much larger question about who should speak for the consumer. Explain your views on the matter. (See Ralph Nader, "The Great American Gap," *The New York Review of Books*, 21 November, 1968, pp. 27—34. Ralph K. Winter, Jr., "The Consumer Advocate Versus The Consumer," (Washington, D. C.: American Enterprise Institute, 1972) pp. 1—16. Hiram C. Barksdale and William R. Darden, "Consumer Attitudes Toward Marketing and Consumerism," *Journal of Marketing*, October 1972, pp. 28—35.)

C) HOME TOOL COMPANY PRODUCT LIABILITY

The president of the Home Tool Company calls upon you to give him advice concerning what he should do about product liability. His company manufactures various hardware products for home use. While not the largest company in the industry, his firm distributes nationally, and his products can be found in millions of homes. One reason for the success of Home Tool is that the company has continuously developed new products. Indeed, at the present time it has forty new products in various stages of development.

One of the competitors of Home Tool was recently sued by a customer who purchased a power lathe and was seriously injured when set screws that held the parts together became loose and permitted the block in the lathe to fly loose. The competitor lost the suit and almost went bankrupt as a result.

While Home Tool has always been concerned about the safety of its products, it now feels that a much tighter rein should be held on product design, development, and distribution.

CASE QUESTIONS

1. What are the facts about increasing manufacturer liability for product safety? (See *Greenman vs. Yuba Power Products, Inc.*, 59 Col. 2d 57, 377 P. 2d 897, 27 Col. Rpts. 697 (1963). David L. Rados, "Product Liability: Tougher Ground Rules," *Harvard Business Review*, July—August 1969, pp. 144—153, and Conrad Berenson, "The Product Liability Revolution," *Business Horizons*, October 1972, pp. 71—80.)

2. What do you recommend to the Home Tool Company as the best way to meet legitimate demands of consumers and at the same time reduce its product liability?

3. Hypothesize some consequences for consumers in terms of new product innovations, costs, and quality as manufacturer liability for product defects becomes tougher.

D) PUFFERY OR PREVARICATION IN ADVERTISING

On July 14, 1971 the Federal Trade Commission ordered seven automobile manufacturers to back up claims made in their advertising. Ford Motor Company, for instance, said its Ford LTD was "over 700 percent quieter." The Chevrolet Chevelle ads claimed that the car had "109 advantages to keep it from becoming old before its time." Chrysler claimed that its Dart Demon was "not a minicar, but saves like one." American Motors said its Matador "has more room inside than any other car its size." Toyota Motors claimed that owners of its Corolla Fastback "won't spend a cent on chassis lubes." The FTC gave these and other automobile companies sixty days to send in any tests or studies that would substantiate claims regarding safety, performance, quality, and price. The information would then be made public. The FTC said also that it would institute legal proceedings in cases involving false advertising. (False advertising exists in the judgment of the FTC when there is inadequate substantiation of claims.) Also, the FTC said it was not seeking substantiation of advertising claims that were "puffery." Puffery advertising, said the FTC, would be statements asserting, for example, that an automobile "is a terrific car" or "improves your virility."

CASE QUESTIONS

1. Do you think the FTC is correct in its actions? Explain.
2. Where can the line between false advertising and puffery be drawn?

References

Theodore Levitt, "The Morality (?) of Advertising," *Harvard Business Review*, July—August 1970, pp. 84—92.

For a short resume of the history and nature of deceptive advertising see: Gaylord A. Jentz, "Federal Regulation of Advertising," *American Business Law Journal*, January 1968, pp. 409—427.

Ralph Nader, ed., *The Consumer and Corporate Accountability* (New York: Harcourt Brace Jovanovich, 1973), chapter 3.

E) SMOKEY CIGARETTE COMPANY

You are the president of the Smokey Cigarette Company. A delegation of community leaders has just left your office after declaring in the strongest language possible that you have a deep social responsibility to stop advertising your products because advertising does in fact induce young people to start smoking and also maintains demand among those who are now smoking. You know the FTC has stopped all cigarette advertising over TV. You feel that the Surgeon General's Report on the relationship between cigarette smoking and cancer does present convincing evidence of the connection. Yet you still have some doubts. You know there is a close correlation between cigarette advertising and sales by brand. If you stopped advertising, sales would drop, and there would be a serious impact on earnings and stock prices. Furthermore, many farmers and your own employees are dependent on your company.

CASE QUESTION————————————————————————

1. What do you think your social responsibilities are in this case?

F) HYPO PHARMACEUTICAL COMPANY PRICING

The Hypo Pharmaceutical Company (HPC) is a medium-size producer of drugs, offering at present perhaps 500 items. Increased laboratory research costs, together with a slowdown in business, have created a moderate financial squeeze on the company, which may force it to abandon dividend payments this year. The company has produced a new vitamin tablet that has received high public acceptance in test-marketing runs. The tablet will cost $5 per thousand, but, because of its acceptance plus heavy advertising, the company is sure it can be sold in bottles of 100 for as much as $5. The demand is calculated to be such that at this price, and considering advertising and other marketing expenses, HPC will net for the next year a profit after taxes equal to, if not somewhat over, the average for the industry. HPC feels this pricing formula is acceptable, since a good seller should logically be expected to offset costs of poorer sellers so that the overall operations of the company are profitable.

CASE QUESTIONS————————————————————————

1. If you knew about all these facts would you feel you were cheated in paying $5 per 100 for the vitamins?
2. If your answer is "yes," explain how you would price items if you were the president of HPC.

G) WISCONSIN TELEPHONE COMPANY

The Wisconsin Telephone Company launched an advertising campaign in 1971 to get households to install a second telephone for the convenience of the very young members of their families. The advertising featured a seven-year-old named Lori Busk, who urged mothers to make a second telephone investment. A hidden voice asks Lori: "Hey, what do you like most about extension phones?" Lori answers: "All the colors," and adds, "They're convenient." Explaining what convenience means, she says, "It means that when you're busy coloring in your room, you don't have to run downstairs to answer the phone."

The telephone company is happy with the results of its campaign: since launching it in 1971, it has installed 15,000 new extension phones. State Representative Harout Sanasarian says, however, that the customers of the telephone company should not be obliged to pay for this kind of advertising.[1]

CASE QUESTION

1. Explain your reaction to this advertising, assuming you are: (a) a stockholder of Wisconsin Telephone Co., (b) a non-stock-holding-consumer, (c) Representative Sanasarian, (d) a member of the Wisconsin Utility Commission, and (e) an FTC commissioner.

DISCUSSION GUIDES TO CHAPTER CONTENT

1. What are the major motivating forces behind the current wave of consumerism in the United States?

2. Identify a few types of legislative actions that the federal government has recently taken to protect consumers. Do you favor them?

3. What are "consumer advocates"? What is your view of Ralph Nader and his organization?

[1] *Time*, 3 April 1972, p. 12.

4. Do you think that businessmen in your area have responded properly and satisfactorily to consumer complaints? Explain.

5. Classical economics says that producers react to consumer wants, but Galbraith says that business forces consumers to buy what business wants to sell them. Who is right in your judgment?

6. Do you approve the FTC's regulation of advertising? Be specific in your evaluation.

7. Argue the pros and cons of the FTC's regulation of cigarette advertising.

8. Manufacturers probably can build most products to last a lifetime. Why don't they?

9. How does manufacturing's liability to consumers differ today than from, say, twenty-five years ago?

10. Deaths resulting from automobile accidents increased up to the time of the speed slowdown in late 1973, which was brought about by the energy crisis. Even so, the death level is still very high. Many critics say the high percentage of deaths and injuries on our highways has been due to the negligence of the automobile producers. The automobile producers claim their products have become increasingly safe and that causes other than automobile quality are most responsible for rising accidents. What are the main issues in this debate? Who is to blame for rising automobile accidents? Have the automobile companies been negligent? Argue the issue from the point of view of a consumer. From the point of view of the chief executive officer of a major automobile company.

MIND-STRETCHING QUESTIONS

1. The President of Motorola (maker of TV sets) asks your advice about what policies his company ought to adopt in response to consumer complaints. What would you advise him to do?

2. Where does the government's obligation to protect its citizens end and interference with free enterprise begin? Just how far should the government go in protecting the consumer?

16

BUSINESS, COMMUNITY PROBLEMS, AND DISADVANTAGED MINORITIES

A) THE MULTI-MILLION DOLLAR MISUNDERSTANDING: AN ATTEMPT TO REDUCE TURNOVER AMONG DISADVANTAGED WORKERS

This is a case history of a failure. It documents one company's very ambitious, very expensive, and very unsuccessful attempt to solve a problem confronting an increasing number of companies in urban areas—the problem of reducing turnover among economically disadvantaged workers.

The company studied was a large, partially diversified, multi-plant, and multi-city—one engaged principally in heavy manufacturing. In spite of the company's geographical and product diversity,

This case was prepared by and is reproduced with the permission of Robert P. Quinn (Survey Research Center, University of Michigan); Teresa Levitin (Russell Sage Fellow at Yale University Law School); and Dov Eden (Tel-Aviv University). It is based upon research supported by a contract with the Manpower Administration, U. S. Department of Labor, under authority of the Manpower Development and Training Act. Researchers undertaking such projects under government sponsorship are encouraged to express their own judgment. Interpretations or viewpoints stated in this case do not necessarily represent the official position or policy of the Department of Labor.

the heart of its heavy-manufacturing activities was located in a single city. In the decade preceding this case report, major demographic changes had been taking place in this city. These changes had radically altered the composition of the labor force available to the company to fill its entry-level positions. An increasing proportion of new recruits were black and many were from the population of the economically disadvantaged. Confounded with racial and economic differences were generational ones. The result was what the company felt was a "new breed" of recruit who was far less tractable than had been the recruits of previous years.

In order to fill its entry-level jobs, most of which involved the assembly of heavy machinery, the company was hiring increasing numbers of workers who had been officially classified as "hard-core unemployed." The pay levels of the entry-level jobs to which these workers were assigned were high. In principle, by securing a job in the company, a disadvantaged worker left the ranks of the hard-core unemployed and began to collect a base pay that averaged considerably over three dollars an hour. For many men, however, this change was short-lived. *42 percent* of these newly-hired disadvantaged workers left the company within their first six weeks of employment. This turnover was far in excess of what the company had previously considered "normal" turnover on its entry-level jobs.

An "Obvious" Solution

The company management was, therefore, confronted with increased turnover without any apparent parallel deterioration of working conditions to which the increased turnover might be attributed. As a result, it attributed the increased turnover to personal characteristics of the new recruits—their lack of skills, their unfamiliarity with the demands of jobs in heavy industry, and, above all, their lack of the "right attitude" toward work. From the company's point of view, the solution to its turnover problem was obvious: institute a training program that would somehow "correct" what the company felt were "defects" that limited the adaptability of their new recruits to their jobs. Such a program might both solve the company's increasing manpower problem and also express concern for disadvantaged workers in the local community. Furthermore, the company's management had already pledged to co-operate with the federal government in securing jobs for the disadvantaged. Through several contracts with the Manpower Administration the company had obtained, at the time of this study, the largest such financial underwriting that had ever been accorded a single company conducting a training program for the disadvantaged.

The company's vestibule training program provided each recruit certified as hard-core unemployed with approximately six weeks of instruction in classes of 15—25 men. Classes were held five days a week, for approximately eight hours a day. Trainees were paid $2.50 for each hour they spent in training. Each trainee was told upon beginning this pre-employment training that he would be guaranteed a job with the company contingent upon his successful completion of the training program.

The training program was staffed by a male adviser and female teacher for each class and a job counselor for several classes. The teachers, most of whom were black and had been clerks or secretaries in the company, provided basic educational instruction. The advisers, most of whom were black and had been community workers outside the company, provided various types of counseling for the trainees, served as role models, and conducted class discussions that ranged in subject matter from black history to values and attitudes about life and work. The job counselors, most of whom were white, were available to assist men who had completed the program with whatever problems they might have on their subsequent company jobs.

Each adviser-teacher team was able to structure the class and to define its own role, except that standard programmed basic educational materials for language and mathematical skills were used in all classes. Advisers and teachers reported that their goals for the program ranged from teaching the trainees a few limited skills from these standard educational materials to encouraging the trainees to develop better attitudes with regard to more inclusive matters such as their feelings of achievement and self-esteem. Although a six week period seemed insufficient time to effect such psychological changes, the staff nevertheless appeared committed to fostering the "personal growth" of trainees and tended to describe as successful any trainee they felt had evidenced such growth.

One thing was conspicuously absent among these very ambitious goals—teaching trainees specific skills that would be relevant to their imminent company jobs. This deficiency resulted in part from the uncertain future job placement of the trainees. The advisers and teachers had no advance knowledge of the particular type of company job to which a trainee would later be assigned. Consequently, there was no way of defining what skills could appropriately be taught him. Moreover, union regulations prohibited men from receiving "hands on" training on the assembly line while they were still in training. To overcome this road-block, the company began to set up a "mini-plant" where trainees would obtain some familiarity with the types of machines they might soon operate. At the time of this study this mini-plant was in an early stage of development and the trainees in the sample had limited acquaintance with it. Not being able to teach specific skills, the staff attempted instead to orient trainees to more general aspects of employment in the company, such as industrial safety, how to deal with foremen, the importance of being on time, how not to "lose your cool" in emergencies, and how to dress for work.

The company's training program appeared on the surface to be a quite reasonable solution to its problem of high turnover among diadvantaged workers *if this turnover were attributable principally to characteristics of these workers rather than to characteristics of their jobs.* The training solution was therefore based on the assumption that the major cause of turnover was the work-related beliefs and attitudes of entry-level employees as well as their general and specific skill levels. Little consideration was given in the development of the training program to the possibility that this turnover might instead be due to matters that could *not* be modified by pre-employment training.

How effective was the company's training program in reducing turnover? To answer this question, turnover statistics were obtained for 290 men who had been certified as hard-core unemployed. A random sample of 90 such men was selected from among all those entering the training program during a three-month period. Sixty-three of these men completed the training program and were subsequently placed on company jobs. The job turnover of these 63 trainees was compared with that of a control group of 227 men who had been recruited by the company at the same time as the trainees but who had received *no* special pre-employment training. Men in the control group were selected so as to be equivalent in terms of age and education to the sample of trainees. All were black men who had been certified as hard-core unemployed. Men in both samples lived in the same urban community and were placed on similar entry-level jobs in the same plants. Trained and untrained workers were compared in terms of the percentage of each group who remained on the job for at least six weeks. For both samples the six weeks were counted beginning with their first day of work. For the trained group this had been preceded by several weeks of training.

Sixty-eight percent of those who had completed the training program stayed on their later jobs for at least six weeks. According to the standards by which the successes of training programs are sometimes evaluated, this 68 percent figure could be regarded as evidence of the effectiveness of the company's vestibule training. This evidence was, however, undermined by the finding that the comparable job-retention figure among *untrained* workers was 58 percent. There was no statistically significant difference between these two percentages. Although the company's training program graduated many men who kept their subsequent company jobs, *precisely the same effect would have been achieved, and a few million dollars saved, had each disadvantaged worker been placed directly on the job without any vestibule training.*

What Went Wrong?

Several conditions appeared to limit the efficient functioning of the training program. Some of these may have been peculiar to the particular program studied. Others may have more general applicability to other job training programs for the disadvantaged. Prominent among these conditions were overambitious and unrealistic training objectives which assumed that the psychological patterns of a lifetime could be undone within a few weeks; restrictive contractual obligations with the Manpower Administration that tended to discourage necessary experimentation and program development; an overestimation of the number of men that could be trained within the contracted time period, resulting in a preoccupation with *how many* men could be trained at the expense of *how well* they could be trained; a graceless handling of racial issues that at times crystallized rather routine staff conflicts into racial confrontations; inadequate separation of program planning from program operations; inadequate power allocation to the training program; and inadequate ongoing program evaluation.

The Sources of Turnover

Suppose that none of the latter conditions had existed. Would the company's training program therefore have been successful? Probably not. This assertion is based on data obtained from a related study of the sources of job turnover among disadvantaged workers.

This study of turnover was conducted in the same company, at the same time, and by the same investigators as was the training program evaluation described above. The sample consisted of 66 men, many of whom were also part of the untrained control group in the training program evaluation. All men in both the turnover study and the training program evaluation were black, had been certified as hard-core unemployed, lived in the same community, and were assigned to similar entry-level jobs in the same company plants. The 66 men in the turnover study differed from the trainees in the program evaluation in that the former had been placed directly on entry-level jobs without any special vestibule training.

Twenty-seven of these 66 men had left the company, either voluntarily or involuntarily, within six weeks of their induction into the company. They were interviewed in their homes within two weeks after their terminations. The remaining 39 had entered the company at the same times as the 27, but they were still on their jobs when they were interviewed. The two groups were equivalent in terms of their ages, the company plants to which they were assigned, and the number of weeks that had elapsed from the times of their entering the company to the times they were interviewed. Topics covered by the interviews, all of which were conducted by young black men, dealt with: characteristics of the worker's job; his perception of his supervisor; his demographic characteristics and biographic data; selected aspects of his beliefs and attitudes, particularly his self-confidence, sense of personal efficacy, and his ascription to middle-class values concerning work; and his beliefs and attitudes concerning selected racial issues.

The total sample of 66 workers was divided into two groups representing those that had high and low scores on each of the measures obtained from these interviews. These two groups were compared in terms of their rates of turnover. The turnover figures are shown in Figure 1 and are expressed as the percentage of each "high" and "low" group who left the company within their first six weeks of employment. The first line of the figure shows, for example, that among the workers who indicated that the type of work they were doing was "pretty good," the percentage leaving within six weeks was 28 percent; the comparable percentage for those who indicated that their type of work was *not* "pretty good" was 54 percent.

Almost all of the measures that were associated with turnover at an acceptable level of statistical significance (.05) involved either characteristics of the worker's job, the supervision he received, or his demographic and background characteristics. The many measures of beliefs, attitudes, or other aspects of personality were not at all related to turnover. Ironically, the training program for the disadvantaged attempted to alter many of these beliefs and attitudes in order to reduce turnover.

If one single factor were to be singled out as *the* major cause of turnover among disadvantaged workers on entry-level jobs, it would certainly be the poor quality of their working lives, including both characteristics of the workers' jobs and characteristics they attributed to their supervisors. But Figure 16.1 shows only the *associations between* turnover and some of these conditions. It communicates no sense of just *how* bad these conditions actually were. Generally, the physical working conditions of entry-level jobs in this company were no worse than those in the industry as a whole—that is, dirty, noisy, overcrowded, and dangerous. Of the workers interviewed, 35 percent had been injured at work during their first *six weeks* in the company. Supervision, while of course highly variable in quality, could often become capriciously unfair in its punitiveness. One supervisor, for example, matter-of-factly offered to arrange for us the discharge of a worker who for reasons unknown had failed to keep an interviewing appointment.

Many people succeed in adapting to poor working conditions no matter how bad these conditions may be. Successful adaptation presupposes, however, some consistency or dependability in the conditions to which one is trying to adapt. For workers interviewed in this study, the *lack* of such dependability was commonplace. They could not predict the particular conditions to which they

Figure 16.1
TURNOVER AMONG GROUPS OF DISADVANTAGED WORKERS
Percentage Who Left Job Within First Six Weeks of Employment

Left side (%)			0	Right side (%)		Description
28%				54%		Workers who regarded the kind of work they were doing as "pretty good" / Workers who did not regard the kind of work they were doing as "pretty good"
32%				61%		Workers who did not often have to work too hard or too fast / Workers who often had to work too hard or too fast
	18%			63%		Workers who were never bored by their jobs / Workers who were sometimes bored by their jobs
24%				64%		Workers who did not feel that it would be hard to have their job assignments changed if they did not like them / Workers who felt that it would be hard to have their job assignments changed if they did not like them
	18%			63%		Workers who felt that it was at least somewhat likely that they might someday get the company job they most wanted / Workers who felt that it was not at all likely that they would ever get the company job they most wanted
33%				56%		Workers who were assigned to only one work station / Workers who were moved from work station to work station
36%				64%		Workers who started each day with at least some idea of what their work routines would be like / Workers who started each day with no idea of what their work routines would be like
	18%			51%		Workers who had a good idea of how their work fit in with that of other workers / Workers who did not have a good idea of how their work fit in with that of other workers

Scale: 75% 50% 25% 0 25% 50% 75%

	75% 50% 25% 0 25% 50% 75%	
Workers whose supervisors never told them to do something that they did not know how to do	28% — 63%	Workers whose supervisors told them to do something that they did not know how to do
Workers who liked the shift to which they were assigned	33% — 67%	Workers who did not like the shift to which they were assigned
Workers reporting to only one foreman	31% — 57%	Workers reporting to more than one foreman
Workers who were not "put in the middle" between two foremen who wanted different things	34% — 56%	Workers who were "put in the middle" between two foremen who wanted different things
Workers who reported having received good supervision	32% — 62%	Workers who reported not having received good supervision
Workers 21 years old or older	37% — 50%	Workers under 21 years old
Married workers	29% — 51%	Unmarried workers
Workers who paid most of the household bills where they lived	21% — 55%	Workers who did not pay most of the household bills where they lived
Workers who had been out of work only twice a year or less in the two years prior to joining the company	25% — 55%	Workers who had been out of work more than twice a year in the two years prior to joining the company

would be exposed (although they could generally assume that the conditions would be bad). They had no control over what might happen to them from day to day. Fifty-four percent reported that they were moved from work station to work station rather than spending most of their time at one station. 28 percent said that they had no idea *at all* at the beginning of each day as to what their work routine was going to be like. Forty-eight percent indicated that there was more than one man whom they considered their foreman. A newly-hired worker was treated as a cipher of "replacement personnel." He was often moved, like a pawn, from job to job, station to station, or supervisor to supervisor in response to highly unpredictable fluctuations in company absenteeism and production quotas.

The Multi-million Dollar Misunderstanding

It was asserted earlier in this case report that even if the company's training program had been unencumbered by a number of existing administrative and operational difficulties it would *still* not have been successful in reducing turnover among disadvantaged workers. The justification for this assertion should be clear in light of the turnover data just presented. These data suggested that turnover was almost exclusively determined by characteristics of the worker's job or by generally immutable properties of the worker's background. *Neither of these sources of turnover can be altered by training.* That the company's training program failed to reduce turnover was less a function of shortcomings of the program's design or execution than it was a function of the total irrelevance of the program to the social problem it was designed to solve. No amount of employee training can make working conditions objectively less noxious or change man's history. In this light, the above suggestions of how the training programs might have been improved appear akin to suggestions for the best way to tilt against windmills.

Why, then, have job training programs for the disadvantaged attained their current vogue? Part of the answer lies in the fundamental American faith in education as the solution to ills. Whenever a social problem occurs and its sources can be attributed to both social systems and people within these systems, efforts to solve the problem more often involve attempts to alter the behavior of the people rather than to modify the systems themselves. This is particularly true when the social system is a large industrial establishment. Confronted with high turnover, management can more comfortably attribute the turnover to shortcomings of its workers than to shortcomings of their company. Lest the organizational *status quo* be altered—or, for that matter, even seriously questioned—an employee training program is then instituted to help employees "adapt" to an environment which management is likely to accept as a fact of life. The training is designed to mold workers to fit the existing industrial system, thereby side-stepping the possibility of modifying the organization to make it more compatible with the needs of the workers. Where organizational changes *are* made they are generally grudging concessions to workers' insistent demands.

Present practices of the federal government do little to encourage companies to attempt organizational change and job redesign as a means of providing workers, disadvantaged or otherwise, with decent jobs. Many millions of dollars are spent on the development of job-training programs for the disadvantaged. Little is spent on the improving of the quality of the jobs to which the disadvantaged are assigned after they have completed training.

Despite the business and government canard about job-training programs, it is clear that such programs cannot be the dramatic successes they are claimed to be so long as the target of proposed change is only the trainee and not also the organization or social system within which such training is taking place. Perhaps this study should have asked not why many disadvantaged workers *left* the company, but why any of these men *remained* at all. Why did they remain in entry-level jobs that offered little reasonable chance for promotion, that were monotonous, physically exhausting and often dangerous? Why did they remain in jobs that provided few opportunities for satisfying personal needs and goals? One answer may be that the alternatives available were even more distasteful—unemployment, illegal activities, or other similarly unrewarding means of self-support.

It is fatuous, however, to expect men to adjust docilely to the kinds of entry-level jobs that the men in this study were given. To try to train men for these jobs is both naïve and a grave misdirection of energy. Paradoxically, if training is successful in that a trainee demonstrates academic competence, high self-esteem, and job skills, as well as the possession of achievement values and goals, he can hardly be expected to be satisfied with the entry-level jobs offered him. Yet training is also a misdirection of energy because it assumes that the *trainee* alone rather than the job *situation* is the appropriate target for change in order to reduce turnover—an assumption vitiated by the findings of the present study. Change must be directed toward the elimination of barely tolerable working conditions rather than toward the modification of those who are victimized by these conditions.

CASE QUESTIONS

1. Do the results of this study surprise you? Explain.

2. The National Alliance of Businessmen was launched in 1968 to find job opportunities for the disadvantaged worker. Report on the success which NAB has achieved up to the present time (document your findings). (See Allen R. Janger, *Employing the Disadvantaged: A Company Perspective* (New York: National Industrial Conference Board, 1972), Philip H. Mounts, *Business and the Hard-To-Employ: A Study of a Metropolitan Office of the National Alliance of Businessmen.* Los Angeles: Institute of Industrial Relations, University of California, 1972.)

3. If you were establishing a program for a company to improve hiring and retention of the disadvantaged, what are some of the major things you would suggest? (See Elmer H. Burack, F. James Staszak, and Gopal C. Pati, "An Organizational Analysis of Manpower Issues in Employing the Disadvantaged," *Academy of Management Journal*, September 1972, pp. 255–271; Louis E. Davis, "Readying the Unready; Postindustrial Jobs," *California Management Review*, Summer 1971, pp. 27–36.)

References

Three relevant and important books are:
Harland Padfield and Roy Williams, *Stay Where You Were: A Study of Unemployables in Industry* (New York: J. B. Lippincott, 1973).

A Special Task Force to the Secretary of HEW, *Work in America* (Boston: The Massachusetts Institute of Technology Press, 1973).

Theodore V. Purcell and Gerald F. Cavanagh, *Blacks in the Industrial World: Issues for the Manager* (New York: The Free Press, 1972).

DISCUSSION GUIDES ON CHAPTER CONTENT——————

1. Do you believe that business today has made a "commitment" to improving the position of disadvantaged minorities? Explain with specific illustrations.

2. What is "equal opportunity and affirmative action"? What if your evaluation of the GE program given in the book?

3. In what ways has business become involved in training and employing the disadvantaged?

4. Why do you think the proportion of minority enterprises to total business enterprises is so small? Do you approve present private and public programs to raise this proportion? What would you recommend be done that is not being done? Defend your position.

5. There is little question that this nation has not met needs for housing for low-income groups. Why is this so? What do you think should be done about it? Defend your position.

6. If you live in an urban area, describe the significant ways in which business in your community is doing things to help the community resolve some of its major problems.

7. What guidelines do you suggest for a company that is interested in doing more to improve the community and help it deal with major problems?

MIND-STRETCHING QUESTIONS——————

1. Identify the ten most significant socioeconomic problems in your community.

2. You are appointed a member of the Committee of Twenty-Five. This is a group of civic-minded leaders—business, educational, religious, philanthropic, legal, and technical—in the community who have joined together to help solve its major problems. The immediate question is to establish policies and programs to deal with the major problems identified in question 1. What would you recommend?

17

BUSINESS AND EDUCATION

DISCUSSION GUIDES ON CHAPTER CONTENT————————

1. Should business continue to support education? Explain.
2. What methods are currently being used by business to support education?

MIND-STRETCHING QUESTIONS————————

1. Many business schools have visiting committees composed of top executives from nationally known firms such as Ford Motors, Time-Life, etc. What should be the function of these committees?
2. William Day, president of the Michigan Bell Telephone Company, said that his company had "adopted a school." When asked about his activity he said he wanted to help prepare the students for the business world. "We think we can make a real difference in public attitudes," he explained. To what extent should business try to influence values in the educational world? What is the basic purpose of education? Is it more likely that business values will impregnate the educational world or that values from the educational world will influence business?

18

BUSINESS AND THE ARTS

A) PHILADELPHIA GAS WORKS ADOPTS PHILADELPHIA CIVIC BALLET

Four years ago the Philadelphia Gas Works adopted the struggling Philadelphia Civic Ballet. Company grants enabled the troupe to hire additional dancers and buy new equipment. Then PGW put the show on the road—literally, in free performances at 20 neighborhood centers where audiences had never before seen ballet. Promotion department staffers designed and wrote promotional material. Market researchers studied their files to help the ballet company choose appropriate selections for each neighborhood. Accounts receivable stuffed announcements into monthly gas bills. Even the commissary department got into the act; it served refreshments at meet-the-dancers receptions after the shows.

CASE QUESTIONS————————————————————

1. Should a corporation like PGW do this?
2. Who pays the costs? Who benefits?
3. How does the cost/benefit equation balance out among

Business Week, 15 May 1971, p. 102. Reprinted with permission.

those concerned, that is stockholders, consumers, company managers, hourly employees, the community generally, the public utility commissioner, and so on? (See Richard Eells, "Executive Suite and Artist's Garret," *Columbia Journal of World Business*, Fall 1965, pp. 37-44. *The Corporation and the Arts* (New York: Macmillan, 1967) Alvin H. Reiss, *Culture and Company* (New York: Twayne Publishers, 1972.) Armand G. Erpf, "Interface: Business and Beauty," *Columbia Journal of World Business*, May-June 1967, pp. 85-90: Joanne Wojtusiak, "In Support of the Arts, Companies Know What They Like," *The Conference Board Record*, January 1970, pp. 62-65.)

DISCUSSION GUIDES ON CHAPTER CONTENT————

1. How do you define "the arts"?

2. What are the pros and cons of business support of the arts?

MIND-STRETCHING QUESTION————

1. You are asked by the chairman of the board of the American Telephone and Telegraph Company to set forth basic policies that his company should use in making financial contributions to the arts. What would you suggest?

19
BUSINESS AND TECHNOLOGY

A) PLANE DEAL?

On the morning of February 7, 1974, the *Los Angeles Times* first broke the story of complex and largely confidential negotiations between the Russian government and three American manufacturers of wide-bodied commercial jets.[1] Although discussions between the Russians and each of the aircraft manufacturers differed slightly, the broad outlines of the proposed agreement were clear—even if their implications were shrouded in uncertainty. In a climate of warming trade relations Russia sought to secure from U.S. firms the technical knowledge to build a massive commercial jet aircraft complex capable of turning out 100 wide-bodied jetliners a year. In return for the export of American expertise the Russians offered to purchase up to thirty of the big planes from American manufacturers.

The *Times* revealed that Soviet teams had visited Boeing, Lockheed and McDonnel Douglas in October 1973 and that Boeing and Lockheed had recently reciprocated by sending groups to Russia. McDonnel Douglas was scheduled to do so soon. And on

(This case was prepared by John F. Steiner, Assistant Professor, California State University, Los Angeles and is used with permission.)

[1] Benjamin F. Schemmer, "Russ Seek U.S. Jet Expertise to Build Huge Airliner Plants," *Los Angeles Times*, February 7, 1974.

January 30, Daniel J. Haughton, Lockheed's chairman of the board, publicly announced that his company had signed a commercial protocol agreement with the Soviet Union which prefaced cooperation in the construction of civilian aircraft and helicopters.

The jet plant envisioned by the Russians would greatly enhance their capability in the commercial aircraft field. Described as a seven-plant complex, it would not only design and build up-to-date wide-bodied jet transports but their engines and electronic equipment as well. Additional facilities would be provided for the maintenance and overhaul of aircraft. The integrated facility would employ over 80,000 workers when in full operation.

The sale of 30 jets to the Russians, in return for help in constructing this manufacturing-maintenance complex, would be a boost for U.S. manufacturers. In 1973, for example, Boeing sold 30 747's in foreign markets, Lockheed exported 39 L-1011s and McDonnel Douglas delivered 57 DC-10s. The sale of 30 additional planes would be a sizeable percentage of total sales. In addition, the free-world market for wide-bodied jets was saturated for the time being and an opportunity was provided for American manufacturers to penetrate the potentially enormous but heretofore off-limits market of the Soviet bloc. The official Soviet airline, Aeroflot, for example, is the world's largest, with approximately 1,720 planes.[2]

On the other hand, some problematic considerations cropped up.

First, concern was manifest by government and industry officials that U.S. commercial jet expertise, the primary remaining element of American dominance in the aviation field, would vanish. The proposed Russian construction complex would allow the Russians to develop a competitive capacity for foreign markets which might have a depressing effect on the future sale of American-built planes.

Second, officials feared an adverse effect on the nation's trade balance. In 1973, for instance, U.S. Commerce Department figures indicated that aerospace products totaled 8 percent of all U.S. imports and were the largest single contributor to America's positive trade balance. More than 27 percent of the industry's production

---

[2] In contrast, America's largest domestic air carrier, United Airlines, has a fleet of 364 aircraft. Thirty-six of these are wide-bodied jets—18 747's and 18 DC-10's.

was sold abroad, totalling $5.3 billion. Included in these figures is the sale of approximately 160 planes at over $2 billion. Throughout the world 72 percent of all commercial jets are manufactured in the United States.

Third, the Russians asked that their manufacturing complex be licensed to produce substantial segments of any jet aircraft purchased. To this proposal one American manufacturer advanced a counter-proposal limiting any licensing agreement to 50 percent of total aircraft body weight. In addition, the Russians approached the manufacturers about the prospect of cooperating on the production of entirely new aircraft based on advanced technology and the lessons learned from production of the current generation of wide-bodied jets by U.S. manufacturers. The companies were cool to this idea, feeling that it might affect the foreign sales of current American models. Both government and industry spokesmen indicated that one major difficulty would be defining exportable technologies.

Fourth, the Russians asked that a bilateral airworthiness pact between the United States and Russia be concluded. This agreement would permit Soviet planes to fly and be sold in the fifty states if they met Federal Aviation Administration (FAA) standards for airworthiness. Such an agreement would also work to the Russians' advantage in competitive aircraft markets abroad. A traditional appeal of American aircraft has been certification by the FAA, which is known for its strict standards. And in the past, Russian planes have not been certified. From a practical standpoint, government officials expressed doubt about the possibility of concluding such an agreement in the near future—even to accommodate the sale of aircraft.

Fifth, government officials worried about a possible "whipsaw effect" as Russian teams negotiated separately with the three U.S. manufacturers. It was already known that their proposals differed slightly in dealings with each of the three companies. In December 1973, Commerce and Treasury Department officials had, in fact, called representatives of the three together and asked each to spell out what technical knowledge each felt was appropriate for export. The companies answered in writing in January 1974 and differed widely in their viewpoints.

Government officials feared that since commercial aviation benefited from the spin-off from military research and development, some military technology might inadvertently be sold to the Russians. Although the official government attitude on trade negotiations between private manufacturers and foreign governments is one of non-interference, government can exercise a veto over proposed exports. Aircraft manufacturers, on the other hand, favored completion of the deal because they estimated its potential to be in excess of $500 million in sales. Although there were problems, they were eager to find solutions. The *Times*, however, quoted one government official as summing up the chances of such a deal being approved as "less than zero, if you can find such a number."

Further opposition came from the newspaper itself. On February 8 the *Times* ran an editorial stating that the deal was meritricious. The *Times* favored selling the Russians all the planes they wanted to purchase outright, but argued that "the U.S. aerospace industry should not, for short-term profit considerations, become involved in arrangements that could seriously undercut this country's competitive position in the long run."

CASE QUESTIONS

1. It is understandable that the Russians wish to develop a commercial aircraft manufacturing capacity for wide-bodied jets that would be competitive on a world-wide scale. Are U.S. manufacturers justified in providing all the help the Russians ask for?

2. What should the position of industry be on the deal? The position of government? (See *United States* vs. *Curtiss-Wright Export Corp.*, 299 U.S. 304, 1936.)

3. In its editorial, the *Los Angeles Times* pointed out that wide-bodied jets could be used to carry troops and military equipment as well as paying civilian passengers. Where national defense interests and private business interests conflict, what principle or principles can you suggest for reconciling such a conflict? Alternatively, are such conflicts possible in theory or practice?

4. It has long been thought in some circles that the tensions which exist between the United States and Russia

would eventually ease when the two nations stepped up their economic interrelationships, particularly in trade. In 1973 the detente between Russia and the United States seemed to herald that era. Is it likely that tensions between the two nations will ease as such economic interrelationships increase? Is this proposal likely to advance that chain of events?

B) TECHNOLOGY ASSESSMENT OF SUBSONIC AIRCRAFT NOISE

The Aeronautics and Space Engineering Board (ASEB) of the National Academy of Engineering was asked to undertake an experiment in technology assessment. It chose for study the impact of subsonic aircraft noise on the growth of civilian air transportation services. Such a survey, it reasoned, could be conducted at minimum cost and by people who were knowledgeable about the subject. Also, aircraft noise is a subject of important environmental attention. Pressures for regulating aircraft noise are likely to increase, and abatement will be costly.

The ASEB, before undertaking the study, said that "a technology assessment should include an appreciation of the entire spectrum of social consequences as well as of technical and economic impacts." The ASEB outlined the following steps for technology assessment:

1) Identify and define the subject to be assessed.

2) Delineate the scope of the assessment and develop a data base.

3) Identify alternative strategies to solve the selected problems with the technology under assessment.

4) Identify parties affected by the selected problems and the technology.

5) Identify the impacts on the affected parties.

6) Valuate or measure the impacts.

7) Compare the pros and cons of alternative strategies.

CASE QUESTIONS ─────────────────────────────────

1. What major purpose do you see for technology assessment? (See the Report of the National Academy of Sciences, Committee on Science and Astronautics, *Technology: processes of Assessment and Choice*.(Washington, D.C.: U.S. Government Printing Office, July 1969, pp. 8-15.)

2. Do you think "technology assessment" is too narrow a phrase for the purpose of technology assessment as defined by the National Academy of Science?

3. Do you agree with the methodology proposed by the ASEB? Expand a little on what each of these steps means to you. (See Martin V. Jones, "The Methology of Technology Assessment," *The Futurist*, February 1972, pp. 19-25.)

4. Review the assessment made of subsonic aircraft noise by the ASEB and report the findings. (See the Report of the Committee on Public Engineering Policy, National Academy of Engineering, *A Study of Technology Assessment* (Washington, D.C.: U.S. Government Printing Office, July 1969), pp. 76-95, 145-173.)

C) SHOULD GOVERNMENT SUPPORT NONMILITARY AVIATION?

Just beginning to be generally understood is the vital impact of aerospace on our national economy as the primary contributor to a favorable U.S. balance of trade. This is where I should like to concentrate my remarks this afternoon—showing why America's aerospace export capability is now in jeopardy, and the consequences if this threat is allowed to develop unchecked. I will also mention some alternative solutions.

The Commerce Department has summarized the export role of aerospace in its report, "The U.S. Industrial Outlook for 1972."

This government report terms the aerospace industry important to the nation's balance of trade not only in terms of its own exports

From a speech given before the Los Angeles Bond Club, by D. J. Haughton, chairman of the board of the Lockheed Aircraft Corporation, 17 October 1972. Reprinted by permission.

but also for the stimulus it provides to other high technology export industries. And it sounds the warning that "beginning in 1972 aerospace exports are expected to decline while imports will increase."

The Commerce Department notes that major U.S. jet engine and airframe manufacturers are waiting to recoup their investments in new wide-bodied jet transports—that they lack sufficient capital to undertake new major risk programs at this time to meet the competition of existing foreign programs.

This government report then states it is probable that no single company alone will again be able to finance a program as large as the wide-bodied jet transports now under construction.

So much for an overall and generalized look, from the outside, at the aerospace export problem.

Now let's look at some of the details. First, what do aerospace exports mean to the national trade balance?

Looking at the four major trade categories—agricultural products, raw materials, low technology, and high technology products—the U.S. has a sizable stable trade surplus *only* in that fourth category, high technology products. The sale of $750 million worth of U.S. wheat to the Soviets over the next three years, which recently got quite a bit of publicity, will hardly make a dent in the balance of payments. Going back to 1965, high technology exports—including aircraft—have averaged a little over $9 billion a year. Obviously, this is our best bet for future export business.

About 80 percent of the aircraft in world aviation today were built in the U.S., most of them in Los Angeles County and the state of Washington. In the five years ending in 1970, aerospace had an overall total trade surplus of nearly $10 billion, of which West Coast jet transports were the major part.

In 1971 alone, aerospace produced a trade balance of $3.86 billion, up 25 percent from 1970. The leverage is great. Export of one wide-bodied trijet such as a California-built L-1011 or DC-10 counterbalances about 8,000 small car imports. Yet this aerospace leverage—a favorable balance of $3.86 billion—couldn't raise the U.S. out of its overall 1971 trade deficit of $2.88 billion—America's first in nearly 80 years.

U.S. Secretary of Commerce Peterson is quoted as sounding the warning at a White House conference earlier this year: "The days when America dominated international trade are over—our competition is tough and it is numerous."

One problem the U.S. aerospace industry faces in continuing to meet tougher international competition is the history of constraint on aerospace profits that has made it difficult to build up an adequate equity base for financing today's expensive development programs.

The SEC reports that the rate of profit decline in aerospace is twice as great as in other industries. Aerospace net profit after taxes as a percent of stockholders' equity dropped by nearly half, from about 10.6 percent in 1969 to 5.8 percent last year.

To illustrate the kind of investment I'm talking about I might note here that Lockheed's investment in the TriStar jetliner—exclusive of suppliers' and customers' outlays—climbed to nearly a billion dollars before we delivered the first airplane.

Compounding this problem has been a shrinking business base in recent years as defense procurement was cut. A look at employment trends underscores the depth of the reductions. In 1968 America had 1,500,000 jobs in aerospace. By mid-1973, that figure will be down by 39 percent—two out of every five jobs in the past five years. That represents the combined lost capacity and employment in five years of a Boeing, *plus* a General Dynamics, *plus* a TRW, *plus* a Grumman, *plus* a Lockheed.

I was disturbed by the false impression created when one of the wire services reported that the fiscal 1973 defense appropriations bill as passed by the House is, quote, "the largest since World War II." True, on the surface. But what are the facts behind that simple statement? Funds for procurement, research, and military construction have increased by only 4 percent in the past nine years. In terms of *real buying power*, they have *actually decreased by 24 percent*.

In fiscal 1953, the final year of the Korean War, about 49 cents of every tax dollar—federal, state, and local—went for defense. The 1973 figure is about 20 cents, *lower by more than half*.

In fiscal 1953, defense spending was nearly double that of all other federal agencies combined. Today that is *more than reversed*— other federal agencies spend *more than twice as much as defense*.

In fiscal 1973, defense will account for about 31 percent of federal spending and just over 6 percent of Gross National Product—the lowest shares since well before Pearl Harbor.

Paralleling reduced government spending has been the falloff in the rate of airline traffic growth, which just this year has begun to make a reversal. The world's airlines started experiencing losses in 1970 and had a record $400 billion loss in 1971 as a result of the lowest passenger and cargo traffic growth for more than a decade. Losses like these slowed airline orders for new equipment to a walk during 1971 and most of 1972.

What does it look like from here on out?

The aerospace downtrend is bottoming out, and only about a 1 percent further job loss is forecast by mid-1973. In California, aerospace jobs have already shown a small upturn, and a period of slow improvement may be in prospect. But, as Washington Redskins coach George Allen says, "The future is now." It is *now* that California airframe manufacturers need to start planning and developing new commercial transports for the decade of the 1980s. And for the reasons I've cited, they are unable to do so, except for evolutionary developments from their present models.

Meanwhile, European nations are making a clear and determined bid to challenge U.S. dominance in the world aviation market. They're very open and outspoken about their intentions. They have good technology, and their research has been growing at about 13 percent annually, while U.S. research has been essentially marking time.

Britain's aerospace exports jumped 60 percent in the 1965-1970 period, France's 40 percent, West Germany's more than 100 percent. But that was only the beginning.

Western European governments are now investing about $4 billion in four major commercial transports aimed at a near term $30 billion market. The Concorde SST, for example, is fully financed by Britain and France. The French-German A-300B airbus, powered by U.S. engines, is 85 percent government sponsored, and will compete with the two U.S. wide-bodied trijets for a considerable segment of not only the European but also the U.S. market. The new French Dassault Mercure transport is 66 percent government financed, and the German-Dutch VFW-Fokker transport 80 percent.

A big advantage, besides government funding support and aid in the form of various write-offs for research and production facilities, is the lower labor rate—in Western Europe about half the U.S. rate. And labor amounts to about 75 percent of the total cost of aircraft development and production.

What will be the result of the determined European challenge? How will it affect the contributions of today's U.S. aerospace industry to the national trade balance?

The Commerce Department, assuming that present European aircraft projects are successful, predicts that U.S. made commercial airliners—and remember we're speaking of California and Washington products—will drop from 80 percent of the world total to about 64 percent by 1980, and that the U.S. share of the world military aircraft market will drop form 60 percent in 1970 to 47 percent by 1980.

These forecasts assume that the U.S. will not do enough—on time—to counteract the European competition. I don't think that's going to happen. Airline health prospects over the longer term are good. World air traffic is forecast to increase by 274 percent by 1980, generating a market for nearly 2,500 large new jet transports.

U.S. competition in new programs needed in the 1974-1985 market can double the present aerospace sales level to a yearly average of $9.8 billion. Besides achieving a higher employment, this sales level would add about $7 billion a year to Gross National Product and, perhaps most important of all, would contribute about $4.9 billion yearly to the trade balance. I believe this is so clearly in the national interest that a way or ways will be found to make it possible.

The world market for commercial aircraft is estimated at $148 billion in the 1974-1985 period.

Aviation is an international industry in every sense of those words. It crosses international boundaries as routinely as pedestrians cross an intersection. The kind of enterprise needed to assure the U.S. aerospace industry's ability to continue exporting its high technology products must be *not only* "free" but also *able* to compete on an international scale for an essentially international market. The Europeans have recognized this fact by providing government support for a significant trade sector that will benefit them.

These days it's not the "giant" Lockheed or "giant" Boeing against smaller competitors. Rather, it's the relatively limited resources of a Lockheed, a Boeing, or a McDonnell-Douglas against the virtually unlimited financial resources of a European government or a combination of them.

The European Common Market Commission has recently proposed an overall streamlining of Europe's aerospace resources *specifically* for the purpose of competing on a broader scale against *not* the U.S. government—but against individual U.S. aerospace companies. It may well be that the methods that have brought U.S. aviation to its present international eminence simply will not work in the future. This is a problem that the financial community, particularly in Southern California, might want to think about and take an interest in.

There are several possible ways of approaching the problem of financing a new development in commercial aviation for the 1980s.

One, of course, is the European way—a consortium of manufacturers backed by government financing for development, manufacture, and sale.

Another is some form of airline cooperative, some way of pooling airline resources, to provide the necessary developemnt funds. Competition within the airline industry is fierce, and like aerospace, airlines have been profit starved by government regulations. But there are signs that this kind of remedy is not impossible.

Or—in some situations, one or more U.S. manufacturers or the U.S. government—or perhaps manufacturers *and* the government—could join with similar foreign groups in international consortiums for research or even for new model development. The drawback is that this could cut into the trade benefits.

We saw an example of this just a week ago yesterday, when Japan announced its intention to enter into the wide-bodied jetliner market in a partnership arrangement with a U.S. company, Boeing. The Japanese will get a boost in jetliner technology and marketing know-how, and the U.S. will lose some trade benefits that might have been saved if other financing was available.

Another alternative—preserving the trade benefits intact—might be found in a strictly U.S. approach—through new methods, not yet worked out, of financing or guaranteeing the needed funds.

Mr. Secor Browne, head of the Civil Aeronautics Board, has

submitted for White House study a proposal to create an aerospace type of reconstruction finance corporation for this all-U.S. type of remedy—and other proposals are being weighed within aerospace industry circles.

The aerospace industry is clearly alert to the threat and has proved over the years that it can and will out-compete European consortiums—given the financing help it needs—by any one of several methods. There's still time to take the actions needed to enable aerospace to continue its beneficial effects on the national trade balance and the national economy in other ways. The only question is what form the action will take.

CASE QUESTIONS

1. Develop a cost/benefit analysis to determine whether or not the federal government should establish a corporation to aid the aerospace industry in developing commercial aircraft.

2. If the federal government will not help directly, what other avenues are open to the aerospace companies in competing against foreign government-business consortiums?

3. In recent years, the federal government has supplied approximately 50 percent of the total national expenditure on research and development. Approximately 80 percent of the government's support has been for military research by the Department of Defense, research by the Atomic Energy Commission, and space research by the National Aeronautics and Space Administration. Can you make a case for a sharp increase in the level of federal expenditures for nonmilitary-connected research and development support to private industry and universities? (See the president's message to the Congress on technology, March 16, 1972.)

DISCUSSION GUIDES ON CHAPTER CONTENT

1. What is meant by "technology"?

2. There is a strong feeling among many people in society that technology is and can continue to be the savior of mankind. A growing groundswell of voices, however, is claiming that technology is destroying society. What are the bases for these conflicitng views? Where do you stand?

3. What is "technology assessment"? To what degree should a company be responsible for detecting and preventing primary impacts when it introduces new technology? To what extent should it be responsible for detecting and avoiding secondary impacts? ("Primary" may be defined as impacts on things such as the landscape, on interrelationships between people, on the way business is done, on ideas and values of people, etc. "Secondary" refers to subsequent impacts.)

4. Since the United States has prided itself on having a private free enterprise system, what justification is there for government-sponsored and financed research and development in industry?

5. Is technological employment to be feared?

6 How has technology affected the structure of and managerial processes in business?

MIND-STRETCHING QUESTIONS ────────────

1. In the short run, technological unemployment is a real threat to some workers. To what degree should companies that are introducing labor-saving improvements be responsible for the retraining of displaced workers and for placing them in jobs suitable to their new talents?

2. Should the federal government have continued its funding of research and development for the supersonic transport? Develop a convincing case for your answer. (For arguments pro and con see Chapter 10 in George A. Steiner, *Issues in Business and Society* (New York: Random House, 1972.)

20

AFFLUENCE GROWTH AND THE POST-INDUSTRIAL SOCIETY

DISCUSSION GUIDES ON CHAPTER CONTENT —————

1. What is meant by the phrase "affluent society"? Explain why you do or do not think today's society in the United States is an affluent one.

2. What are Galbraith's attitudes toward public and private expenditures?

3. There are many people today who believe that the rate of growth of this society should be slowed down. What are the arguments they give? What are some major criticisms of these arguments? What is your evaluation of the arguments?

4. Explain the fundamental impacts that you see for business under conditions of zero population growth.

5. It has been suggested that a new index called Net Economic Welfare (NEW) should be used to supplement GNP. What is NEW?

MIND-STRETCHING QUESTION———————————

1. What arguments can you advance for and against the establishment of a Department of Technology in the federal government?

V

BUSINESS AND GOVERNMENT

21

GOVERNMENT - BUSINESS INTERRELATIONSHIPS: AN OVERVIEW

A) SOUTHERN CALIFORNIA EDISON TRIES TO BUILD A POWER PLANT

Southern California Edison Company is a large electric utility supplying power to Central and Southern California. The market served is over 50,000 square miles and contains a population of over 7,000,000 people.

The Southern California region has been among the fastest growing in the country in the post-World War II period. Consequently the system load (electricity demand) on Southern California Edison has been increasing at the rate of approximately 9.4 percent annually since 1950. The growth rate has been decreasing in recent years, but SCE forecasts a growth rate of 7.3 percent annually. The current capacity of the system is 8000MW. The forecasted requirements are 17,000MW by 1980 and 34,000MW by 1990.

SCE was able to meet all of its system requirements prior to 1945, by utilizing a series of remotely located hydroelectric plants in the Sierra Nevada mountains. These plants, in addition to providing power, enhanced flood control capability and provided controlled inflow to the irrigation of the San Joaquin Valley agricultural area. The reservoirs provided recreational facilities.

Confronted with the population boom in Southern California, the company quadrupled its output between 1950 and 1965. The decreasing number of feasible hydroelectric sites and increased emphasis on reliability of power created a need to locate plants near the area of greatest demand, and SCE turned to developing new oil-and gas-fired steam electric generating plants in its Southern California customer area.

While these plants were not always welcomed enthusiastically by the local residents, the general reaction was that they were a necessary part of an industrial society. In addition, the generating plants added to local property tax bases, helping to finance local education and community improvements.

SCE was an early developer of nuclear generating plants and its San Onofre plant, in Orange County, was opened in 1968.

The development of these local power sources has been supplemented by remote sources and purchase of surplus power from other West Coast systems. Power is purchased from hydroelectric projects in the Pacific Northwest and from the California State Water Project. In addition, power is imported from Hoover Dam hydroelectric plants in the Northern Sierras. SCE is participating in a multiutility development of coal-fired generating stations in the New Mexico/Nevada area. This power, imported over high-voltage transmission lines, will account for about 15 percent of the total SCE system capacity.

With the rise of extreme environmental concern in the mid-1960's, the nation's electric utilities became highly visible targets. SCE, however, developed a reputation as one of the industry's leaders in pollution abatement. The Council on Economic Priorities, a consumer research group, reported:

> Southern California Edison, which supplies power to one of the most notoriously polluted areas of the country, was one of the cleanest power companies in the United States throughout the 1960's. Under intense pressure to abate air pollution at its ten California fossilfuel plants, the company has actively sought out low-polluting fuel sources and played an extremely innovating role in developing new pollution control technology.[1]

In 1967, SCE moved to provide the power that had been projected as needed for the continued growth and development of

[1] "The Price of Power," *Economic Priorities Report*, Vol. 3, No. 2, May/June 1972, New York: Council of Economic Priorities, 1972, p. 36.

the Orange County area. Orange County is a rapidly growing urban area directly south of Los Angeles. SCE projected that the area would account for one-third of its total system demand and one-half of its system growth in customers during the 1970's. About 20 percent of the county's power requirements is now being filled by imported power. If new units within the county are not installed, SCE projects that 70 percent of the power required in 1975 will be imported.

Several different sources were evaluated to meet this demand. The first, importation of power from the Navaho project in New Mexico, was rejected as both too indefinite and not meeting the need for generation within the area to provide reliability. The Navaho project was a joint venture with other Southwestern power companies to build a series of six coal-fired generating plants on the Navaho reservation in the Four Corners area of New Mexico and Nevada. The plants were to be fired by coal which was strip-mined from the Black Mesa area. Many problems appeared likely in the project including permit approvals and court action by both Indians and environmental groups. (These plants were built later and SCE imports power from them.)

Also considered, but rejected, was the option of providing the needed power through the "Bolsa Project." As envisioned, this project would be a joint venture in constructing a "nuclear island" containing both generating plants and desalinization plants in the Pacific Ocean between Seal Beach and Huntington Beach off the Orange County Coast. This option was rejected as unlikely to succeed due to both funding uncertainties, anticipated regulatory agency difficulties, and objections by environmental groups.

The third alternative considered was the expansion of SCE's Huntington Beach facility. The Huntington Beach property had been acquired in 1956, and SCE had built five generating units there. It was proposed to build two additional units on the site. They would be 790MW oil- and gas-fired units.

The first step taken in the planned expansion was to contract with the Environmental Safeguards Division of NUS Corporation to perform an atmospheric study to determine air quality effects of the proposed expansion. The study indicated that even with two additional units, the plant would be operated at a level of NO_2 discharge of .04 ppm (parts per million) hourly, leaving a residual of .21 ppm from other sources before the .25 ppm ambient air standard would be violated. In addition, it was indicated that the maximum hourly ground level concentrations of NO_x would actually be reduced to one-half the 1968 standard. At the same time, SO_2 levels would be reduced by two-thirds. This would occur because of the greater efficiency of the newer units, coupled with a decreased load on the older, less efficient, units.

In addition to this study, an evaluation was made of the effects of the cooling procedures—the Huntington Beach site utilizes the ocean for cooling—and of aesthetics. The results led to the decision to proceed.

At this point, design engineering and construction scheduling was begun. One of the principal factors affecting scheduling of construction of generating plants is the lead time on purchase of the generator and boiler. Purchase orders were placed in September of 1968 for the turbine generator from the English Electric Company at $12 million per unit. The boilers, with a shorter lead time, were ordered in October of 1969 from the Foster-Wheeler Company at a cost of $11 million apiece.

A large number of regulatory agencies must approve the construction of a power plant (Table 21.1). In mid-1969 the first approaches were made to the various agencies involved. Among the groups contacted were the Army Corps of Engineers, the California State Resources Agency, the Santa Ana River Basin Regional Water Quality Control Board, the Orange County Air Pollution Control District, the California State Lands Commission, the State Division of Highways, and the California Public Utilities Commission.

Although the initial discussions about the expansion with the Orange County Air Pollution Control District had been favorable, the Huntington Beach project was not public knowledge. A newspaper story in the *Los Angeles Times* (Aug. 2, 1969), however, made the area residents aware of the planned expansion. The result was pressure put upon the OCAPD form four major directions to stop the expansion.

Local property owners opposed the expansion. They complained of increased pollution in the neighborhood, aesthetic degradation, and increased "fallout." This "fallout" is the negative effect of the stack emissions on the property and such things as plant life and wear of paint on the houses. SCE's response to this last point was that the effect was due to both the emissions and the sea breeze.

TABLE 21.1

PRINCIPAL AGENCIES CONCERNED WITH POWER PLANT SITING

Agency	Jurisdiction	Authority[a]
	United States Government	
Federal Power Commission	Hydroelectric power development along navigable rivers; interstate power transmission; interstate sale and transportation of natural gas	National wildlife refuges, impact on fish and wildlife Authority[a] Exclusive authority to license hydroelectric power projects; regulates rates and allocation of interstate shipments of natural gas; regulates interstate sales of electricity at wholesale.
Atomic Energy Commission	Development of nuclear power; control of fissionable materials; regulation of reactors; disposal of radioactive waste; safety of radioactive materials	Licenses construction and operation of reactors, fuel reprocessing plants; regulates transportation of radioactive materials; establishes standards for safety, release of radioactive materials, and public exposure to radiation (in conjunction with EPA).
Department of Army, Corps of Engineers	Construction or disposal of waste in navigable waters	Authorizes or issues permits for construction, dredging or disposal of waste in navigable waters (waste permits after consultation with EPA).
Environmental Protection Agency	Air quality, water quality, radiation, environmental impact	Administers federal laws and programs for air and water pollution (including approval of state standards and programs); establishes certain minimum standards for emissions and ambient air and water quality; recommends radiation standards for public exposure and environmental concentrations.

Agency	Jurisdiction	Authority[a]
Federal Aviation Administration	Hazards to air navigation	Assesses hazards to air navigation and issues permits for stacks, towers.
Dept. of Commerce, National Oceanographic and Atmospheric Agency (NOAA).	Commercial fisheries, navigation	Evaluates obstructions to navigation and aids to navigation.
Land Management Agencies Dept. of Agriculture, Forest Service	National forests	Issue Federal Land Use Permit for facilities on federal lands.
Dept. of Interior: Bureau of Land Management	Federal lands, offshore rocks Parks, monuments, national recreation areas	
National Park Service		
Fish and Wildlife Service	National wildlife refuges, impact on fish and wildlife	
State of California		
State Power Plant Siting Committee (representing various departments of the Resources Agency, Dept. of Public Health)	Environmental and resource impacts of power plants	Reviews thermal power plant sites and site development plans; establishes agreement with utility to insure protection of environment through appropriate research, monitoring programs, and plant design.
Public Utilities Commission	All areas of public interest not preempted by AEC	Reviews site, site development, alternative sites, need for power, etc.; issues certificate of public convenience and necessity.

TABLE 21.1 - Continued

Agency	Jurisdiction	Authority[a]
Resources Agency		
State Lands Commission[b]	State-owned lands, tide and submerged lands	Reviews site development and issues leases for use of state tidelands and submerged lands.
Air Resources Board[b]	Air quality	
State Water Resources Control Board[b]	Water quality and water rights	Coordinates water quality investigations of state agencies. Reviews actions of regional boards upon petition or by its own initiative; certifies water-quality standards, establishes policies.
Regional Water Quality Control Boards[b]	Waste discharge and water quality	Prescribe and enforce new discharge requirements on cooling waters and other wastes. Prescribe monitoring programs before and after construction.
Dept. of Fish and Game	Fish and wildlife, living marine resources	Establishes programs for ecological monitoring of plant sites.
Dept. of Water Resources	Water resources: supply and conveyance; hydroelectric power generation	
Dept. of Navigation & Ocean Development	Boat harbors, beach maintenance, marine resources	
Dept. of Conservation	Forestry; geology and seismic hazards	
Dept. of Parks and Recreation	State beaches, parks and reserves	Approves easements for cooling water conduits across site-owned beaches, shores, and parks.

Agency	Jurisdiction	Authority[a]
Dept. of Public Health	Public health, radiation hazards	Reviews site locations and development plans; advises utilities and state agencies of historic values.
Division of Industrial Safety	Safety of workmen	
California Heritage Preservation Commission	Historic areas	
Local Government		
County Board of Supervisors, County Planning Commission, Engineering, etc.	County land use, construction (unincorporated areas)	Reviews site location and development; advises on issuance of permits, required zone changes, or other approvals.
Air Pollution Control District	Air-pollution control	Grants construction permit and operating permit for discharge into atmosphere; sets emission standards; monitors and enforces.
City Governments, Planning and Zoning Body, Building and Safety Dept., etc.	City land use; building and construction permits	Grants zone changes (where necessary); issues building permits, grading permits, street closures, etc.

[a] In addition to actions listed, most agencies have responsibility to review Environmental Impact Statements that affect their area of concern or in which they have expertise; the primary agency issuing a permit, or otherwise involved in a project, must also prepare an Environmental Impact Statement and circulate it for comments before issuing the permit.

[b] These elements of the Resources Agency are governed by separate, independent boards.

A second opposition group was the environmental group S.O.S. (Stamp Out Smog) which was composed of a number of environmentally concerned residents of Orange County and advised by Professor Haggen-Smit of Caltech, the Chairman of the State Resources Board. The group argued against any increased pollution sources.

A third vocal opponent was a private citizen, Paul Rykoff, who espoused the view at a number of public meetings that the expansion was negating Orange County's growth and thus adding to the problems which already existed there.

A fourth opponent was Orange County Supervisor Robert Batten. (Orange County is governed by a Board of Supervisors.) Batten proclaimed that: "My obligation to the people in Orange County now is much greater than my obligation to the people moving in."

On September 25, 1969, five days before the formal permit application to the OCAPD was submitted, SCE received a letter from the OCAPD Officer Fitchen denying permission. It read:

> must deny the authority to construct any additional power plants, as they are known sources of air pollution and cannot be operated without emitting contaminants in violation of . . . the OCAPD rules and regulations.

On October 22, led by Supervisor Batten, the Orange County Board of Supervisors adopted a resolution which supported the OCAPD position and recommended that the California Public Utilities Commission place a moratorium on all construction of fossil-fuel plants in the state until it could be proved that no new pollutants would be discharged.

On November 18, the OCAPD formally turned down the permit application. SCE then appealed to the District Hearing Board. On December 23, the OCAPD issued a new stricter set of rules limiting emissions from stationary sources.

Meanwhile, on December 17, public hearings began before the California Public Utilities Commission on the SCE application for a certificate of public convenience and necessity to construct and operate the new facilities. The hearing required a total of 19 days of testimony ending in early March of 1970. In addition to SCE representatives, the OCAPD, property owners, S.O.S. and others appeared.

The PUC filed its decision on June 23, 1970 ordering immediate commencement of construction on the first of the two Huntington Beach units and authorizing the construction of the second. The decision dealt with three basic issues, as follows:

1) The need for additional generating capacity to meet demand in Orange County.

2) The effect of the proposed plants on air quality.

3) The conflict in jurisdiction between the PUC and the OCAPD.

The decision acknowledged the need for additional generating capacity to maintain the quality of life in Orange County. The PUC also held that its authority in matters of public utility regulation was paramount over the OCAPD and cited legal precedent to support this position.

On August 27, 1970, the OCAPD, with the blessing of the Orange County Board of Supervisors, filed in the Supreme Court of the State of California a "Petition for a Writ of Review" to determine the lawfulness of the PUC action.

On May 26, 1971, the Court ruled that the OCAPD and the PUC have concurrent jurisdictions—the directives of both agencies must be met. SCE then filed, along with the PUC, for a rehearing. On June 23, 1971, this petition was rejected.
SCE then abandoned the project.

As of the writing of this case (March 1973), some three years later, the issues still remain.

Edison, despite a revised load requirement estimate and some success at obtaining power elsewhere, is still predicting the likelihood of shortages in the period after 1974. Because of a slowing growth rate in Orange County, the 1974 required load projection was reduced by over 300MW, leaving a shortage of about 400 to be made up from the failure to obtain generating expansion at Huntington Beach for 1974, with increasing shortages continuing thereafter.

The Four Corners joint project has become a reality, despite the efforts of conservationists. Two of the six plants have been built and Edison is planning on utilizing 100MW from this project toward Orange County power needs in 1974 and an increasing amount to follow, depending upon the continued success of the project.

A technological advancement has been made by Westinghouse Corporation in the development of combined cycle units which are less polluting than the older units and also meet the standards of both Orange and Los Angeles Counties' codes. Consequently, Edison plans to install these units in place of some older ones at its Long Beach plant in southern Los Angeles County. Edison is also continuing to explore the expansion of several non-Orange County sites and possibilities of building some coal-fired non-urban facilities. Efforts have been initiated to revive the Huntington Beach expansion, utilizing six of the combined cycle units to add 1400MW of generating potential. On September 21, 1972, the OCAPD granted certification but an Edison official was pessimistic about chances for successful installation because of the changed priorities in a number of the state regulatory agencies.

Edison's abilities to expand generation through building nuclear plants would appear to be decreased since the time of the case. The long-running debate about plant safety, especially the ability of the emergency cooling systems, and a large earthquake in the Los Angeles area in February 1971, have brought a significant public reluctance to build such plants. An April 1972 Environmental Initiative, voted on and defeated by a closer margin than commonly expected, went so far as to require a five-year moratorium on construction of nuclear plants.

The regulatory apparatus has also expanded since the original case was written. A Coastline Initiative, passed by voters in November 1972, provided for a board to review all construction in California's coastal zones to preserve the coastline and prevent environmental degradation. The 1970 National Environmental Protection Act, in addition to establishing the Environmental Protection Agency as another part of the regulatory chain, requires an Environmental Impact Statement to be prepared and filed for all significant construction, the preparation of which is costly.

While short-range forecasts for power are being slightly reduced, the growth in demand continues. According to Edison, brownouts and blackouts are only a matter of time.*

*For further information, see Arthur M. Louis, "Southern California Edison Struggles to Bring Power to the People," *Fortune*, May 1973, pp. 212 ff.

B) THE L-1011 FEDERAL LOAN GUARANTEE

On February 1, 1971, Daniel J. Haughton, chairman of the board of the Lockheed Aircraft Corporation, held a meeting of his board of directors to digest a loss of $484 million, before taxes, on four defense contracts. He left immediately for England, where he expected to hear a routine presentation of the status of the new Rolls-Royce RB-211 jet engine designed for Lockheed's L-1011 commercial transport. Two hours after his arrival, he was told that the next day Rolls-Royce would appoint a receiver and declare bankruptcy. If nothing were done the Lockheed Aircraft Corporation, together with many of the L-1011 suppliers and perhaps some airlines, would also be forced into bankruptcy.

The Lockheed Aircraft Corporation

Lockheed at the time of these events was the largest defense contractor in the nation, with sales of approximately $2.5 billion in 1970. At the end of 1970, employment was almost 85,000. The company had built a long succession of successful aerospace products, including the Polaris and Poseidon missiles, the Agena space rocket, antisubmarine aircraft, the supersonic reconnaissance airplane (SR-71) and the Constellation and Electra commercial aircraft. Lockheed airplanes had achieved many new records and pioneered many new technical innovations.

Why the L-1011?

The last Lockheed commercial aircraft was produced in 1961. In a few years the company found itself with over 80 percent of its sales in United States government programs, 90 percent of which was with the Department of Defense. Because the company foresaw declining markets in these areas, and because it wanted to become less dependent on the military market, it decided to reenter the commercial aircraft market. The basic decision was made about 1964 and took the form of entering the supersonic transport competition held by the Federal Aviation Agency. Lockheed did not win and decided to build the L-1011, a medium-range, three-engine, wide-bodied jet. No other aircraft manufacturer at the time was in this market.

In March 1968 Lockheed had initial orders for 144 TriStars (the L-1011), at a total market value of $2.1 billion. This was enough to make Lockheed commit itself to production.

Financing the L-1011

From 1965 to 1970 the company spent about $400 million on fixed assets to produce a commercial transport. Much of this funding came from current cash flows. In 1967, however, a debenture bond issue of $125 million was marketed. Once the L-1011 design was settled, the airlines advanced progress payments, reaching $263 million by 1971. In May 1969 a group of banks extended a credit of $400 million. In light of the potential of the airplane and projected operating cash flows, the company felt its financial position was acceptable.

Why the Rolls-Royce Engine?

Lockheed was a good customer of the General Electric Company, which was developing the type of engine needed on the L-1011. So, why go overseas to Rolls-Royce? The reasons given were that the British engine promised to be around 300 pounds lighter than the GE engine, a very important factor if indeed it proved so. Also, the British engine was to be shorter, easier to install, operative at somewhat lower temperatures, and quieter than GE's; moreover, it would yield more thrust in succeeding developments. As it turned out, many of these advantages did not appear.

To complete a contract with Rolls-Royce, Lockheed had to avoid mandatory direct foreign investment controls established by the president to reduce the United States balance of payments deficit. The company surmounted the problem by persuading the British to create an Air Holdings Company that was committed to buy fifty TriStars. The British government extended the company a 40 percent guarantee against loss. Thus, United States income from the purchase of these aircraft would far exceed the payments for the engines. This move also reduced the threat of competition for sales by a consortium, which was being discussed to produce a comparable two-engine "airbus" for the European market.

Problems with the Engine

One of the reasons for the promised lower weight, lower noise level, and higher thrust of the RS-211 engine was the use of Hyfil fan blades. Hyfil is a composite material of carbon fibers bonded with epoxy resins. Unfortunately, rain and hail proved to erode the tips of these blades, and no suitable remedy could be found. Also, ingestion of large birds by the engines broke the blades. Rolls-Royce then had to turn to titanium, a demanding new technology.

One result was a heavier engine. A far more serious result was heavier financial load. The original contract price for each engine was $840,000, but now the cost jumped to $1.1 million. This added cost for the 555 engines under contract, plus heavy penalties for missed delivery dates, was more than Rolls could bear.

The British government originally had agreed to contribute 70 percent of the research and development cost, and by February 1970 it had contributed $240 million. It would not, however, meet the new costs.

Crisis

Lockheed naturally turned now to GE. However, it was estimated that to install the GE engine in a 220 plane program would entail a cost of perhaps $150 million above the costs associated with the higher-priced Rolls engine. Everyone, including GE, agreed that to make the switch would be too expensive. Thus, every effort had to be made to resolve the Rolls-Royce problem.

The British government created a new, nationalized company, Rolls-Royce (1971) Ltd., to carry on negotiations with Lockheed. A higher price of $1,020,000 was negotiated for each engine, as well as more realistic delivery dates. The British government agreed to pay for increased development costs. By June 1971 the commitment was $310 million. United States banks accepted these negotiations. However, Lockheed calculated that it needed $250 million more to finance the program. The British government wanted to make sure that Lockheed would not collapse and demanded that the United States government guarantee the $250 million loan from the banks. Furthermore, the British government demanded that the United States guarantee the loan by August 8, 1971.

The Lockheed Problem

Lockheed had no recourse but to ask the federal government for help. The company felt that prospects for the sale of the airplane were excellent and that under normal circumstances it would not have needed additional cash—and if it had the banks would have extended it. But things were not normal, because the company had suffered major losses in its defense contracts.

At the time of the loan guarantee issue, there were 178 TriStars ordered by the airlines. Estimates of the market for this type airplane ranged widely, but there was agreement that it could be betweeen 700 and 800 by 1980. Lockheed management originally thought it could sell 350 TriStars by the end of 1980. (The McDonnell Douglas DC-10 also competes for this market.) At the time of the guarantee dispute, it still clung to this figure despite a rosier estimate of 409 submitted by its technical staff. The breakeven point, argued the company, was far below the more conservative sales estimate.

The company argued that with such numbers it could have managed with its current financing. However, because of a dispute with the Department of Defense, it had to return to the money well for $250 million. The dispute with the government was settled when Lockheed accepted a loss of $484 million on four programs. This settlement resulted in a net loss after taxes of $86.3 million for 1970, and reduced the net worth of the company from $371 million at the end of 1968 to $235 million by the end of 1970.

The dispute with the government was over cost overruns, cancellations, and performance standards. The most publicized was that of the C-5A, a giant cargo carrier built for the U.S. Air Force. The loss for this airplane was $247 million. A rigid rotor helicopter lost $124 million. On navy ship programs a loss of $89 million was accepted, and for a rocket engine the company suffered a $24 million loss.

Lockheed did not agree with the government that it was to blame for these losses and wanted to take the issue to court. The Pentagon, however, decreed otherwise. In effect it ruled that the company had to accept the losses or get no further defense contracts. There is no doubt but that Lockheed made important mistakes. But, as C. J. Medberry, chairman of the board of Bank of America, testified before the Congress: "It is apparent from Mr. Packard's [deputy secretary of defense] testimony and our own observation . . . Lockheed was not solely responsible for its difficulties with the government contractual work."[1] The government, therefore, was deeply involved in Lockheed's financial problems.

[1] U.S. Congress, Senate, *Emergency Loan Guarantee Legislation, Hearings Before the Committee on Banking, Housing and Urban Affairs, On S. 1567, S. 1641, Etc.*, 92nd Cong., 1st Sess, p. 385.

S. 1891 and H.R. 8432

These two bills were introduced in the Congress in June 1971 to provide the loan guarantee. In early August 1971, a few days before the deadline for decision demanded by the British government, the Senate voted on and approved a bill that was identical with one previously passed by the House of Representatives. The measure passed in the Senate by one vote!

The new law established an emergency loan guarantee board, headed by the secretary of the treasury, with authority to guarantee loans up to $250 million, following a finding that the guarantee "is needed to enable the borrower to continue to furnish goods or services, and failure to meet this need would adversely and seriously affect the economy of, or employment in, the nation or any region thereof." The law does not specify Lockheed, although there was no doubt in anyone's mind that the provisions of the law applied solely to this company.

Arguments Advanced in Favor of the Legislation

The Nixon Administration and Lockheed argued, of course, that the guarantee was desirable because there would be highly beneficial results. If the bill were defeated, the losses would be substantial.

To begin with, it was pointed out that the guarantee would cost the government nothing. The loan was made by the banks, and in the event the company failed, the government would have first claim on all the company's assets, which could be sold at well over the guaranteed figure.

The company said that as many as 60,000 jobs would be lost if it went into bankruptcy. Of this number Lockheed would be forced to lay off 17,800, and an additional 16,000 in thirty-five states who were working for suppliers would lose their jobs. Applying a conservative multiplier to these direct losses, it was argued, the total job loss would be over 60,000.

Approximately $1.4 billion in direct investment would be lost. Tools and facilities might have resale value, but most of the inventory would be valueless. The banks would lose their $400 million. Suppliers would lose $354 million. The airlines would lose their advance payments of $263 million. Some 70 percent of the company's 35,000 suppliers were small businessmen, many of whom would go bankrupt. Lockheed stockholders would, of course, lose their equity.

No less a figure than Arthur Burns, chairman of the Board of Governors of the Federal Reserve System, testified that such a loss could well stem the tide of rising economic activity, with enormous losses to the nation's econonomy.

Losses in income taxes to the federal government (from workers and companies) could reach $500 million a year, said Treasury Secretary Connally. Losses to the unemployed could not be calculated, but they would be huge. Many of those unemployed would not readily find new jobs, said Lockheed.

If Lockheed went bankrupt, the result would be to give McDonnell-Douglas a monopoly in the market served by the L-1011, because there would be no competitor for the DC-10. This decline in competition, it was asserted, would not be in the national interest.

If Lockheed went bankrupt, the receiver in bankruptcy, it was said by Secretary Connally, would not accept current military contract prices with Lockheed and would renegotiate them. The net result could be to increase contract costs to the federal government as much as $500 million. Deputy Secretary of Defense Packard said, for instance, that the cost of the C-5A to the government alone would rise from $100 to $300 million.

In sum, the failure of Lockheed would be a major financial catastrophe, with associated disaster to the people, to companies, to the government, and to the entire economic system.

Arguments Opposed to the Legislation

Senator Proxmire argued that thousands of small businessmen are faced with bankruptcy each year, and the government does not bail them out. Why then should it bail out a big company? He and others argued that the claimed loss of jobs would not take place, because those who ordered the L-1011 would now turn to the DC-10, and more workers would be hired to produce them.

Senators Proxmire and Cranston charged that Lockheed management was not efficient and that if the government saved the company from bankruptcy it would, in effect, be rewarding poor management. It was argued that to lose the "stick" of bankruptcy would be a serious blow to our economy, because it would reduce the incentives for American businessmen, at least "big business," to be efficient. Those who argued this way said that the proof of the pudding was in Great Britain. There, government had assumed a responsibility for bailing out financially distressed companies—and the British economy was not known for its efficiency.

Many argued that the basic objective of our competitive system is to make sure that resources are used most effectively in producing the goods and services that people want at prices they are willing to pay. If a firm fails, it is not doing this. It is using resources inefficiently, is not using resources for the right purposes, or both. To keep it from failing is to perpetuate waste. Subsidizing a failing company, therefore, undermines the very purposes of the competitive system.

Guaranteeing the Lockheed loan would set many bad precedents, not the least of which was government interference in decisions on whom to help, what produce, and how private resources should be used. Not only could the government not do this efficiently, but interference by government in these spheres would be contrary to the basic philosophy of our economic system. We have relied on the marketplace to do these things in the past, continued the opposition. This is far more efficient than allowing government to do it.

It was argued that federal loan guarantees would inevitably increase government control over business. If business runs to government every time trouble appears, the government will get more involved in the decision-making process.

Others felt that if the government supported Lockheed, it would naturally place defense contracts with the company rather than with competitors. (Lockheed, however, felt the result would be just the reverse.)

Mr. Borch, chairman of the board of General Electric, suggested that if the British government sought a guarantee for the Lockheed loan, the British government could and should make that guarantee. He felt that the British government was now a competitor of GE, not only because it had nationalized Rolls-Royce but because it had subsidized the RB-211 engine. Indeed, he said, had not the British government subsidized the engine, Lockheed would have bought GE engines. Furthermore, he said, the British government extended very favorable financing to several American airlines in the purchase of the Rolls engine. This, he argued, made things difficult for American competitors.

Opponents argued that Lockheed's management obviously could not control costs, as indicated by the huge C-5A and other defense program cost overrruns. Since the Department of Defense would not condone this evidence of poor management, why should the taxpayer bear any burden for cost overrruns in Lockheed's commercial business?

Bankruptcy for Lockeed need not be a disaster. The company would still continue to operate. Only parts of the firm would be liquidated.

The monopoly issue was nothing to worry about. The issue in this case was simple: There was an adjustment being made in an industry to declining demand conditions. Given Lockheed's past history of mismanagement, it was not surprising that this was the company threatened with exit from the industry.

The Core Issue

Dean Phil C. Neal, of the University of Chicago Law School, testified that:

> The whole objective of the competitive system is to maximize economic productivity by channeling resources into the most efficient hands. The failure of a firm, assuming that it cannot be made profitable through the restructuring of ownership and management that will flow from reorganization proceedings, is a signal that it represents an inefficient or wasteful combination of resources.[2]

The inference is, of course, that society would be much better off if those resources were used in ways that were more profitable and, therefore, more beneficial to society. The bankruptcy of an unprofitable firm in the end serves the public interest.

On the other hand, Ezra Solomon, then a professor at the Standford University Graduate School of Business, testified:

> The case for approving a loan guaranty seems very clear to me; by so doing, we avoid potentially large losses in employment, output, and exports, which society would suffer as a result of Lockheed going into bankruptcy. Given existing employment conditions in the manufacturing sector of the economy and in the capital markets here and abroad, the adverse effects of such a business failure could be serious indeed. Certainly the cost to the government of offsetting such adverse effects, after the fact, would be many dozen times larger than the likely

[2] *Ibid.*, p. 794.

cost of extending a loan guaranty now. Indeed, given the various safeguards incorporated in the terms of the loan guaranty, the likely cost of positive action is close to zero.[3]

Another observer noted, "The old profit test of survival works beautifully in a simple society. In today's extremely complex world that simple formula should, on occasion, be replaced by a cost/benefit analysis."

----------------------------References----------------------------

For two short articles, pro and con, see:

John B. Conally, "The Case for the L-1011 Lockheed Transport Loan Guarantee," George A. Steiner, ed., *Issues in Business and Society* (New York: Random House, 1971), and William Proxmire, "The Lockheed Bail-Out: A Threat to Free Enterprise," in *Issues in Business and Society*.

For a detailed discussion see:

U. S. Congress, Senate, *Emergency Loan Guarantee Legislation, Hearings Before the Committee on Banking, Housing and Urban Affairs on S. 1567, S. 1641, etc.*, 92nd Cong., 1st Sess., Part 1, 7–16 June 1971; and Part 2, 17–22 June, 7–9 July 1971.

U. S. Congress, House, *To Authorize Emergency Loan Guarantees to Major Business Enterprises, Hearings Before the Committee on Banking and Currency, on H.R. 8432*, 92nd Cong. 13, 14, 15, 19 and 20 July 1971.

C) STUDEBAKER CLOSES A PLANT AND THE PENTAGON CLOSES AN AIR BASE

In December 1963 the Studebaker Corporation closed its South Bend, Indiana, automobile assembly plant, thereby putting 6,000 employees out of work. This closing was no surprise, for the company had been ailing since 1954. At about the same time, the secretary of defense announced the closing of the Rome Air Material Command, in Rome, New York, with the loss of about 4,250 jobs. After the secretary made this announcement, the maximum pressure that could be exerted was directed at him to keep this base open. When Studebaker closed, however, no public official protested. The

[3] *Ibid.*, p. 1189.

event was accepted, and efforts were directed toward finding employment for those who had lost jobs.

CASE QUESTION

1. What does the contrasting response mean to you? Should events such as a plant closing be treated the same as the closing of a public facility—and vice versa?

DISCUSSION GUIDES ON CHAPTER CONTENT

1. Briefly describe the major constitutional provisions that permit the federal government to regulate business.
2. It is often said that the federal government and business are partners. What does this mean to you? Is it a good or bad thing?
3. What are the basic ways in which government influences business?
4. What is the "principle of comparative performance"? How useful is it in assuring the "right balance" between government and business?
5. How can the principle of marginal social cost/benefit analysis be applied in assuring a better relationship between business and government?
6. What other guides would you suggest for bringing about, and maintaining, a proper relationship between business and government?

MIND-STRETCHING QUESTIONS

1. Does the United States today have the right balance between government and business? If you think it does, describe some of the principal characteristics. If you disagree, explain why and suggest ways to assure the right balance.
2. The Postal Service is seeking to charge all users of its service a price that will cover its costs. This philosophy has been attacked by those who believe, as did George Washington and Thomas Jefferson, that it is to the advantage of the country to encourage the dissemination of information and

ideas. If this involves a postal deficit, then that is what we should have. Senator Barry Goldwater says, as he reads the Postal Reorganization Act, "When it comes to a choice between the ability of the public to obtain a wide range of educational, literary and news information through a variety of publications, or the ability of the Postal Service to be totally self-sufficient, I am certain Congress intended for the function of information to prevail."[1] Explain where you stand and why.

[1] *The Wall Street Journal*, 18 March, 1974.

22

THE POLITICAL ROLE
OF BUSINESS
IN PUBLIC AFFAIRS

A) THE CANDIDATE'S DECISION

Jonathan Conrad, Republican candidate for the United States Senate, paced nervously back and forth in his dimly lit, downstairs study. His campaign for high office in a southern state would draw to a close in less than two weeks with the general election, but the most difficult decision of the campaign, indeed of his career, loomed before him. Now, with the house nearly darkened, his wife and two children in bed, Conrad discovered that the repose and detached reflection he had promised himself were not forthcoming.

Conrad, a native son and prominent big-city banker in his state, had been a reluctant candidate. Although he had served on the city council in his hometown for four years, been elected to the State Assembly for a term, and spent an additional year as chairman of the state's Republican Central Committee, his reputation as a fair and reliable politician stemmed partly from lack of ambition for higher office. He earned a yearly salary of $50,000 as president of Midland City Bank. This was supplemented by income from several businesses in town which he owned plus the earnings of bank shares in

*This case was prepared by John F. Steiner, Assistant Professor, California State University, Los Angeles and is used with permission.

his name. He led a gentleman's life and valued the time he was able to spend away from politics with his family.

Several years ago, however, state leaders became concerned about the growing influence of Alvin "Big Toe" Weaver. Weaver had captured the sentimental attachment of the voters in a race for a seat in the House of Representatives by touring his district in shoes with holes in the front to dramatize the plight of poor sharecroppers who would be displaced from their land by construction of a dam. Weaver, a Democrat, had so skillfully exploited this issue in speeches filled with purple oratory that he was elected by a margin of almost two to one.

The landslide fed Weaver's ambition, and during three terms in the House of Representatives he curried the favor of party professionals and placed cohorts on party committees across the state. Two years ago, when Joshua Ironwright, the popular Democratic senior Senator from the state, announced his retirement at age 81, the dominance of the so-called "Weaver machine" in Democratic party politics assured Weaver's nomination for the seat.

In anticipation of the forthcoming election Weaver had spent more time at home than in Washington during the last year and a half, criss-crossing the state with a proposal to cut unemployment in the state's huge pool of unskilled labor. In speech after speech Weaver proposed a three-step plan, which he referred to as "a new Bill of Rights for the working man." Step one would require all major corporations operating in the state to reinvest capital gains from state operations in programs for training and hiring the hard-core unemployed. Step two called for each business employing more than twenty-five workers to hire an additional labor force of not less than 5 percent of the total number of workers. And step three provided for the establishment of a "Citizen Overseer Body" to enforce reinvestment and the hiring of minority workers.

Businessmen, including Conrad, had opposed this plan by calling it unworkable, inefficient, and probably unconstitutional, but Weaver persisted in its advocacy and his charismatic appeal met with success. A statewide polling organization determined that as a result of Weaver's canvassing, 55 percent of the voters approved the plan, 30 percent disapproved, and 15 percent were undecided.

Approximately a year ago, however, doubts about Weaver began to grow—even among Democrats. He launched a bitter attack against businessmen, educators, and politicians who opposed the plan by branding them bigots and exploiters. The issue, already hotly debated, developed dark racial overtones. It was then that a bipartisan committee of state politicians, businessmen, and professionals had come to visit Conrad.

Weaver was dangerous, they explained. His ability to incite the base emotions of the population on the race issue was feared. Furthermore, there were unconfirmed but widely circulated rumors that Weaver was mentally unstable. Aides reportedly swore he had delusions of grandeur and late at night would lock himself behind his office doors and rage at the demons that tormented him. "We have come to you," the committee spokesman explained, "to enlist your service to the state. We want you to oppose Weaver in the upcoming senatorial race because your reputation for fair-play and popularity with voters make you the only candidate with which to oppose a demagogue like Alvin Weaver." Conrad had consented, but now he half-wished he had not.

With the support of all factions of his party and the endorsement of some prominent Democrats, Conrad breezed through the June primary. The first polls of the Conrad-Weaver match-up in early July, however, showed Weaver leading in voter preference with 64 percent and Conrad trailing miserably with only 28 percent and 8 percent undecided. With only three months until the general election the situation seemed bleak.

Conrad chose a staff, set up headquarters operations in the capitol, and conducted fund-raising campaigns netting a total of $450,000. Throughout the remainder of July and well into August he conscienciously attended teas and rallies, spoke before large but reserved audiences, and earnestly solicited funds.

Much of the money was allocated for staff expenses and mass mailings. Volunteers went door-to-door and telephoned houses. Billboard space was purchased to insure that Jonathan Conrad became a household name. Some radio and television spots were purchased, but emphasis was placed upon reaching "influentials" in the electorate, or prominent community leaders who supposedly could swing others' votes.

This effort produced inadequate results. A poll in the first week of September revealed that Weaver still held a substantial lead, although the margin had narrowed somewhat to 61 percent for

Weaver versus 33 percent for Conrad and 5 percent undecided. Throughout September Conrad's attempts to diminish the large gap, although successful in a small way, lagged behind projections and it appeared that Weaver's magnetic personality was sufficient in itself to overcome even the most concerted effort and widespread party support. Then it happened.

Weaver and Conrad had shared a platform together at the dedication of a new textile plant. At the conclusion of his speech Conrad had pivoted to return to his chair when an angry Weaver jumped up and confronted him. With noses barely inches apart a debate between the two ensued much to the delight of the roaring crowd. Then, after an angry exchange of words, Weaver spat on Conrad in full view of the audience. This action was greeted with a loud chorus of boos and Weaver's bodyguards were forced to struggle to lead him to safety.

The incident was widely reported in the press, and the public—it's sense of fair play violated—began to listen to what Conrad had to say. His measured tones and carefully thought out proposals suddenly gained new support and now, ten days from the November 5 election, the polls showed that he had closed to within five percentage points of Weaver. In a meeting with his advisers earlier in the day, however, there had been a shared feeling of impotence, even in the face of such great gains.

A privately commissioned poll showed that although Conrad had closed to within five points of Weaver, the gain capped a leveling off trend and the rise was not likely to continue without increased effort. It was time for a major media blitz to push Conrad over the top, but not enough money remained. Advisers estimated such a campaign would cost $215,000, but the cost was academic since campaign coffers held only $48,610. It seemed too late to organize further fund-raising efforts.

After the meeting with his advisers Conrad returned home, where he received a telephone call from a Ralph Watson. Mr. Watson explained that he represented a wealthy industrialist who would rather remain anonymous but had large business interests in the state. Watson explained that the candidate's problem had come to the attention of his boss, and Watson was instructed to send a blank check for the candidate's war chest. The reason for the magnanimity, Watson assured, was that Conrad and his possible anonymous benefactor agreed closely on most issues. Watson explained that if Conrad gave the go-ahead signal, he would soon receive the check. If he preferred, a number of different checks in smaller amounts could be sent to separate "campaign committees" to make up the total amount needed. The checks would come from businessmen around the state at the "request" of the benefactor, and in this way could be disclosed without fear of adverse repercussions. What did Conrad wish to do?

Conrad replied that he would return the call the following morning.

CASE QUESTIONS_____

1. If you were in Conrad's position, what would you do?
2. If Conrad accepts the money will he be beholden to the wealthy donor when he votes or otherwise exercises his influence as senator; In all areas of public policy? In some?'
3. Are present campaign financing and spending laws adequate to regulate practices that might later lead to subtle forms of political blackmail?
4. Do businessmen with large economic holdings have the right to use their wealth for political influence?

B) BUY AMERICAN

Section 724, the "Buy American" provision, is amended to include the words "specialty metals" in the list of items which are prohibited from being purchased outside of the United States. The Committee held hearings in which this proposal was made by representatives of the specialty metals industry. The Committee was favorably impressed by the evidence presented and wrote to the Department of Defense with regard to this matter. The Assistant Secretary of Defense for Installations and Logistics replied that in general the Department of Defense was in agreement with the

*From Section 724 of the *Department of Defense Appropriation Bill of 1973*, PL 92-92nd Congo, H. R. 16593, 26 October 1972.

statements made by the witnesses concerning the need of the Department of Defense for a viable specialty metals industry in this country. The Secretary further pointed out that the Defense requirements for these materials are currently only a small percentage of the U. S. consumption, and that an action such as that recommended by the Committee would not in and of itself solve the problems of this industry. The Secretary did state strongly that his domestic capability must be preserved.

Further, hearings were held by the Subcommittee on General Legislation of the Committee on Armed Services of the United States Senate with respect to specialty steels and their essentiality to national security and a favorable report was issued in this regard.

The action recommended by the Committee means that no part of any appropriation contained in this Act shall be available or be expended for the procurement of any article containing any specialty metal not melted in steel manufacturing facilities located within the United States or its possessions, except to the extent that the Secretary of the Department concerned shall determine that a satisfactory quality and sufficient quantity of any such article containing specialty metals melted in steel manufacturing facilities located within the United States and its possessions cannot be procured as and when needed at United States market prices and except for procurements outside the United States in support of combat operations.

For the purposes of this Act, the term "specialty metals" is defined as follows:

1) Steels where the maximum alloy content exceeds one or more of the following limits: manganese, 1.65 percent; silicone, 0.60 percent; or copper, 0.60 percent; or which contains more than 0.25 percent of any of the following elements: aluminum, chromium, cobalt, columbium, molybdenum, nickel, titanium, tungsten, or vanadium;

2) metal alloys consisting of nickel, iron-nickel and cobalt base alloys containing a total of other alloying metals (except iron) in excess of 10 percent;

3) titanium and titanium alloys; or

4) zirconium and zirconium base alloys.*

CASE QUESTION────────────────────────────

1. Colt Industries, which controls Crucible Steel Company, lobbied for this provision. What is your reaction to: (a) the right of a company to lobby self-serving legislation, and (b) the action of Colt Industries in this particular case?

C) A TRIUMPH FOR THE PORK BARREL

The House of Representatives voted solidly the other day to continue spending $225 million a year on a little-known farm subsidy program that President Nixon wants to end because it has long since outlived its usefulness.

The vote, it seems to us, was simply another victory for pork-barrel politics, though quite naturally the House chose to regard it as something quite different. As one member put it, eloquently if not necessarily accurately, nothing less was involved than "a reaffirmation that Congress is a coequal branch of government." Defined in those pulse-quickening words, the issue took on the significance of a major skirmish in the contest for authority between the legislative and executive branches, while the vote itself was transformed into a triumphant assertion of congressional independence and a barrier against ever-expanding presidential power.

Well, maybe. It all depends on your point of view. Our point of view is that it was still pork-barrel politics, and a good example of why Congress is in trouble.

---

*Note the wording "any such article containing specialty metals melted in steel manufacturing facilities located within the United States and its possessions cannot be procured." If strictly interpreted, this could mean that the only United States supplier of titanium mill products to military aircraft would be the Crucible Steel Company. No other titanium producer could qualify as a supplier, since no others are also steel-manufacturing facilities. Similarly, International Nickel Corporation's Huntington, Virginia plant, which supplies 75 percent of all high-temperature alloys for defense production, could not qualify as a supplier because it does not make steel. Ironically, Eastern Stainless Steel Company, which produces International Nickel Corporation alloys under a license agreement, would be a qualified supplier. Ed.

The program that the House voted to continue is called the Rural Environmental Assistance Program, or REAP. It was started during the Depression as a conservation measure. Farmers were paid to reseed grassland, enrich their fields with lime, construct drainage projects and the like. The program undoubtedly helped, and it won wide popularity among farmers, limestone suppliers and others. Little wonder. So far it has cost $8 billion, money spent in every one of the nation's 3,060 farm counties. Subsidies like that develop large and loyal constituencies, and their weight is felt in Congress.

But, popularity aside, is the program still needed? The last four Presidents have tried to cut back on it, without luck. Finally, last December, Mr. Nixon ordered the Agriculture Department to stop spending money on REAP. The Administration concluded that farmers would take conservation measures on their own because it is good business to do so; that, with net farm income at an all-time high of nearly $19 billion, farmers could do without this subsidy, and that there are more important things needing scarce budget dollars. It was a sensible decision.

The House disagrees, as is its right, and the Senate almost certainly will, too. Whether votes can be found later to override the promised Nixon veto of the REAP bill is another matter, and also largely beside the point.

CASE QUESTION

1. Why were four presidents unable to stop this form of subsidy?

DISCUSSION GUIDES ON CHAPTER CONTENT

1. Does business have a right to exert political power?
2. What is the difference between business involvement in the electoral process and business involvemnet in day-to-day activities of government?
3. What major trends are discernible in the current political activities of business?

*From an editorial, *Los Angeles Times*, February 11, 1973. Copyright, 1973, Los Angeles Times. Reprinted by permission.

4. In what ways are local businesses exerting political influence in your community? Do you accept what is being done as in the public interest?

5. Develop a case to support the involvement of business in political activities. What is the case against it?

6. Where, and under what circumstances, does business in general have great power in government? Give examples of instances in which particular business interests have gotten their way in government. Cite also instances where they have not.

7. Is it beneficial to business, and to the country, to have businessmen move in and out of government as managers or staff experts?

8. Are business pressure groups evil? Explain your position.

MIND-STRETCHING QUESTIONS ————————————

1. Is it possible to assure that pressure groups will act in the best interests of the public instead of in their own selfish interests? How would you assure this?

2. It is the right and duty of every individual citizen of the United States to support the political candidates of his choice. Yet, this is considered unethical for corporations, which are regarded as individuals in the eyes of the law. Is this just? Why?

23

THE CONVERGENCE OF BUSINESS AND GOVERNMENT PLANNING

A) PLANNING FOR TWO-WAY CABLE TV

The age of two-way cable television is here. Experiments are now in progress that permit homeowners to request specific programming, information, or services from a computer. This is a development that private industry can readily finance, because it has so many potentials for profit. Linking a computer to an unlimited number of cable TV channels can make available in a homeowner's living room a very large number of commercial, entertainment, and educational services. It is not at all inconceivable that this new technology will serve the public as library, newspaper, post office, classroom, theater, sports arena, mail-order catalog, bank, and communications center. Its potential benefits to society stagger the imagination.

Professor Stanley Scott takes the position that two-way cable TV must not be developed by private industry without careful government supervision. He claims that commercial broadcasting, which has been developed by private industry with only overall governmental policy guidance, has become enslaved by the need to appeal to mass audiences. The trivial, he says, smothers the significant. "Probably never before," he writes, "has technology been more in need of informed and intellectually inspired guidance than it is now, as we move into the era of the all-pervasive 'wired city.' "[1]

"We must not blow this opportunity," agrees Professor Semour Clearwhistle, "to build a truly magnificent, cheap, and influential educational system for masses of people who cannot under our present system receive the knowledge they need and thirst for." He continues, "If we do not plan the development of this new utility with care the 'great wasteland' which has characterized our current commercial broadcasting will be like a green garden in comparison. This utility must be planned by government, in cooperation with industry. No other way makes sense."

On the other hand, Miles Flemming, who is the general manager of a major national TV network, asserts that this new development must remain solely in the hands of private industry. He accepts the fact that some government regulation is necessary to prevent abuses. "We need the powers of the Federal Communications Industry to be expanded," he says, "to encompass this new development. But the FCC authority and operation should be about the same as it is today."

CASE QUESTIONS

1. What arguments pro and con can you advance concerning this proposition: two-way cable TV must be planned carefully by the federal government, with the cooperation of private industry?

2. The president of the United States asks you to outline for him a plan for the development of two-way cable TV that, in your judgment, will provide the maximum benefit to the government, the public, and private enterprise in the United States.

DISCUSSION GUIDES ON CHAPTER CONTENT

1. What is meant by "planning" in business and government?

2. Trace the evolution of long-range planning in business and government.

[1] Scott, "Lessons From The History of American Broadcasting," *Science*, 22 December 1972, p. 1265.

3. Describe the principal types of governmental plans. How was the French Five-Year Plan developed?

4. Argue the proposition: The United States should prepare comprehensive national plans along the lines of the French system.

5. On the assumption that the United States will not develop single comprehensive national plans, what do you think ought to be done to assure better planning by the federal government?

6. What is meant by "privatizing" the public sector? What are the propositions upon which it is based?

MIND-STRETCHING QUESTION

1. It is altogether likely that in the United States the federal government will work closely with private industry in undertaking major projects that neither can carry out alone. What basic principles would you suggest to assure that as the two work more closely together, each will devote to an undertaking that influence which it is best able to make, and each will avoid potentially significant problems that such a partnership can easily bring?

24

ECONOMIC CONCENTRATION AND PUBLIC POLICY

DISCUSSION GUIDES ON CHAPTER CONTENT————

1. How do the views of businessmen, lawmakers, economists, and political theorists differ concerning competition? In what ways are they similar?

2. Identify: the Sherman Act; the Clayton Act; the rule of reason; conglomerate; price competition versus other types of competition; concentration ratios; reciprocity; entry barriers; and horizontal versus vertical mergers.

3. Identify the most significant Supreme Court decisions up to the 1960s concerning firm size and mergers.

4. What is the difference between the structure school of thought concerning mergers and size, and the performance and behavior school? Which side are you on? Explain.

5. Is aggregate concentration growing or remaining relatively constant? How about micro concentration?

6. It has long been accepted conventional economic wisdom that market concentration is indicative of monopoly power, collusion, price inflexibility, high prices, and high or excessive profits. More recent data do not confirm this. Explain.

7. Explain the reasoning of the Supreme Court in these recent decisions concerning conglomerates: Brown Shoe, Reynolds Metal, Procter and Gamble, El Paso Natural Gas, and Von's Grocery. Do you think these decisions were in the right direction?

8. Has it been proven or disproven that conglomerates lessen competition, add to aggregate concentration, and are less efficient than smaller companies?

9. Outline those basic public policies which you think should govern the growth and merger of business enterprises.

MIND-STRETCHING QUESTION ————————————

1. The business ethic of the United States has always stressed efficiency, becoming the best in one's field, and outstripping the competition. Why, then, when a company does just this and eliminates all or most of its competition, do we penalize it for becoming a monopoly?

25
BUSINESS AND INTERNATIONAL POLICY

A) THE BURKE-HARTKE BILL: FOREIGN TRADE AND INVESTMENT
Foreword

On September 28, 1971, the Foreign Trade and Investment Act of 1972 was introduced into the Congress by Representative James A. Burke (D-Mass) and Senator Vance Hartke (D-Ind). This proposed legislation is commonly referred to as The Burke-Hartke Bill.

The bill's introduction occurred at a time when sentiment toward "protectionism" and "isolationism" was rapidly growing. That trend has continued, though it still does not represent a majority viewpoint.

In 1971 the United States suffered its first balance of trade deficit since 1960. Despite the currency realignments of 1971, the United States merchandise trade balance deteriorated sharply. The trade deficit came to a record $6.8 billion for the year 1972, about two and one-half times the 1971 figure.

The United States rate of unemployment during this time was also a major factor in the bill's introduction. Overall domestic unemployment rates moved up from 4.5 percent for 1970 to 6.8 percent for 1971, and then receded to 5.8 percent for 1972. Even though overall employment for 1972 increased 3.4 percent as opposed to a historical annual growth rate of 1.7 percent, unemployment rates still received a great deal of attention and were of major concern to business, labor, and government.

The Burke-Hartke Bill takes an extreme position in attempting to alleviate these national problems. Nevertheless, it represents a state of mind toward national policy beset with deep and contradictory views.

The measure generated heated opposition from the Nixon administration and business groups, who viewed its provisions as a retreat from our traditional free trade policies. This retreat, it is argued, has in it great potential damage to United States and world economic activity.

The main premise of the bill is that by reducing the incentive for United States corporations to invest overseas and increasing the acceptance of domestically produced goods over foreign imports, both foreign trade and domestic employment in the United States will be drastically improved.

The bill contains provisions aimed at:

1) Massively overhauling corporate tax laws affecting United States-based multinational corporations and their propensity to establish and continue substantial overseas operations.
2) Establishing restrictions severely limiting foreign investment by United States corporations, in an effort to stimulate domestic investment and create more jobs for American workers.
3) Curtailing various practices relating to the export of American technical know-how to increase our competitive advantage.
4) Establishing a new agency representing American industry, labor, and the public to set import quotas.

While this specific bill seems unlikely to be passed into law, similar bills, or certain of its provisions, could easily be adapted in the near future.

Major Provisions of the Burke-Hartke Bill

On September 28, 1971, the Foreign Trade and Investment Act of 1971 was introduced simultaneously in the Senate (S. 2592) and the House of Representatives (H.R. 10914). The bill provides for a comprehensive restructuring of legislation relating to the overseas operations of United States corporations. It also embodies substantial governmental control over foreign trade.

Major provisions can be identified as follows:

1) Taxation of United States overseas operations.
2) Formation of a Foreign Trade and Investment Commission.
3) Imposition of import quotas.
4) Antidumping law revisions.
5) Revisions to the 1962 Trade Expansion Act.
6) Foreign investment controls.
7) Patent transfer restrictions.
8) Labeling of foreign components.
9) U.S. Tariff Code revision.

TAX CHANGES. The bill proposes major changes in the Internal Revenue Code of 1954 relative to the tax treatment of United States companies producing goods in foreign nations. It would:

1) End tax deferral on earnings of foreign subsidiaries. Taxes would be levied at the time of generation of earnings, not upon repatriation. This would remove incentives to operate in low tax areas.
2) Repeal the existing United States income tax credit for payment of foreign income taxes or for taxes on royalties received for patents used outside the United States. This would increase costs through double taxation.
3) Require companies to use stricter guidelines in estimating depreciation on foreign machinery and property. This would create an increased tax and cash flow burden during development of overseas facilities.
4) Tax a United States company's income from licensing and transferring patents to foreign corporations. This would eliminate the means of syphoning earnings from high tax areas to low tax areas.
5) Eliminate tax exemptions for United States citizens who work overseas for a subsidiary of a United States company. This would increase the cost of managing foreign operations.

The net effect of these provisions would be to substantially raise the cost of foreign operations. The return on investment that could be generated on capital invested overseas would in most situations be equal to or less than for domestic operations. If the added risk of such activities is considered, the likelihood of United States firms establishing, or even continuing, foreign operations is rather remote.

TRADE COMMISSION. The bill would create a three-member Foreign Trade and Investment Commission with broad powers to regulate foreign trade and investment. The commission would assume functions now performed by the U.S. Tarriff Commission and sections of the Treasury, Commerce, and Labor departments.

The three members, appointed by the president with the advice and consent of the Senate, would be representatives of labor, industry, and the public.

IMPORT QUOTAS. Under the bill, the new commission would be empowered to set quotas on all imports except those in four categories: goods covered by a voluntary agreement with another government; goods covered by existing quotas; goods needed but not produced in the United States; and goods produced by a domestic industry that had failed to modernize its equipment.

On all other commodities, quotas in the first year would be set equal to the average annual imports during the period 1965-1969. In succeeding years quotas would be adjusted by the commission to maintain the initial ratio between imported and domestically produced goods. Quotas would change automatically as United States production increased or decreased. The lead time required to adjust to supply and demand conditions would cause increased prices and significant shortages.

ANTIDUMPING LAW. The bill includes a provision revising the existing law, which levies penalties on foreign exporters who injure United States firms by selling goods in the United States at prices below their home market prices (the Anti-dumping Act of 1921).

The bill would make the new commission responsible for handing complaints against dumping, and require that they be disposed of within four months. Under existing law, complaints are dealt with by both the Tariff Commission and the Treasury

Department, and proceedings sometimes take more than two years to complete.

ESCAPE CLAUSE. Another provision of the bill would ease requirements for assistance to industries harmed by increased imports. Under the new provision, increased imports need only substantially increase the threat to domestic industry rather than be the main cause (as under the escape clause of the 1962 act). The new commission would have power not only to determine the existence of the threat, but to revise import quotas to provide relief. Under existing law, the president must make the decision. The president still would decide whether or not to grant adjustment assistance, however.

INVESTMENT CONTROLS. The bill provides the president with new authority to regulate the transfer of capital from the United States to other nations if he determines that such a transfer would reduce United States employment.

Existing foreign investment controls were instituted under authority given the president in the Trading With the Enemy Act. In 1968, President Johnson imposed such controls to protect the United States balance of payments. The president's authority to impose such controls depended on the continued existence of the state of national emergency declared by President Truman in 1950.

This new authority given the president eliminates the need to relate the capital transfers to national defense or national emergency situations. This added flexibility, coupled with severe penalties, permits more rapid and effective executive response.

PATENTS. Another section of the bill would authorize the president to prohibit any holder of a United States patent from producing a patented product abroad or from licensing its production in another nation.

LABELING. The bill would require that all products made with foreign-produced components and marketed within the United States be so labeled. In addition, advertisements of such products would have to disclose the use of imported components and the nations that produced the components.

TARIFF CODE. The bill would repeal existing provisions of the U.S. Tariff Code that permit United States companies to set up operations overseas to assemble components manufactured in the United States into finished products for export back to the United States. This would repeal legislation enacted to promote Domestic International Sales Corporations (DISC'S).

The existing code alolws companies to use cheap labor (e.g., in Mexico) in their assembly operations and to pay only duty on the value added by such labor to the final product.

Proponents of the Bill

Labor leaders and the rank-and-file membership of unions hardest hit by import-related job losses not only support the provisions of the bill but were the prime movers behind its introduction.

The United Steelworkers of America, United Rubber Workers, National Maritime Union, Seafarers' International Union, International Union of Electrical Workers, Glass Bottle Blowers Association, International Brotherhood of Electrical Workers, Textile Workers of America, International Association of Machinists, International Ladies Garment Workers' Union, and International Alliance of Theatrical and Stage Employees are solidly pushing the bill. The United Automobile Workers Union has taken a somewhat moderate approach to the legislation because its membership is divided on the issue. In the auto industry, hard hit by imports, the rank-and-file sentiment is for protective legislation to save jobs in domestic plants. But in the defense and agricultural equipment industries, where jobs are often dependent on export sales, the pressure is against the stiff quota regulations proposed under the Burke-Hartke Bill. Both of these industries are heavily organized by the UAW. Consequently, the major thrust of the UAW trade position is an attack on the multinational corporations. But the effect of the position would clearly force a "buy American" policy on the United States economy.

Significantly, only a few business concerns—such as Latrobe Steel, a specialty steel maker hard hit by imports—have expressed approval of the bill. Others will probably follow, but the general business reaction has been decidedly negative.

Opponents of the Bill

Opposition to passage of the bill was very strong within the Nixon administration, the international business world and academia. The administration has been rushing out studies on the economic benefits to the nation of international corporations, and the globe-girdling companies are busy making similar defensive statements. International Telephone & Telegraph, currently one of the more visible United States-based international concerns, recently hired the New York public relations firm of Harshe-Rotman and Druck to visit thirty large cities and publicize the virtues of international companies.

Such business groups as the Emergency Committee for American Trade (ECAT), the National Association of Manufacturers (NAM), and the U. S. Chamber of Commerce are engaging in a flurry of activity to inform the public about the issues. They are trying to answer union arguments and are publicizing government and private studies on multinational companies. ECAT is urging its members and other companies to analyze the Burke-Hartke Bill and communicate their concern to their congressmen. And NAM is organizing a broad, grass roots campaign to alert American business concerns and their employees to the dangers of the measure.

Individual companies are also getting into the act. Caterpillar Tractor, for example, has taken full-page ads in several major newspapers proclaiming its free trade sentiments and opposition to the Burke-Hartke Bill. American Cyanamid has made public a study of the drastic effects passage of the bill would have on its foreign operations. Honeywell, Inc., and Minnesota Mining & Manufacturing have discussed the measure in their employee publications. Other companies, following the example of the Bank of America, have raised the subject with their corporate clients.

Impact of the Bill

Most of the controversy surrounding the Burke-Hartke Bill is concerned with these questions:

1) Do multinational companies export American jobs?

2) Will the bill increase employment in the United States?

3) Is a free trade policy in the best interests of the United States?

4) Will other countries retaliate and foment a trade war?

Do Multimational Companies Export Jobs?

The authors of the bill are convinced that high unemployment in the United States is a direct result of the growth of the multinational corporation.

Representative Burke stated this contention when he introduced the bill. He said:

> American jobs are being exported, as huge amounts of money are shipped abroad to build plants to make goods for sale in the United States. American jobs are being lost, also, because that foreign production often takes the place of possible U.S. exports. Products as varied as airplane parts and shoes, clothing and automobiles—all kinds of jobs are at stake.[1]

In 1962 when labor supported the Trade Expansion Act, which followed a philosophy of free trade, George Meany, the head of the AFL-CIO, concluded that export-related jobs totaled more than 4 million, while jobs "adversely affected" by imports were no more than 400,000. Today, however, the AFL-CIO concludes that during the past six years 900,000 jobs have been lost because of imports. In the past, more jobs were gained each year through exports than were lost. But in 1971, much to labor's despair, there was for the first time a net loss of 200,000 jobs. A particular concern to labor unions has been the reduction of membership in import-vulnerable industries. Workers whose jobs are displaced by imports are hurt more than business firms, contend the unions, because investment can be reallocated more easily than workers, especially if they are older, unskilled employees. The AFL-CIO points to the expanded role of imports in some of our most basic industries: 20 percent of the market for steel, 25 percent of auto sales, 35 percent of television set sales, 60 percent of phonograph sales, 86 percent of radio sales, and nearly all tape recorder sales. The union report also put much of the blame on large American firms that shipped their technology, know-how, and money abroad to produce goods.

Government officials admit that many industries have been

---

[1] *Congressional Record—House*, September 28, 1971, p. 8785.

severely hurt by the increased flow of imports. However, they strongly disagree that multinational corporations are to blame.

The multinational corporations' favorable impact on United States employment usually is ignored by critics. Exports from the United States by such corporations increased 180 percent between 1960 and 1970, compared with a much smaller increase in all United States exports. At the same time, multinational corporations increased their domestic employment by an estimated 31 percent, over 2 1/2 times more than the 12 percent increase for all jobs in the United States.

Additionally, very few of the goods manufactured abroad by foreign affiliates of United States corporations are shipped to the United States. Only 6 percent of all foreign-affiliate sales in 1957, and only 8 percent in 1968, became United States imports. Some proponents of foreign investment restrictions have claimed that United States foreign-owned companies export heavily to the United States. Actually, imports from subsidiaries of United States companies remain a small part of aggregate imports in the United States. Our foreign investments also reward us in many less obvious ways. A recent survey of seventy-four multinational corporations conducted by ECAT pointed up a number of the more obscure benefits of foreign investment. Among other facts, the ECAT survey revealed that during the 1960-1970 period the corporations examined:

1) Increased their total sales from facilities in the United States from $58 billion to $113 billion, a gain of $55 billion.

2) Increased their export from the United States from $4.3 billion to $12.2 billion, a gain of $7.9 billion. (Their rate of export to production in 1970 was 10.8 percent, or double the national average for manufacturing firms.)

3) Increased their domestic payrolls from $2.4 billion to $3.3 billion, a 37.5 percent gain. (By comparison, the average rate of increase for the nation during the same period was only 10.3 percent.)

The ECAT survey suggests that those United States companies which are most vigorous abroad are also the most dynamic at home. ECAT argues that efforts to restrict these companies overseas in order to force them to invest more at home would be counterproductive. These restrictions would reduce the vitality of multinational corporations both overseas and in the United States by reducing their revenue, income, and opportunities.

Individual companies insist that their foreign investments actually boost United States employment. Says General Electric vice-president J. Stanford Smith; "We recently received an order from Brazil for 80 diesel locomotives to be assembled in Brazil, but with 50 percent of the content to be supplied by our plant in Erie, Pa. We would never have received this order without establishing facilities in Brazil." And Caterpillar Tractor executive vice-president Lee L. Morgan recently noted that since the company established subsidiaries in Britain in 1950 and France in 1960, its exports to those countries have increased by factors of 15 and 4, respectively.[2]

A recent study by Brookings Institution economist Lawrence Krause concluded that between the first quarters of 1970 and 1971, when total unemployment in the United States rose by 1.7 million, changes in exports and imports resulted in the loss of some 410,000 jobs and the gain of 393,000 others, making for a total loss of only 17,000 jobs. A recent series of case studies by Harvard Business School researchers indicates that most multinational corporations invest abroad to prevent the loss of markets to foreign competitors and that their moves tend to create jobs for Americans.

Will Employment Rise after the Burke-Hartke Bill is Passed?

Supporters of the bill feel certain that employment will increase steadily after its passage. The provisions of the bill, it is claimed, will in effect insulate the American workers from the pressures of foreign economies, in particular, "cheap labor." If the United States economy is in an expansionary cycle, the rest of the world will be allowed to continue to participate on an increasing basis. If, however, the economy is declining, the rest of the world must realize that it will have to reduce exports to the United States.

It is strongly argued that if multinational corporations are given

[2] Dan Throop Smith, Lee L. Morgan, and Elizabeth R. Jager, "The Foreign Trade and Investment Act of 1972, Three Points of View," *Columbia Journal of World Business,* March-April, 1972, p. 14. Reprinted by permission.

the same advantages for investments at home and abroad, they will probably elect to invest at home because of risk considerations.

Additional investment domestically will, of course, increase United States employment. Likewise, if United States-developed technology remains here, American-made products will be given a competitive advantage.

Opponents agree that probably the most destructive part of the proposed legislation from the standpoint of innovative American companies is the weakening of incentives to discover new products and processes. Under the Burke-Hartke Bill, the president could remove United States patent protection from products made or licensed abroad. Thus, the choice for United States companies would be to manufacture the products they invent either at home or abroad. They could not do both, as they do today.

The Burke-Hartke legislation, by effectively preventing overseas use of United States patents, would enable producers abroad to profit from discoveries revealed in United States patents. If foreign markets were cut off, United States research costs would have to be recovered from a lower volume of sales at home. This would help to push prices higher.

Any restriction by tax or regulation on foreign investment, it is argued, eliminates rather than creates jobs in the United States. Opponents argue that the net gain in employment in the United States, if the bill is passed, would by far fail to offset job losses arising from United States housed foreign company purchases in the United States. Retaliation from abroad would further cost jobs in the United States. The net loss of jobs, it is argued, would be very great.

Free Trade?

Most of the labor movement has supported every liberal trade initiative since the first reciprocal trade agreement in 1934. In 1962 labor participation was crucial to the passage of the Trade Expansion Act. However, with the loss of hundreds of thousands from union rolls as a result of import penetrations, free trade notions in many unions are a thing of the past.

Elizabeth R. Jager, AFL-CIO economist, summed up the union position on free trade, as follows:

In today's "real world"—a far cry from the never-never land of the textbooks—a combination of factors are threatening the U. S. position at home and abroad. Among these are the managed economics of modern nations, foreign government-sponsored subsidies and services, multinational firms, rapid technology transfers and uncounted capital flows. The fear slogans of the 1930s and 1940s have been used to mask these factors and their impact on the United States. Cries of "protectionism" and "Fortress America" have little relevance in our jet age with its telecommunications and programmed production whereby imports rise during a recession. Thus isolationism is impractical in a modern world. . . . Today, U.S. multinational firms and others cry "free trade," which really means keeping U.S. markets wide open for their low-wage, foreign-made goods, and thus for their ever-greater profit, regardless of the eventual destruction of the U. S. markets, U. S. industries, and U. S. workers' jobs.[3]

Dan Throop Smith, Senior Research Fellow, Stanford University, stated the opposing viewpoint in the same article:

The arguments in favor of free movements of goods and capital are familiar. The relative costs of production and relative rates of return on capital vary in different parts of the world. The most efficient use of the world's resources requires flexibility to permit goods to be produced and purchased where the costs are lower, and for capital to go to the places where it is most productive—that is, where capital is most needed.

The proposed freeze on the proportion of imports to total consumption would be as stultifying as it would have been to "protect" employment on railroads by prohibiting airlines and buses from providing any greater proportion of transportation services than they represented in, say, the period from 1920 to 1925; or, to go further back, to have set a quota for automobiles in proportion to their output compared to horse-drawn carriages in 1900. . . .

An attempt to deny U. S. consumers the opportunity to buy cheaper and better goods from foreign sources would be properly and bitterly resented if it were proposed by business groups. It is a strange and ironic twist of logic when it becomes respectable, though no fairer or more reasonable, when proposed as a general policy to "protect" certain jobs. And in the long run, workers are frozen into less productive, and hence less well-paying jobs. Would employees generally be better off if we had kept hod-carriers employed by outlawing the adoption of mechanical hoists for building materials? As a practical matter, quotas on imports would remove a competitive source which not only lowers prices to consumers but forces increases in productivity

[3] *Ibid*, pp.16, 17.

by U. S. producers, thereby providing the only solid basis for increases in real wages.

As a final practical point, how are import quotas to be allocated? If foreign costs are lower, as they must be to make quotas significant, those importers who receive quotas will have windfall profits as they get the advantage of the spread between lower costs of foreign products and the prices necessary to cover the higher costs of U.S. producers.[4]

Opponents further argue that by protecting inefficient industries, import controls not only force consumers to pay higher prices, they allow protected industries to become less efficient. This leads to still higher prices, greater distortion in resource allocation, reduced consumer choice, and, inevitably, declining employment.

The U. S. Department of Commerce estimates that the Burke-Hartke quotas would reduce imports by about $12 billion a year, or more than 25 percent from the 1972 level. An internal department report says that declines would be as much as 36 percent for products from Japan and 27 percent for those from the Common Market nations. This report also estimates that color television imports would drop by 65 percent from the 1971 level and auto imports would decline 52 percent.

Trade War?

Labor unions dismiss the notion that a trade war will follow if the bill is passed. "These arguments simply are out of date," contends Elizabeth Jager. "For 25 years we've shown concern for other nations, and now they're just going to have to realize it's in their self-interest to do the same for us," she says.[5]

Other union officials indicate that some retaliation is possible, but assert that it is unlikely it would be significant or long lasting. On the other hand, the Commerce Department study says there would be "immediate retaliation," since the "political and economic pressure" abroad "would be so great as to make such retaliation unavoidable." Competition among countries for portions of quotas leads to retaliation and loss of export markets. Then, one retaliation leads to another and so on, until trade is strangled. Restrictions of

[4] *Ibid.*, pp. 11-12.
[5] *Ibid*, p. 16.

this kind encourage the formation of monopolies and cartels, anticompetitive international groups that the United States has worked to eliminate.

The worst thing about the bill, argues Senator Javits, is that it will not remedy the problems it addresses. Instead it will invite retaliation by other nations and result in a destructive trade war. Passage of the proposed import quotas, he warns, "would proclaim to the world that the United States is copping out of the Free World's economic system and going isolationist."

CASE QUESTION

1. If you were in the United States Congress, would you vote for this bill?

References

For sources for this case and short articles containing arguments for and against the bill, see:

Henry J. Heinz II, "The Burke-Hartke Bill," *Vital Speeches*, 1 October 1972, pp. 750-752.

Albert Hunt, "That Burke-Hartke Bill," *Wall Street Journal*, 15 May 1972. "The Raging Fight Over Burke-Hartke," *Business Week*, 12 February 1972, pp. 14-15.

Implications of Multinational Firms for World Trade and Investment and for U.S. Trade and Labor (Washington, D.C.: U.S. Government Printing Office, February 1973).

Irwin Ross, "Labor's Big Push for Protectionism," *Fortune*, March 1973, pp. 92 ff.

Stanley H. Ruttenberg, "Updating the World of Trade," *The American Federationist*, February 1973, pp. 1-7.

"The Foreign Trade And Investment Act of 1972: Three Points of View," *Columbia Journal of World Business*, March-April 1972, pp. 11-18.

DISCUSSION GUIDES ON CHAPTER CONTENT

1. Identify and/or define: multinational company, balance of payments, free trade, nontariff trade barriers, balance of payments (trade and total), expropriation.

2. Why do American companies invest in foreign production facilities?

3. Explain some of the major sources of conflicts between multi-national companies and the host countries in which they do business.

4. What can and should be done to reduce these conflicts?

5. What are the more important conflicts that the federal government has with multinational companies whose headquarters are in the United States?

6. Explain the principal provisions of the Burke-Hartke Bill.

7. Do you believe that multinational companies export jobs? Explain fully.

8. What is the case for free trade? What is the case for tariff protection?

9. All things considered do you see the multinational company as beneficial or harmful?

MIND-STRETCHING QUESTIONS———————————

1. There are many observers who think that in the next thirty years a few hundred of the largest multinational companies will virtually control world trade and production. Others think that the problems facing the multinational corporation will bring about an important decline in its influence. Which side are you on? Explain.

2. There are many observers who think that the multinational corporation has virtually unlimited capability for doing "good things" in the underdeveloped countries of the world. What good can a multinational company do and still keep its stockholders happy?

26

OTHER ISSUES IN GOVERNMENT REGULATION OF BUSINESS

DISCUSSION GUIDES ON CHAPTER CONTENT —————

1. The author says there is a regulatory crisis. What does he mean? Do you agree with the textbook on this matter? What can and should be done to remedy the main deficiencies in current government regulation of buisness?

2. Do you agree with Galbraith that the solution is to socialize industry?

3. Distinguish between the short-term and long-term energy problem in the United States. What has been done to remedy the problems in both the short and the long run? Do you think that what has been done to date is appropriate? The best that can be done?

4. In 1971 the federal government guaranteed a $250 million loan to the Lockheed Aircraft Corporation. This was a very controversial action by the government. What were the arguments for and against it? Where do you stand on the issue?

5. Do you think American corporations make enough information public about their activities? Explain.

6. What are the arguments for and against corporations making public forecasts of their activities?

7. How can profit figures be changed by using current acceptable accounting standards?

8. Do you favor federal incorporation of businesses? Explain.

9. What is meant by "full employment policy"?

10. Have the objectives of the Employment Act of 1946 been met?

11. What were the fundamental causes of price inflation in the United States following 1965? Was the action taken by the federal government to counteract inflationary forces effective? Explain.

12. Are you in favor of direct wage and price controls to control inflation? Explain your position.

13. Is inflation inevitable in the future in the United States?

VI

BUSINESS AND ITS EMPLOYEES

27

THE CHANGING
ROLE OF
PEOPLE
IN ORGANIZATIONS

A) STAN SHELDON AND THE "JOINING UP" PROCESS

Everyone in Division X agreed that Stan's brief employment with
the company was disastrous—and so did Stan. Now quite happy in a
job with another company, he described his tenure this way:

"I was recruited on my college campus and joined Division X
because the company enjoys an excellent reputation back there. I
began work in June, was given a supervisor, a project, and part-time
training. For the first few weeks I felt anxious and lost, but very
enthusiastic about the whole thing. It's hard to say, but I think that
it was after about a month that I began to get a little upset—because I
wasn't getting the direction I needed to work on my project. I felt so
helpless. I didn't know where facilities were, or how to get
information, or how to get things done. I felt guilty about having to
go to my boss and ask questions all the time, so I didn't until I got
frustrated. It was usually difficult to find him, and that just used up
more of my time and made me more upset.

"I'm still not sure exactly what it was about the way that he
answered my questions, but it wasn't very helpful. He gave very terse

From John P. Kotter, "Managing the Joining-Up Process.
Reprinted by permission of the publisher from *Personnel*, July/August 1972 ©
1972 by the American Management Association, Inc.

answers. He would do things himself, which got something done at the time, but didn't teach me anything. I'm probably not being completely fair, because he did occasionally try to coach me, but he did it by making me read things, and that's not the way I learn. I'm sure I told him that but he never heard me. I managed to locate some good resources in our group, some guys who really know their stuff and didn't mind answering my questions. This kept me going for the first four months, more than anything else.

"Two things in particular happened in about the fifth month that brought things to a head. I was directed to Curt Smith for some help on a certain aspect of my project. I hadn't met Curt before. After talking for a while, he got this puzzled look on his face and said that my project looked very much like something that was tried and abandoned about seven years ago. I just didn't know what to think, especially since I had gotten the impression from Phil Davis, my boss, that the project was new and important."

"At about the same time I found out that John Mathis, who was hired the same time as I, had just gotten a raise. I hadn't heard about the possibility that I might even get a performance review, much less a raise. At this point I was confused, hurt, and a little mad. I started to go immediately to Phil and confront him, but I didn't; I just didn't have the kind of relationship where I felt free to talk to Phil. At the time I felt a bit guilty, because a friend of mine told me that I sounded as if I wanted a father, not a boss. Well, I don't feel that way anymore, but when you're new in a big organization, you are a bit like a child. You're lost, anxious, and need others to help you; you do need a father figure."

"Anyway, I tried in my own way to find out what was going on, but I got nowhere. When I mentioned salary administration, people began to whisper, and no one gave me the same story. When I tried to find out how well people thought I was doing, I began to realize that I didn't really understand at all what the company expected from me besides so many hours a week. When I finally confronted Phil he tried to make me feel better, but he really didn't give me any information. So I finally said to hell with it and went to the assistant division head and asked for a transfer."

"Well, as it turned out, going above two levels of management on any issue like this is a cardinal sin in the company. Faces started turning red everywhere and people began to get defensive, and nobody, including the assistant director, was talking about what I thought the issues were. About two days later I took all my notebooks and put them through a paper shredding machine, posted notices of my resignation on about ten different doors, and left."

Stan's boss, Phil Davis, agrees now that the whole episode was poorly handled and he personally regrets it:

"I think it was four days before Stan arrived when I was told about him. I went to Ken (Phil's boss) and he suggested that since we had no obvious projects for Stan, I choose one that used the best approach we had come up with for solving our problems. I chose one that we gave up on a few years back, and while it wasn't a great project, it was better than the one I was given when I first arrived ten years ago. I know I probably didn't spend enough time with him, but I'm awfully busy myself, and, to tell you the truth, managing the new man is not what Ken Thomas talks about when he gives me a raise."

"In retrospect, I don't think that I've been particularly well prepared for managing a new employee. I know that Stan complained that I didn't give him enough feedback; well, I thought I was giving off cues all the time about how I felt he was doing, but he didn't seem to see them. I can certainly do without another incident like that one. It affected my other work and even my home life. The company has got to be on guard to avoid that sort of thing."

Finally, Phil's boss, Ken Thomas, reacted:

"This is an example of a real goof on our part. Stan cost us over $14,000 in the obvious costs of recruiting, pay, and equipment, and gave us nothing in return. He took up a good deal of other people's time and energy. He obviously upset some people and caused others unnecessary pain. Stan himself probably suffered a great deal. This kind of incident has got to be avoided in the future."

CASE QUESTIONS

1. Who is to blame for this situation, Stan Sheldon or the managers of Division X? Compare what Stan Sheldon wanted from Division X with what Division X wanted from Sheldon. Was there a mismatch?

2. What corrective actions do you recommend? (See John P. Kotter, "The Psychological Contract: A Concept for Managing the Joining-Up Process," *California Management Review*, Spring 1973, pp. 91-99. See also Donald M. DeSalvia and Gary

R. Gemmill, "An Exploratory Study of the Personal Value Systems of College Students and Managers," *Academy of Management Journal*, June 1971, pp. 227-238.)

―――――――――――――References―――――――――――――

Harry Levinson, "What An Executive Should Know About his Boss," *Think*, March-April 1968, pp. 31-33.

B) WHISTLE BLOWING AT HI-QUALITY AIRCRAFT

James Sinclair, president of Hi-Quality Aircraft, was pacing in his office, deep in thought and obviously concerned. He was pondering what to do to stop the controversy raging in the press about the safety of his new Exec-Six airplane. Somehow he did not seem able to stop this controversy, and if it did not stop, sales were not likely to reach the breakeven point, with a resulting substantial loss to the company. What could he do? What should he do?

He had somehow lost control of the situation. He still couldn't believe it had happened. Maybe if he tried to review this terrible fiasco again it would help. Yet after reviewing the problem so many times before, this seemed like an exercise in futility.

The newspapers had called Phillip Evans a "whistle blower." Sinclair had never liked that term and, in most cases, the people associated with it. Evans was becoming a hero around the country, with Hi-Quality Aircraft playing the role of corporate villain. Before this incident was closed, many people would be hurt.

Success Story

James Sinclair had assumed the presidency of Hi-Quality late in 1969. Jim had an engineering background, but his impressive credentials in corporate finance assured his appointment. He had established a reputation with two other aviation firms as a hard-driving, competent manager.

During the last ten years, Hi-Quality had grown from obscurity to become the major producer of executive aircraft. Superior engineering, coupled with attractive pricing, enabled the firm to record constantly rising sales and profits. The firm had always followed a policy of generously supporting its research and development programs. It took pride in its engineering and design excellence.

Project HQE-12

Early in 1970 Hi-Quality embarked on Project HQE-6—the design and manufacture of the Exec-Six aircraft. This airplane would be the most advanced and fastest six-passenger executive aircraft yet conceived. It would also be priced at least 10 percent lower than its closest competitor. As always, design and engineering would be the best Hi-Quality could offer. Profit margins would be the lowest in ten years, however, because of the low price tag. And competitive pressures would exert much more influence on cost-benefit analysis of engineering design requirements than ever before.

This new project necessitated a 20 percent increase in personnel in the engineering section. Phillip Evans was hired as a project engineer in March of 1970. Evans was twenty-eight years old and had already established himself as a real "comer" in aircraft fuselage and airfoil design. His previous experience had been with a large military contractor in the aerospace industry. Some of his designs were largely responsible for the speed and superiority of American fighter-bombers.

Cost versus Design Considerations

The HQE-6 prototype was completed in late 1971. Preliminary testing indicated that it was indeed a superior aircraft. Bernard Collins, the veteran senior project engineer, was very pleased with the work his engineering section had done. He was especially happy with Phillip Evans, whose wing design enabled the aircraft to take off and land in 25 percent less distance than conventional aircraft. Also, the cruising speed of 625 miles per hour was well above design requirements and the competition.

Keith Mitchell, general production manager, was not quite as enthusiastic as Collins. The accounting department had just completed costing the HQE-6 and found that its construction costs were 15 percent higher than the targeted price. While costs exceeded projections on several features of the aircraft, the wing design was estimated to be 60 percent over budget. In addition, manufacturing lead time on the wing construction was estimated to be three times original projections.

Mitchell and Collins had always been able to work out such problems in the past, and it looked as if it would be possible to bring costs into line on most of the sections of the aircraft except the wing section. Collins agreed that substantial redesign was in order for the wing section.

Quality Level Becomes Critical

Evans seemed to accept the situation that Bernard Collins presented to him. He began redesign work immediately, but did seem somewhat puzzled as to why the original design was unacceptable.

After two weeks of long work days, the engineering section presented two proposals for redesign. The first design, worked out almost entirely by Evans, was a substantial departure from the prototype design. It was potentially a dramatic breakthrough in design characteristics, but once again costing estimates indicated that it would be around 30 percent over budget.

The second proposal was a joint effort of three engineers in the section, working closely with senior project engineer Bernard Collins. This proposal involved using the original design with modifications. These modifications involved: (a) reducing the number of reinforcing stringers between the inner and outer skins of the wing assembly; (b) changing the material specifications from steel and inconel to titanium-steel construction; and (c) increasing the angle of jet flap on the trailing edge of the wings.

Preliminary wind-tunnel experiments indicated that the second proposal would meet accepted safety factor limits of five to one at cruising speed and three to one at take-off and landing.

Proposal 2 was given the go-ahead for final testing and manufacture, since the modifications brought the construction costs within budget limits.

Confrontation

Mr. Sinclair recalled the conversation that Bernard Collins said he had had with Phillip Evans the following week. Collins was in his office going over test results of the revised design, when Evans abruptly charged in.

"Mr. Collins, I've got to talk to you about this new design," said Evans.

Collins: "Sure thing, Phil, what's on your mind?"

Evans: "Well, to put it simply, that wing design won't do the job. As a matter of fact it's so bad it's not safe."

Collins: "I don't understand, Phil. All test results show that it meets safety requirements, and after all, it's only a modification of your own design, which we know was far superior to anything in the industry."

Phil: "Mr. Collins, that's just the problem, it's not the same design. Those modifications virtually destroy the design of the prototype. I've made some trial experiments with models of the proposal, and my suspicions are confirmed. Its wings exhibit slight vibration characteristics on steep ascents and descents and during prolonged flight at low altitude. Likewise, temperature rise approaches the danger level on the leading edge of the wing, which could cause skin separation. Most importantly, the friction drag coefficient transfers from the laminar flow curve to the turbulent flow curve because of the change in material specifications and trailing edge design."

Collins: "Wait a minute, Phil, we've had several engineers running tests on the model, too, and they have all been favorable. From what you've told me, it seems that you don't really understand how this plan will be used in actual service. It doesn't have to be capable of operating like a navy fighter-bomber."

Evans: "But Mr. Collins, what about emergency situations? Operating characteristics must be considered there also."

Collins: "They are. That's why we calculate in a safety factor. Look, Phil, we've been in business quite a while now, and we take it seriously. We stand by our planes, our record speaks for itself!"

Evans: "Maybe so, but I know about wing design, and I say that in certain situations, conditions may exist to cause the wing sections to separate from the fuselage. And if that happens, someone is going to die, and it will be too late. I don't want any part of it."

Evans immediately left Collins's office without giving him a chance to answer. Evans resigned that afternoon.

The Engineer Takes Other Action

The first flight of the airplane was made in early 1972, and by the fall of 1972 the airplane had recorded 750 hours of flight time. In

October of 1972 all tests had been made, and final certification by the Federal Aviation Agency was given. This meant that the airplane had passed all federal air regulations and requirements.

At the time of FAA certification, the company had received orders or options for 50 airplanes. This was enough to convince the company it should proceed. The breakeven point was calculated to be 150 aircraft, and it was hoped that this number of aircraft would be sold by the end of 1973. The total sales of the airplane were conservatively estimated to be 410 over a five-year period.

Manufacture of the Exec-Six began in November 1972, with the first deliveries to be made in early 1973. A few days after production began, Sinclair received a registered letter from Phillip Evans that outlined his objections to the project and demanded that production be stopped. Sinclair again reviewed the situation with his top management and the engineering department, and a decision was made to continue production. In his letter Evans stated that if production was not halted, he would present his case at the annual stockholders meeting to be held in three weeks.

Sinclair could hardly forget what happened at the annual meeting. Evans, a stockholder, demanded to be heard. Sinclair had been prepared for the confrontation and was convinced he could handle it effectively.

Evans began: "Mr. Sinclair, as president of Hi-Quality Aircraft, isn't it true that you have been aware for some time of the potentially dangerous design specifications of this new aircraft?"

Sinclair: "I am thoroughly familiar with the design specifications of the Exec-Six, and I am convinced that the aircraft meets all existing safety standards. It indeed is a superior aircraft."

Evans: "Mr. Sinclair, I worked on the design of that aircraft and I know of several weaknesses that can cause structural damage under certain conditions."

Sinclair: "Ladies and gentlemen, I must emphasize that these allegations are unfounded. The aircraft has successfully passed all model testing and prototype experiments by us and the government and clearly meets or exceeds standards for design performance. We all know that under severe testing it is possible to fail any design if the conditions become too extreme. This aircraft is built for specific civilian functions, and it is inappropriate to evaluate its performance in extreme experiments meant for military aircraft, which is what Mr. Evans has done."

Evans: "Then you admit the plane did fail design tests."

Sinclair: "No, I don't."

Evans: "Do you admit that under certain conditions, even though abnormal, the design could fail?"

Sinclair: "I can simply restate that no aircraft can perform perfectly under *all* conditions. The cost to build such an aircraft would be so high that no one could afford to build it or buy it."

Evans: "Then you're saying you can't build a safe plane because it costs too much."

Sinclair was able to bring the argument to an end, but the damage had been done. He hoped that his persistent, rational arguments had prevailed. After watching the local TV newscasts of the proceedings, however, he wasn't so sure. The newscasts, while accurate, seemed to raise doubts in the viewer's mind about the safety of the airplane. The story was picked up by national news media and was continuously in the news as a result of what amounted to a crusade by Evans to stop production of the airplane. Evans kept writing letters to Hi-Quality management, its board of directors, newspapers, and the FAA.

The Crises

In June of 1973 a recently delivered Exec-Six crashed on landing. In the airplane were three engineers employed by the company owning the plane. Neither they nor the pilot were injured, but the airplane was seriously damaged. The official determination of what caused the accident would not be known until the National Transportation Safety Board made its report some months hence. The engineers in the airplane, however, all agreed that pilot error in slowing down the airplane too much had caused an engine stall.

The crash gave impetus, however, to Evan's public outcry against the airplane. A national consumer activist group joined Evans, and once again the story of Exec-Six was featured in the headlines.

Sinclair was still absolutely sure of the reliability of the aircraft and sought in every way possible to counter assertions by Evans and all others now involved in the debate. Sinclair obviously was not completely successful. While the Exec-Six was still being sold, the orders were far below the projections. Some of the original options were not picked up, and new orders were slow. Indeed, by the fall of 1973, only seventy-five firm orders had been received, one-half of what was anticipated. There was no doubt in Sinclair's mind that poor sales were directly attributable to Evans's campaign.

CASE QUESTIONS

1. Did Phillip Evans handle his grievance appropriately?
2. What should be management's strategy in handling such incidents?
3. What would be the effect on business enterprises if this type of whistle blowing became recognized as appropriate employee behavior?
4. Analyze in general terms the cost-benefit trade offs generated in this case. Who comes out ahead? Who loses?

References

Ralph Nader, Peter Petkas, and Kate Blackwell, *Whistle Blowing* (New York: Bantam Books, 1972).

Charles Peters and Taylor Branch, *Blowing the Whistle: Dissent in the Public Interest* (New York: Praeger, 1972).

C) CONFLICT OF INTEREST POLICY

Inorganic Chemicals Company has prepared the following policy statement for its employees:

General Statement of Policy

The company expects and requires directors, officers and employees (herein "employees") to be and remain free of interests or relationships and to refrain from acting in ways which are actually or potentially inimical or detrimental to the Company's best interests.

From Sorrell M. Mathes and G. Clark Thompson, "Ensuring Ethical Conduct in Business," *The Conference Board Record*, December 1964, p. 22. Reprinted with permission.

Application of Policy

1. "Conflicts of Interests" Defined

A conflict of interests exists where an employee

A. has an outside interest which materially encroaches on time or attention which should be devoted to the Company's affairs or so affects the employee's energies as to prevent his devoting his full abilities to the performance of his duties.

B. has a direct or indirect interest in or relationship with an outsider, such as a supplier (whether of goods or services), jobber, agent, customer or competitor, or with a person in a position to influence the actions of such outsider, which is inherently unethical or which might be implied or construed to

   i. make possible personal gain or favor to the employee involved, his family or persons having special ties to him, due to the employee's actual or potential power to influence dealings between the Company and the outsider,

   ii. render the employee partial toward the outsider for personal reasons, or otherwise inhibit the impartiality of the employee's business judgment or his desire to serve only the Company's best interests in the performance of his functions as an employee,

   iii. place the employee or the Company in an equivocal, embarrassing or ethically questionable position in the eyes of the public, or

   iv. reflect on the integrity of the employee or the Company.

Practically, conflicts of interests of the types just mentioned are reprehensible to the degree that the authority of the employee's position makes it possible for him to influence the Company's dealings with the outsider; thus, for example, the situation of those who buy or sell for the Company, or who can influence buying or selling, is particularly sensitive.

C. has any direct or indirect or relationship or acts in a way which is actually or potentially inimical or detrimental to the Company's best interests.

2. Examples of Improper Conflicts

There follow a few obvious examples of relationships which

probably would run afoul of the foregoing definition, but any relationship covered by the definition is subject to this policy:

A. Holding an outside position which affects the performance of the employee's work for the Company.

B. Relatively substantial (whether with reference to the enterprise invested in or to the employee's net worth) equity or other investment by the employee or members of his immediate family in a supplier, jobber, agent, customer or competitor. Under normal circumstances, however, ownership of securities of a publicly held corporation is not likely to create a conflict of interests unless the ownership is so substantial as to give the employee a motive to promote the welfare of that corporation and unless the employee, through his position with the Company or otherwise, is able to promote such welfare.

C. The acquisition of an interest in a firm with which, to the employee's knowledge, the Company is carrying on or contemplating negotiations for merger or purchase. In some cases, such an interest may create a conflict even though the interest was acquired prior to the time the Company evinced any interest in merger or purchase. Similar considerations are applicable to real estate in which the Company contemplates acquiring an interest.

D. The receipt of remuneration as an employee or consultant of, or the acceptance of loans from, a supplier, jobber, agent, customer or competitor of the Company.

E. The acceptance by the employee or members of his family from persons or firms having or seeking to have dealings with the Company of any cash gifts, or of gifts or entertainment which go beyond common courtesies extended in accordance with accepted business practice or which are of such value as to raise any implication whatsoever of an obligation on the part of the recipient.

F. Speculative dealing in the Company's stock on the basis of information gained in the performance of the employee's duties and not available to the public, or other misuse of information available to or gained by the employee by reason of his employment.

CASE QUESTIONS————————————————————

1. Do you approve of a company's making and enforcing a policy statement such as this? Is this in conflict with an entrepreneur's philosophy? Is this in conflict with an individual's rights to privacy?

2. Do you approve of the definition of conflict of interest in this statement?

3. Do you accept the examples of improper conflicts given in the statement?

4. If you do not like this conflict of interest policy, what policy would you suggest that would protect the interests of the corporation?

D) BIG COMPANIES: OPPRESSORS OF INDIVIDUAL EXPRESSION OR SOURCES OF SELF SATISFACTIONS?

A Case For Role Playing

Businesses in general, but large companies in particular, have for a number of years been strongly attacked for forcing conformity, stifling self-expression, thwarting creativity, repressing natural drives, and in numerous other ways oppressing the individuals whom they employ. Businessmen themselves, however, do not accept this picture. They say that an individual can lead a very satisfying life in a large company. They say there are many institutional arrangements present in large companies that not only permit but stimulate individual creativity, innovation, and participation.

Role 1. You are on the side of the critics of business: You accept the basic thesis in the first part of the introductory paragraph. Your assignment is to talk with your friends and read to build up a concrete list of ways in which large companies do, in fact, repress the individuals who work in them.

Role 2. You take the position that "life can be beautiful in a large company." Your task is to explain exactly how large companies today do help individuals to lead more satisfying lives.

Role 3. You take the position that there is truth in both statements. Your assignment is to think ahead and explain what a big company can do, aside from what it is now doing, to improve the personal self-satisfactions of individuals who work there and also advance the welfare of the company. *Note*: In the development of these three positions, it may be useful to classify people in groups, such as blue-collar workers, white-collar workers, lower-level managers, middle-level managers, and top managers.

--------------------References--------------------

Chris Argyris, "The Individual and Organizations: Some Problems of Mutual Adjustment," *Administrative Science Quarterly*, June 1957, pp. 1-24.

Leonard R. Sayles and George Strauss, *Human Behavior in Organizations* (Englewood Cliffs, N. J.: Prentice-Hall, 1966), chapter 18.

George A. Steiner, "Business Bigness: Benefits and Dangers," *Business Horizons*, October 1971, pp. 57-58.

George Strauss, "Organization Man—Prospect for the Future," *California Management Review*, Spring 1964, pp. 5-16.

E) THE "I AM" PLAN: JOB ENRICHMENT OF WEYERHAEUSER COMPANY

- All people have some creativity.
- All people have personal dignity.
- People want to be responsible.
- An employee can best manage his own job; supervisors are resource persons and coordinators.
- Everyone wants to succeed in whatever he choose to do.
- If a person does not succeed, it is because he does not have the necessary knowledge, skills, or attitudes.

These assumptions about human nature underlie Weyerhaeuser's approach to job design and enrichment. Its job enrichment projects involve all levels of employees. Since job enrichment is viewed as

From Harold M. F. Rush, "The 'I am' Plan," *Job Design for Motivation*, New York: National Industrial Conference Board, 1971, pp. 55-60. Reprinted with permission.

improving work satisfaction at multiple levels, the company sees in it a means of increasing productivity of the total enterprise. In other words, it does not regard job enrichment as an isolated program, but rather as a natural out-growth of a larger organizational improvement or development effort.

The assumptions underlying Weyerhaeuser's program are consonant with those of McGregor's "Theory Y," namely, that people are creative and self-responsible. Therefore, Weyerhaeuser's job enrichment is called the "I Am" plan, shorthand for "I am manager of my job."

Managing effectively involves acquiring certain basic skills relating to the production-technical requirements as well as the interpersonal aspects of the manager's job. Weyerhaeuser has outlined these skills in several ongoing courses. The primary course for key managers is the Weyerhaeuser Management School. In order to understand the "I Am" plan, it is necessary to review the fundamentals of Weyerhaeuser's internal management school, a four-week course conducted by the company's manpower development staff, assisted by outside experts. The school is conducted at a central location for managers, at several levels of responsibility and from many locations, who represent the company's lines of business, including pulp, paper, wood products, etc. Each of the week-long sessions is separated by a month during which the attendees have an opportunity to apply their newly acquired skills. The school, which was started in 1963, has gone through several curriculum changes, but currently the course covers the following subject matter:

First Week

1) Fundamentals of management

2) Modern theories of management

3) The manager's role in society

4) Management and leadership styles

5) Organization theory and organization planning

6) Management of the manager's time

Second Week

1) Problem identification and situation analysis

2) Problem-solving methods

3) Decision-making

4) Goal-setting

Third Week

1) Motivation theories; application of motivation theories to the work situation

2) Communication: theory and practice

3) Creativity: how identify and how release

Fourth Week

1) Conference leadership techniques and principles

2) Practicum in conference leadership and group interaction

Weyerhaeuser's manpower-development staff reports that typically managers begin to explore observable, concrete ways of applying what they have been learning after the third week of the school. In fact, it was at the urging of managers attending the school that Weyerhaeuser began to explore ways to unlock individual creativity and increase employee motivation on a systematic basis. It was felt that much of the actual subject matter from the school is relevant to *any* manager's job, whether he be a professional manager, a working supervisor, or a rank-and-file employee who manages his own job. For this reason the "I Am" plan in its implementation draws heavily on the techniques taught in the management school.

Because Weyerhaeuser is primarily a manufacturing concern with mass production operations, management realized that redesign of jobs could possibly be disruptive to production schedules and cause morale problems among employees if the project were undertaken on a company-wide basis. Therefore, the company began the "I Am" plan with a pilot project in a typical manufacturing plant.

The plant selected—a paper-manufacturing facility with many automated processes—is in the eastern United States. The work force comprises 300 employees. Management at this plant had gone through the Weyerhaeuser Management School and were committed to the goals of the effort. Since the project would have a direct impact on employees at all levels, labor union cooperation was held to be essential; therefore, management not only obtained agreement from officers and stewards of the bargaining units but actively involved union officials in the job enrichment project that eventually developed.

Once the corporate staff was assured of management and union cooperation, it was decided to turn the project over to local management for its actual implementation, while corporate staff made themselves available as consultants and resource persons. This method was chosen because the corporate manpower development staff felt that the effort would probably be more effective if the responsibility rested with the local plants; and it gave corporate staff the perspective they felt they needed to observe and evaluate the project.

The company in 1968 assigned a full-time coordinator to the pilot project. From several candidates interested in the job, the plant manager selected a production worker. (See box.) The coordinator reports directly to the plant manager, who works with him as a two-man team.

The next step was to train the coordinator in job enrichment concepts and in work simplification methods and techniques, because work simplification is integral to Weyerhaeuser's job enrichment. Next, he and the plant manager began a series of programmed steps to implement the "I Am" plan.

Step 1. Select an Employee Committee

A committee of 60 employees, a "diagonal slice" of the work force, was selected for in-depth exposure to "I Am" concepts and applications. They included all of top management, representatives from middle and lower management, clerical workers (both men and women), production workers, union stewards (21), and presidents of the union locals.

Step 2. Get Feedback on Committee's Perceptions

In a series of committee meetings the coordinator gleaned information from the members about the problems and goals of their peer groups, as well as their perceptions of the larger organization's problems. The committee members all were leaders of their peer groups, either by virtue of job status or because they emerged as "natural" leaders.

Step 3. Integrate the Committee into a Group; then Educate

The meat of the course was synthesized to form the subject matter for three monthly seminars for the committee members. First there was a four-hour "appreciation session" to level about the aims, methodology, and schedule of the project. Confrontation and conflict-resolution techniques were used to gain understanding and to help remove any skepticism about the company's motives for undertaking the "I Am" project. Participants, both management and labor, pledged cooperation.

At the first seminar a behavioral scientist explained motivation theory and its relation to the job. Another behavioral scientist conducted the next seminar, a session on creativity. The third month's seminar was devoted to effective communication.

Factory Employee Coordinates Pilot Project

One aim of most job enlargement or job enrichment projects is to create more meaningful work. In the Weyerhaeuser "I Am" plan, a principal goal is to make work more meaningful by enriching the content of the employee's job, as well as to build growth mechanisms into it. A job factor generally accepted as a "motivator" is growth and advancement. Sometimes this means growth within a given job and sometimes it refers to growth through new responsibilities and new challenges.

A dramatic example of personal growth and advancement opportunity exists in the company's selection of the "I Am" coordinator for the manufacturing plant where the pilot study was conducted.

The plant manager invited employees to become full-time coordinators of the job enrichment project. There were volunteers from virtually every level of responsibility and a wide range of occupational categories. Logical choices for the job of coordinator might be a personnel officer, a systems and procedures man, or an industrial engineer. The individual who was finally selected and trained was a fifth-hand (low man) on a paper machine in the shop; he was in his mid-twenties; he had no college or management training; and he was a union steward and vice president of the local.

In his favor were: a history of achievement in high school and in sports; natural leadership among his peers; hard work; and knowledge of his present job. The company provided the additional training he needed because he showed strong motivation to improve his job situation and keen interest in the goals of the "I Am" plan.

A Weyerhaeuser executive comments: "This is a good example of real job enrichment, which implies putting into practice the words we mouth about people being creative and committed to goals with which they can identify. . . . I suspect we have plenty other such 'gems' in the company."

The coordinator is now a manager of manpower resources development for several plants. His job is that of a development specialist and his responsibilities encompass more than job and process improvement.

Step 4. Get Survey of Attitudes and Job Opinion

The company then conducted a plant-wide attitude survey that centered upon job satisfaction and motivation. Responses, which were anonymous, were analyzed by department and categorized as "satisfiers" and "dissatisfiers" in a "motivation-maintenance" model. These data were analyzed and fed back to the group for exploration of conditions that could have caused the problems uncovered by the survey.

The timing of the survey was deliberate. The organization development specialists felt that the survey would produce more openness and straight feedback after employees had learned to trust management's motives in connection with the "I Am" plan.

Step 5. Select Discussion Leaders for Work Groups

The next phase was concerned with gearing-up for process improvement and with job satisfaction/dissatisfaction factors among specific work groups, who would primarily work toward improving their own situation. To do this, the "I Am" coordinator needed discussion leaders for the various units of the organization. Thirty-six volunteered, and 18 were selected. Each discussion leader was also the communication channel to his department or work group, regardless of his official status. Again, though coincidentally, a "diagonal slice" resulted, representing a wide range of job categories, age, tenure, union/ management membership, and education (one was a Ph.D.; another, a grammar school graduate).

Step 6. Train Discussion Leaders

In 1969, the corporate manpower development staff held a week's course on conference leadership and conflict resolution for the 18 discussion leaders. This was the first time the company held the course for nonexempt employees. A corporate trainer remarked that he was not able to tell from their performance in the sessions who were managers or professionals and who were production workers.

Step 7. Hold Small Group "Improvement" Conferences

The discussion leaders held a series of "improvement" sessions with their respective work groups. The sessions, held on the employee's own time, utilized the data uncovered by the attitude survey as well as problems—both "maintenance" and "motivational" in nature—that discussions elicited in face-to-face conferences.

The improvement sessions helped to sense and uncover a wide variety of dissatisfactions, many of which top management had been unaware of. An important feature of the sessions was brainstorming and work simplification techniques. Once the problems and shortcomings were identified, the employees asked, "What can we do about them?" They categorized them into those that only management could eliminate, and those which they, themselves, could resolve or improve.

Step 8. Establish a Steering Committee

Seven managers from the original 60-member employee committee were selected to act as a steering committee on job and process improvement. They advise and recommend changes in job design, processes, and work flow. They also have responsibility for effecting improvements and changes recommended in the data gleaned from the various small group "improvement" conferences, as well as those changes indicated by the attitude survey.

Step 9. Set Up and Train Project Teams

The coordinator puts together project teams of people directly concerned with a particular problem identified for improvement. (For example, a work-flow problem might be tackled by a purchasing agent, a scheduler, a production control man, a production worker, and a quality control man. A problem relating to mechanical bottlenecks might be tackled by a team composed of a millwright, machine operator, foreman, and maintenance man.) "Outsiders" are not included in a task force; the members are persons seeking to improve or enrich their own jobs. The teams are trained in work simplification techniques, problem-solving, and decision-making, and they go through some team-building exercises before functioning as a task force.

A personnel executive reports that several hourly paid workers have been promoted to supervisory jobs, chiefly because of their proficiency with managerial skills that they acquired on project teams. He concludes, "This is a very effective way of developing managers . . . far better than most traditional management development courses."

Step 10. Establish an Ongoing Process

As job and process-improvement problems are identified and as project teams go about making modifications, other problems are uncovered and, in turn, resolved. What started as a problem-solving effort, becomes, in a sense, a self-perpetuating, normal mode of action.

Step 11. Recycle: Repeat Educational Process

The final step, as conceived by Weyerhaeuser, is a refresher course or a recycling of the "I Am" educational process, designed to "lock in" the concepts for employees already participating in job and process improvement, as well as to include new employees or newly selected discussion leaders.

Job Enrichment for the Work Group

Vertical job-loading or "job enrichment" may be summarized as a matter of adding the planning and controlling functions to the actual doing of the job. Sometimes these plan-and-control elements—traditionally the province of the manager—may be delegated to an individual employee in connection with his job or they may be delegated to a work unit or group. In the latter case there is usually some element of group accountability. Weyerhaeuser's "I Am" plan is strongly dependent upon intragroup and intergroup activity.

Examples of job enrichment through group responsibility and accountability may be found in the plant where Weyerhaeuser ran its "I Am" pilot project. For example, once over-all manufacturing objectives are established, the plant's top management communicates them to the foremen. The foremen meet with their respective work groups to communicate the objectives, and to plan the production schedules, work flow, and individual responsibilities. The foremen do not assign specific responsibilities or schedules; the work groups break down the objectives into concrete action plans, daily production schedules, and individual job responsibilities.

Each work group measures itself on its effectiveness in terms of:

1) Productivity of the group

2) Machine and equipment utilization (including down-time)

3) Product quality control

4) Individual productivity and contribution

5) Group behavior (tardiness, absence, interpersonal interaction, etc.)

The company measures effectiveness on a group basis; and each work group evaluates itself as a group, as well as the contributions of each of its members, against its goals and objectives.

Since wage rates are negotiated by the bargaining units, base pay scales are predetermined for each job classification. However, the bargaining contract provides for additional compensation for work groups that are high producers.

Results of Pilot Project

Since Weyerhaeuser undertook its pilot study the pilot plant has shown a rate of productivity exceeding that of comparable plants. The local coordinator also reports that employee grievances have dropped appreciably. A Weyerhaeuser executive comments, "The fact that productivity is higher at this plant could be attributed to a greater market for its products, increased automation, or the introduction of job enrichment via the 'I Am' plan. Since the market isn't greater and since there has been no further automation, I have to conclude that the 'I Am' plan is responsible." Asked whether the upturn in productivity may be due to the "Hawthorne effect,"[1] he replied: "There may be some possibility of the 'Hawthorne effect,' but that doesn't bother me. The fact is that these people are higher producers. Furthermore, the 'I Am' plan is constructed to include

[1] What is popularly called the "Hawthorne effect" denotes higher productivity among workers because they are being noticed.

action phases that will make the job improvement and enrichment factors a part of the everyday operation of the plant."

Weyerhaeuser intends to install the "I Am" plan on a company-wide basis. Twenty-five additional coordinators from as many plants have been through motivation and creativity training, the basic course in job and process improvement, and some organizational development in the form of "appreciation sessions" and team-building with the management group at their home plants. Employees and their unions disliked the term "work simplification," so "job and process improvement" was substituted. The action phases of the "I Am" plan are in various stages at the plants. Because Weyerhaeuser expects to implement the plan company-wide, it has established its own job and process improvement school.

The manager of manpower development found that the coordinators going through training were enthusiastic about the challenge of their new jobs and about the possibilities the "I Am" plan holds for their fellow employees. He reports that they became a "fraternity" and wanted to keep in touch after they returned to their respective home bases. To help bridge the communication gap for them, the manpower development staff publishes a regular newsletter that reports problems and breakthroughs at the various plant locations.

Assessing Weyerhaeuser's success with job enrichment, an organization development specialist at headquarters lists several rules-of-thumb that he feels have helped appreciably:

"1) Be open and clean about your intentions to management and employees alike.

"2) Be sure local management understands the concepts behind motivation and its relation to productivity; then be sure you have their full commitment.

"3) Gain commitment from the union and involve them from the very beginning.

"4) Select a good coordinator from the local work force—and don't just confine your consideration to employees who already have some knowledge of personnel or industrial engineering. The skills he can learn, but he must be someone who can function as a teacher and gain rapport and trust from people at all levels.

"5) Train the coordinator well, both in methods and principles as well as in interpersonal skills.

"6) Expose a large portion of the population to the concepts underlying the project, because the small group is where the real action must take place and each group will need its own leader.

"7) Avoid the trap of treating the effort as a program; programs have stop-and-start times. What you are really trying to do is change a life style of an organization.

"8) Implement change by and through the people whose jobs are affected. This gives them a stake in what happens, and it is neither coercive nor manipulative.

"9) Keep the job content foremost in your goals.

"10) Be patient and go slowly."

CASE QUESTIONS

1. Contrast what Weyerhaeuser is doing with the old authoritarian, bureaucratic business structure in which McGregor's "Theory X" is accepted by management.

2. In your view should job enrichment be undertaken by a company to create "more meaningful work" for people or to assure "better utilization of people and equipment"?

3. Do you believe that the workers you know will be motivated to higher achievement if their jobs are enriched? (See Thomas H. Fitzgerald, "Why motivation Theory Doesn't Work," *Harvard Business Review*, July-August 1971, pp. 37-44. Louis E. Davis, "Readying the Unready: Post-Industrial Jobs," *California Management Review*, Summer 1971, pp. 27–36.)

4. Many people in and out of business are today talking about the "quality of work life." What do these words mean to you? (See *Work in America*, Report of a Special Task Force to the Secretary of Health, Education, and Welfare (Cambridge, Mass.: MIT Press, 1973); Irving Kristol, "Is the American Worker 'Alienated'?" *Wall Street Journal*, 18 January 1973.)

DISCUSSION GUIDES ON CHAPTER CONTENT —————

1. What is work? How have the definitions of work changed over time?

2. Explain Maslow's hierarchy of needs classification. What importance do you attach to this classification?

3. Herzberg says that job dissatisfaction is not the opposite of job satisfaction. What does he mean? Of what significance is this observation?

4. Explain why there is dissatisfaction among blue-collar and white-collar workers, managers at different levels, new MBAs, young workers, women, and minority workers.

5. What is meant by QOWL (quality of working life)?

6. What do you think can and should be done by business to improve QOWL? Explain fully.

7. What are some of the methods that large organizations employ to stimulate individual creativity, innovation, and imagination?

8. Bennis and Slater assert that future organizations are going to be more democratic and temporary. Do you agree with them? Explain.

9. What are the broad interrelationships between business and leisure? Business and the family?

MIND-STRETCHING QUESTIONS —————

1. Many organizations are presently considering adoption of the four-day work week. What implications does this have for business and for society as a whole?

2. It has been stated that today's youth emerging from college and entering business will have a profound effect on organizational structure and goals. How will this come about? How would you, fresh from school and entering a company at or near the bottom of the ladder, go about introducing the concepts you have learned and the values that you hold?

28
LABOR UNIONS AND MANAGERIAL AUTHORITY

DISCUSSION GUIDES ON CHAPTER CONTENT————————

1. Many managers express concern about the power of unions over their "managerial prerogatives." How has union power restricted managerial authority?

2. On the other hand, there are limitations on the exercise of power by unions. Describe some of the more important limitations.

3. Despite the antipathy that often exists between managers and unions, there is an acceptance of unions on the part of managers, and unions are much less militant and more amenable to peaceful negotiations today than ever before. Why?

4. Explain the nature and potential significance of the agreement the United Steelworkers of America made with management not to strike and to submit disagreements to arbitration.

5. Discuss the political power of unions.

6. What might be some of the more significant future demands of labor unions in the United States?

MIND-STRETCHING QUESTION————————————

In Chapter 20, the negative aspects of allowing business monopolies were discussed, and it was conceded that monopolies which act in constraint of trade should be outlawed. Many national labor unions, such as the Teamsters, UAW, and others, could be considered monopolies acting in restraint of trade in that they control all the workers of the nation in their particular fields. Should they also be declared illegal? Why? Why not?

VII

THE
FUTURE

29

FUTURE FORCES AND PATTERNS IN THE BUSINESS - SOCIETY RELATIONSHIP

A) ALTERNATIVE ENVIRONMENTAL FUTURES FOR THE U.S. BUSINESS-SOCIETY RELATIONSHIP

You are about to listen to taped excerpts from a conference held recently to discuss future roles of business in the United States. This conference was conducted not so much to forecast what might lay ahead, but to speculate about possible alternatives.

As a background for the conference, a discussion paper was prepared that set forth some of the major trends which would have the most important impact on the evolution of the business-society interrelationship in the United States. World-wide trends that were discussed in this paper were as follows: rapidly growing population, growing unemployment, a growing income gap between rich and poor nations, rapid urbanization, expanding education, deteriorating environment, economic interdependence brought about by the multi-national corporations, growing political-economic integration (e.g., the European Common Market), price inflation, and political and economic instabilities leading to military engagements. The major trends discussed for the United States were: population slowdown and the changing proportions of age groups, growing economic prosperity and rising per capita income, rising governmental expenditures, the rising tide of education, expanding technology, changing social values, the emergence of the postindustrial society, growing interdependence of institutions, increasing emphasis on individualism, growing pluralism, the equality revolution, growing emphasis on the quality of life, and the redefinition of work-leisure patterns. (For a discussion of these subjects see Carl H. Madden, *Clash of Culture: Management in an Age of Changing Values*. Washington, D. C.: National Planning Association, 1972. Lester R. Brown, "Developing Trends and Changing Institutions: An Overview of World Trends," *The Futurist*, December 1972 pp. 225-232. General Electric, "Our Future Business Environment," *Business Environment*, April 1968, 570 Lexington Ave., New York, New York.)

Since this is a tape you are unable to identify the speakers. But the group was small, and present in it were college professors, businessmen, and students.

The Tape

"Upon the basis of that splendid paper on trends and projections, and your own observations, what 'futures' do you see for the U. S.?"

"What do you want us to do? Forecast?"

"No, the idea is not so much to forecast, but to describe different possible futures. I mean by this to hypothesize, on the basis of possible major trends, what the main outlines of the business environment in the U. S. will be in, say, the year 2000, and what the business role in it will be like. If you want to project present trends that's OK. If you think major new developments will tremendously alter our society that also is OK. I do think that we ought to try to be somewhat realistic, however, in the sense that what we hypothesize has some probability of happening. Before we get started, let's agree to rule out nuclear war. In the event of an all-out holocaust, we shall be back in the Neanderthal age."

"Well, I for one think there is a good chance we shall see more of the same thing that is going on now. I have in mind an extrapolation of current trends. Sure, we will see rapidly expanding technology, growing affluence, and changes in the way people view things. But basically, we will be in 2000 much like we are now."

"I can buy that scenario, but not that we will be much like we are now. We can have in the year 2000 fundamentally the same kind of institutions we now have. Business can exist as a profit-making institution, but maybe we will have more and larger businesses. Business-government relationships may be much as they are today. But even so, pressures of all kinds will so change the way we do things in our institutions that they will operate very differently from the way they do now."

"Can you give us an illustration of what you mean?"

"Sure. Take just the way people are treated. There is a growing trend today to let people get more involved in organizations, to have a piece of the action. This sort of thing will lead to more permissive management. It will lead to new ways of doing things on the production line. It will lead to new business organizations—internally, I mean."

"Your surprise-free description is not realistic. We are witnessing today such basic changes in the demands by people in our society that some major changes will inevitably take place. Take our cities. They are unmanageable today. Government has money and power but can't do anything. Business has the capability of doing something but no power and no profit incentive. The logic of the situation, if reason is to prevail, is to create some sort of 'social-industrial complex.' I think Si Ramo first used that expression. This would be the sort of joint-planning and operating arrangement in the social world that we have in the military-industrial complex."

"Well, that is not 'surprise free' to me. We are beginning to do some of this type thing now. In transportation, for example."

"Yes, but I think many more major changes in the way we do things will occur. We have too many problems that don't seem to get solved the way we do things now. Look at the welfare mess, our inability to control inflation, or the archaic ways Congress does its business. We have got to have a wholesale cleaning up in many areas. When you add this all up, you get something different from an extrapolation of current trends."

"Do you have in mind something of an internal recon-struction?"

"Yes, I guess you could call it that. But It's more than reconstruction of institutions. It's an injection of new experimentation into what we do, a new type of creativity to solve our social problems. I guess decentralization of decision making might also be basic in my scenario."

"As a businessman I think we are going to have a major change, but I don't think you have caught the picture. Look at what is happening to us abroad. Our balance of payments is seriously unbalanced. Competition's getting tougher and tougher. In some areas, we can't compete any more. Why? A major reason is that in Japan, for instance, and in other countries, too, there is a sort of government-banking-industry cooperative planning arrangement. There, industry is in bed with government. Here, the government restrains us. I think this is all going to change. If not, we're going down the tubes. I see a new attitude in government to help business out. I think we will see a much closer relationship between the federal government and business. I would not be surprised to see big labor as part of this arrangement. Maybe even the universities will get in the picture. We have to do this if we are to compete in a world where other nations do it."

"You're talking about Galbraith's 'technostructure.' "

"Maybe so. Galbraith's description of today's industrial structure is something I, a businessman, don't recognize. But it may be something we will come to as a matter of self-preservation."

"I hope you're wrong. Competition has been the central force that's got us where we are. We will lose that motivation with the setup you describe."

"No, I don't think so. Indeed, it could be just the reverse. We can't compete abroad today because of foreign government business arrangements that block us. Domestically, big companies today compete rather aggressively. Why can't they do so under this arrangement?"

"I think what has been said up to now has missed the boat. Some of our students have been telling us—and not enough people are listening—that we now have the capability, and we soon will have the demand, for creating a whole new society that will fulfill the highest expectations of man. The very affluence of this society will permit us to achieve the age-old dream of man to lead a natural, fulfilling life."

"What do you mean by 'natural'?"

"It's not easy to explain. But let me try. The idea that man in a state of nature is free goes back many centuries. Man is a part of nature. Man is central, and natural things enhance his self-fulfillment. In today's society nature is exploited for profit. The individual is subject to authority and his spirit is suppressed. Science and technology are used to make profits for somebody rather than pursued for the intellectual stimulation that natural, unrestrained inquiry would yield. The highest self-fulfillment does not come from the competition and antagonisms in life that are created when people act solely for profit. The good life is one free of pressures, close to nature, in tune with nature: rejecting hypocrisy; emphasizing cooperation rather than competition, being rather than doing; discovering new truths for pleasure rather than profit; preserving the natural environment rather than exploiting it. You see, when you begin with self, and think of self-fulfillment, you have to admit that our institutions simply are archaic. They thwart the very thing society should now aspire to."

"That sounds kind of mystical to me. What happens to our institutions in your scenario?"

"Well, as this consciousness of love, fulfillment, and self-satisfaction spreads, obsolete institutions will simply be abandoned. The natural relationships of people, in communities, will replace them."

"That sounds like Charlie Reich's 'Consciousness III' to me."[1]

"You are describing utopia, aren't you?"

"Call it what you will, that is what I see. Several decades in the future—we no longer will be obliged to work to meet our economic needs. They will be at hand in automated factories. Then, man will have the time and interest to meet his highest spiritual, intellectual, and self-aspirations."

"I'd like to get back to a scenario that is evolutionary from our present stance. I can lay a case for evolutionary change, but at a revolutionary pace that will answer the aspirations that the last two scenarios seek. Our present society has been greatly criticized for being unadaptable to changing needs. I think many of our institutions have shown great capability to change to meet new demands. Both business and government, for example, have been rather flexible—maybe not as flexible as some would want, but

[1] Speaker is referring to Charles A. Reich, *The Greening of America* (New York: Random House, 1970).

flexible and innovative. Various schemes for a guaranteed annual income, for instance, are innovative. We have not yet done this, but we will soon. I think it was Gunnar Myrdal who, when commenting on the future of the U. S., said he was sanguine because no other powerful nation of the world is so capable of rapidly making up its mind to do something that needs doing, and doing it quickly. That's us. Look back just a few years at the extraordinary changes in our institutions, especially business, to meet new societal demands. This sort of thing is going to continue. So, I put my chips on a scenario in 2000 that has us looking and doing things in ways comparable to now, but with such new and imaginative devices and ideas that it really will be a very different society. Maybe this will preserve what we now hold in high value—our productivity, our democratic way of doing things, our organizations—and yet meet the new demands for a higher quality of life for everyone."

"Another possibility would be, of course, authoritarian government. If any of the scenarios suggested in the discussion up to this point fails to achieve its basic purposes, the result could be revolt. That leads to anarchy. Anarchy inevitably leads to some sort of authoritarian government."

"I suppose it is possible, although I don't think probable, that early in the twenty-first century we might well have a world government of some type."

"We haven't talked much about the U. S. and its international relationships. You know, it will make a great deal of difference, for instance, if we pulled in our horns and took a 'Fortress America' position and paid no heed to the rest of the world. I guess the inevitable result of that would be a war of some kind. On the other hand, if the U.S. took a strong leadership position in securing peace in the world and pressed for a powerful United Nations, we might move toward some form of world government."

"All the scenarios so far have been based implicitly on assumptions that we can go on growing in population, using resources prodigiously, raising industrial output, producing foods in sufficient degree to prevent mass starvation, and polluting the air and waters. All these things are growing exponentially. That can't continue. I agree with the Club of Rome study that unless drastic, heroic measures are taken immediately the inevitable result will be ecological disaster. There is no other way. Sometime at the beginning of the twenty-first century, the world literally will collapse. I refer you to *Limits to Growth* by Dennis S. Meadows, Donella H. Meadows, Jorgen Randers, and William W. Behrens II.[2] "

"What heroic measures are you suggesting?"

"Nothing less than a drastic slowdown in population, investment, industrial output, and technology and a cleanup of our polluted environment."

"That's a bleak scenario. What shall we call it? Doomsday?"

"I don't buy it. First of all, I don't think all the things you say will jump exponentially. But I do agree that specific resources are finite. Slowing down technology seems to me to be wrong. We need to speed it up, but on the right things. I suppose that sometime in the great distant future, growth will slow down and stop. But that, it seems to me, is far beyond our time frame. In the meantime, we can do many things within our present system to prevent ecological disaster. I have an article here that I submit for the record to support this view."[3]

"Speaking of bleak scenarios, I suppose it is possible that we simply will not solve our fundamental social issues, which will lead to widespread disorders and an economic and political collapse in this country."

"You fellows with the 'doomsday philosophy' ought to read John Maddox's *The Doomsday Syndrome*.[4] Maddox is a leading English scientist and editor of *Nature* magazine. In this book he flays those who see nothing but disaster from population growth, pollution, and resource usage. He is highly optimistic rather than pessimistic and lays a persuasive case."[5]

"I am not sure this excursion into the future is worth much. So many things can happen to shape events. Aside from major wars or natural catastrophies, for instance, a crusade by the federal government to break up big companies might deny this country the competetive strength of large companies. If this brings about economic deterioration, that chain of consequences could be

---

[2] Meadows, et al., *Limits to Growth* (New York: Universe Books, 1972).

[3] Henry C. Wallich, "Eco-Doom: The Limits to Credulity," *Business and Society Review*, Summer 1972, pp. 103-105.

[4] Maddox, *The Doomsday Syndrome* (New York: McGraw—Hill, 1972).

[5] For a review of this book see Dennis L. Meadows "The Doomsday Syndrome," *Technology Review*, February 1972, pp. 70-71.

catastrophic. On a more optimistic side, a long era of genuine peace and institutional reform could bring about for us an undreamed of opulence, leisure, and indulgence in self-satisfactions. How can we tell what will happen?"

"You are correct that the future holds infinite possibilities. But I think it is good to hypothesize about major trends and the basic types of world they may produce. Doing this serves to draw attention to the larger possibilities for the future. This is, I think, an effective learning tool. If we were to get into details, we would see possibilities that would be missed in general, abstract observations about the future or in merely following each of many different trends. Also, the scenario approach helps us to see how different institutions and disciplines—economic, political, psychological, legal, military, etc.—interact."

"We seem to be building alternative futures with walls or hard lines around them. This bothers me. Whatever happens is not likely to fit into one of the scenarios—the world of 2000 for the U. S. probably will have in it a combination of forces found in all the scenarios so far presented. I have a different idea. Why not start with, say, three basic scenarios? The first would be a reasonably optimistic one. The second would be a moderately pessimistic one. Then, on the basis of these two scenarios, develop possible deviations. This would, of course, give us the possibility of an infinite variety of futures, but it would be more realistic."

"I am not so sure the experiment here is to be realistic. Isn't it rather to be provocative in thinking about possibilities? If we are going to be realistic, we must begin to put probabilities on our thoughts."

"The world of 2000 is too far off to think in terms of probabilities for alternatives."

"I disagree. The real issue, is it not, is whether the probabilities we note today are worth anything?"

"The idea was advanced concerning an optimistic and pessimistic scenario. What is in mind?"

"I advanced those models. Well, in building either one it seems to me you must begin from today's base and then—in light of major goals and objectives of this society, as best one can determine them and projecting them into the future—set forth what you consider to be optimistic or pessimistic outcomes for major economic, political, social, intellectual, and demographic phenomena and so on. For instance, an optimistic economic projection of GNP would be, I suppose, a continuation of the real rate of growth of around 4.5 percent a year. A pessimistic scenario would say that, for a number of potential reasons, the rate of growth would be around 2 percent a year, with erratic ups and downs. Or, to take another area, an optimistic view would be that by 2000 we will have managed our major social problems—pollution, ghettos, racism, discrimination, etc.—in a balanced, rational, and democratic way. A pessimistic view would be that we have not."

"How about your deviations from the basic models?"

"The deviations get you into details about specifics. For example, population fertility rates, inflation, balance of payments, size of government versus business, business size and power, and so on."

CASE QUESTIONS

1. How many fundamentally different scenarios were mentioned in this dialogue? How are alternative futures developed? For a short article on the methodology of making futures forecasts see David M. Kiefer, "The Futures Business," *Chemical & Engineering News*, August 11, 1969, pp. 62-75.

2. Which scenario do you think is most probable in the year 2000? (For extensive discussions of scenarios see Herman Kahn and Anthony J. Wiener, *The Year 2000*, (New York: Macmillan, 1967). Herman Kahn and B. Bruce-Briggs, *Things to Come* (New York: Macmillan 1972). For a short treatment see Harold A. Linstone, "Four American Futures: Reflections on the Role of Planning," *Technological Forecasting and Social Change*, vol. 4, no. 1, (1972), pp. 41-60.)

3. For the most probable scenario, as determined by the class, develop in some detail the changing role of business. (See George A. Steiner, "The Redefinition of Capitalism and Its Impact on Management Practice and Theory," *Proceedings of the Thirty-second Annual Meeting of the Academy of Management*, August 13-16, 1972, pp. 2-11. Neil H. Jacoby, *Corporate Power and Social Responsibility: A Blueprint for the Future* (New York: Macmillan 1973), chapter 12.)

DISCUSSION GUIDES ON CHAPTER CONTENT————————

1. What are the dangers in making social forecasts? Of what value are social forecasts?

2. The author says: "there are deep underlying forces operating in the world that increase complexity, tension, and instability." What are they?

3. Do you agree with all the one hundred trends presented in the textbook that the author says will determine the future business-society interrelationship?

4. Which would you omit as being comparatively insignificant?

5. Are there any that you think are missed in the list?

6. Looking at the list do you see the same emerging society that the author does?

7. The author says that "institutional lags" could prevent the coming of the new "great society." What does he mean? Do you agree?

8. Do you think there will be changes in social values that may prevent our achieving the great society?

9. Do you see any other forces that may prevent the coming of the great society? Explain.

10. The author says that business power will decline relative to that of other institutions. Do you agree? What is this likely to mean for the future business-society interrelationship?

11 If we can land a man on the moon and bring him back safely, why can't we better manage our socioeconomic problems?

12. A number of alternative futures were presented. Appraise the probability of each for the year 2000. The year 2050. The year 2100. Explain why.

MIND-STRETCHING QUESTIONS————————————

1. E. J. Mishan has observed the following:

Whatever the prospects, it is difficult to envisage any decent way of life without a wholesale reversal of the powerful trends—technological, philosophical, economic—that began in the 18th century. The phenomenal expansion of human population, the secular trend toward centralization, the hectic pace of obsolescence, the spread of auto-mobilization and air travel, the growth in mass media, the increasing mobility and uniformity; all such forces will have to go into reverse if such commonly voiced aspirations as variety, order, intimacy, conservation, care, margin, space, ease and openness, are ever to be realized.[6]

What is your reaction to this observation?

2. Which relationships that exist in the business-society nexus in the year 2000 will be most different from today's? What relationships will be much like those of today? Explain your position and the premises upon which it is based.

3. If you were asked to give the author of this textbook your views on what should be done to revise the book what would you tell him?

[6] E. J. Mishan, "On Making The Future Safe for Mankind," *The Public Interest*, Summer 1971, p. 61.